Oxford Rebels

Oxford Rebels

the life and friends of Nevil Story Maskelyne
1823–1911
pioneer Oxford scientist, photographer and politician

Vanda Morton

ALAN SUTTON
1987

ALAN SUTTON PUBLISHING
BRUNSWICK ROAD · GLOUCESTER

First Published 1987

ISBN 0-86299-456-X

Printed in Great Britain

Contents

Acknowledgements

The photographs in this book are all taken by Nevil Story Maskelyne unless otherwise captioned. They are now mainly with dealers or in private hands, although a few Maskelyne photographs can be located in photographic museums such as those at Lacock and Bradford. I would like to thank those private individuals who gave their kind permission for me to see and record the photographs reproduced in this book. These photographs have not been captioned with technical detail because they are used here purely as illustrations to the text. I would also like to thank *The Illustrated London News* Picture Library for their kind permission to reproduce such splendidly lively steel engravings of the period (on pages 15-16, 18, 26, 36-37, 40, 44, 50, 62, 64, 66, 68-69, 78, 80, and 84); and *Punch* for kind permission to reproduce several of their inimitable cartoons (on pages 11, 41, 83 and 92-94). I would like to thank the Museum of the History of Science, Oxford University, for kindly allowing me to reproduce pictures of early chemical equipment (endpapers and pages 19 and 55) and the photograph of Brodie (page 35); and the Bodleian Library, Oxford, for kind permission to reproduce the lecture notice on page 54 (G.A.Oxon 8vo.659(2)) and the illustration from Charles Mansfield's book, *Paraguay, Brazil and the Plate* on page 57 (203 b 236). I would also like to thank Clive Cousins for kindly lending the Mackenzie engraving of the Old Ashmolean Museum, reproduced on page 46, and the engraving of the University Museum on page 147, by J.H.LeKeux.

For permission to make short quotations (from original sources which are listed in detail in the bibliography) I would like to acknowledge the kind permission of the following: Bodleian Library, Oxford; British Museum of Natural History (Mineralogy); Cambridge University Library; King's School, Bruton, Somerset; Fox Talbot Collection, Lacock Abbey; Leicester University Library; Mineralogical Society, London; Museum of the History of Science, Oxford University; Nigel and Pam Arnold-Forster; Rt.Hon.the 18th Earl of Derby (Knowsley papers); Southampton University Library; Wadham College, Oxford.

In addition to warm thanks to all those named in the text of the preface, I would like to thank the following for their kindness, advice, support or practical help: Jill Lake, John Johnson, Nick and Ros Faith, Maĩre Newton, Simon Meade, Loïs Mitchison, Penelope Byrde of Bath museum service, Jake Arnold-Forster and all my immediate family.

Preface

Peering at old photographs one day by the dim light of a Wiltshire cellar, I began to glimpse young eager intelligent faces appearing from the baskets and cupboard shelves where they were stored. The photographs had been taken by my great-grandfather, Nevil Story Maskelyne, but his name itself was daunting and the only portrait I remembered seeing of him had shown him too much of a worthy old gentleman to have awoken curiosity. Basset Down House where he had spent his dying years had long since been pulled to the ground and its once tranquil view is threatened by housing and industrial estates. However, we used to visit my grandmother Mary at Basset Down before it went. She was the second daughter of Nevil Story Maskelyne and she used to enjoy showing us the crystals and other stones with which he had surrounded himself. As a child I would watch her slender hand at a sunlit window, turning a piece of stone until it gleamed a brilliant blue or green. In her stables there still stood the old wicker bath chair in which her father had been trundled about as an invalid in his last years.

A closer look at the photographs though, showed that he had been a young man when he took them, for although there were some older academics among them, the majority of his sitters were attractive men and women in their twenties, wearing clothes ranging from the stove-pipe hats of the 1840s to the crinolines of the 1850s. When was photography invented? For all practical purposes it was invented in 1839, so this collection was very early indeed. The next question was – who were all these interesting-looking people and how did my great-grandfather know them? This was the start to the research for this book, which was to be greatly encouraged in the early stages by the Curator of the Fox Talbot Museum of photography at Lacock in Wiltshire. This well-liked enthusiast, Bob Lassam, had recently become interested in the photography of Maskelyne by finding some copy negatives of his work, so we joined forces for a while – the Fox Talbot Museum staging a summer exhibition of his photographs, for which I did what research I could in the time available.

By this time it was becoming apparent that the true interest lay not so much in the photographs themselves but behind them, in the lives of the men and women they showed. From that time on I began to search the story out, fitting in research on a very part-time basis around my normal work. This drew me into the more obscure corners of Oxford University, where I would find myself clutching huge old keys to a wooden door at the top of a spiral staircase, or maybe descending two floors beneath the Radcliffe Camera or delving into a rank, damp little chamber beneath Broad Street itself.

In Oxford I received particular help from Clifford Davies of Wadham College and also from Tony Simcock, librarian at the Museum of the History of Science, who works in the great vaulted basement where my great-grandfather spent much of his active life. There are many patient librarians in Oxford and it is very generous of Oxford University to allow readership at its great libraries – the Bodleian Library and the Radcliffe Science Library – to a few of us who have no academic qualifications whatsoever. Glancing around at my fellow library users in the decorative timbered Duke Humfreys Library, I was struck by the intense concentration of all these scholars, who had clearly read a great many books already, by the wide use of spectacles and by the sad presence of the one or two on the fringes of sanity, for whom the strain had proved too much. These libraries certainly yield up a wealth of original letters, documents and contemporary books, but Reading University, nearer home for me, held an unexpectedly rich store of nineteenth century and scientific information, and it was a retired chemistry professor, Dr Holt from Reading University, who kindly looked over the scientific part of this book, his blue eyes twinkling as he spotted 'errors' made by the early scientists, with their limited background knowledge. Dr Brock, of the Department of Victorian Studies at Leicester University, has also been an extremely helpful correspondent on the historical aspects of science.

Sometimes the quest for material has led to unexpected adventure, like the weekend when the family travelled to Lacock with tent and research notebook. Arriving in a torrential downpour, we were kindly invited to spend the night in Lacock Abbey. Thirteen-year-old William spent the night in a haunted panelled room overlooking the cloisters and was asked curiously in the morning if the nun had walked through in the night – to which he stalwartly replied that if she had he hadn't seen her. When we visited the remote Devon homestead where our friendly cousins, the Mastermans, harbour some Maskelyne letters and papers, blizzards struck across the moors, howling and beating against the thick walls all night, and we only just got away through the hedge-high snowdrifts before Devon was cut off completely.

The one place where Nevil Story Maskelyne's presence can still be readily sensed is the British Museum of Natural History, even though he never worked in the building. When I first went to see them, the current Keeper and Curator of Minerals, Dr Bishop and Mr Couper, seemed to feel themselves colleagues of his and were fully aware of his work in their department. During a lunch break from the mineralogy library, I learned more from Mr Couper about mineralogy than most people get to hear in a lifetime and I only wished there had been a tablecloth to write it all down on.

Perhaps the most dramatic moment in the research story came when most of the better photographs went to London (unknown to me at first) to be sold. With permission and with the loan of a colleague's camera and the help of a student of photography, I arranged to photograph the collection at the auctioneers' before it was sold and dispersed. It was entertaining seeing Christies' South Kensington salerooms at work, with their armies of young ex-Etonians dressed as removals men hurrying about with trolley-loads of marketable bric-a-brac. We had eight hours allotted for completing the task, spread over two days, and we were working with unfamiliar cameras without built-in light meters, perched over the corners of desks in a little office where fitful sunlight alternated with stormy gloom. We managed to record all the hundreds of items, including the paper negatives, and David Allison himself, Christies' photographs man at the time, chivalrously held his black umbrella over a daguerreotype to help reduce the reflective effect of its silvered surface.

Although in one way those were two of the most exhilarating days, because of the satisfaction of making a record of the photographs, the most fascinating picture by far has emerged through research into the characters depicted in the photographs and into their world of scientific discovery and awakening social conscience. They turned out to be just the kind of lively and interesting people it had struck me they must be, on first seeing the photographs in the cellar, but the story of their rebel radical activities, their creative frontier thinking and contribution to Victorian life went far beyond what anyone could have dared to expect from looking behind the pictures in great-grandfather's family albums.

The Silver Spoon

The shepherd's wife walked home ten good shillings richer, and well pleased with the night's lambing, for in her capacity as midwife to the scattered hamlet of Basset Down, she had just delivered Mrs Story of Basset Down House of a baby son. This child was not only heir to the Basset Down estate, but he was destined to become one of an unusual and active set of young Oxford intellectuals of the mid nineteenth century. Tiny Master Mervyn Herbert Nevil Story (whose name later became Maskelyne, derived from 'masculine') was born on 3 September 1823, only four years after the birth of Princess Victoria, his future queen, and his own life was to encompass the entire Victorian era, bringing him into contact with many other energetic and celebrated Victorians on the way.

The childhood of Nevil Story, like that of his future Oxford contemporaries, was comfortable and well provided-for, and his upbringing gives the background to the struggles in which they were all to become involved. For the time being he was securely cradled within the thick stone walls of his parents' large Wiltshire home which nestled under the escarpment, half way up a north ridge of the Marlborough Downs. Its front windows looked down over miles and miles of rich green pastureland scattered with hedgerow elms, sweeping away into the blue distance of the Cotswold hills.

The Basset Down estate had been left not to Anthony Story himself but to his wife Margaret, only child and heiress of her father the Astronomer Royal. Since their marriage in 1819, Anthony, who had no previous experience of land management, had spent four years learning to run the farms at a profit. In the year of Nevil's birth, because of this profit drive, it can be seen from Anthony Story Maskelyne's accounts that the top-grade farm workers at Basset Down actually took a drop in wages – from one shilling and threepence a day to one shilling and twopence (the top women's farm wage fell from sevenpence halfpenny day to sixpence a day) – and these lower wages were to remain constant despite rising corn prices.

While it became steadily more expensive for Basset Down labourers to buy grain from the Storys for making bread, Anthony Story was achieving bigger profit margins by selling a good deal of his grain to merchants in the late autumn and early spring, when prices were higher. In this way he benefited from the Corn Laws, a price-fixing measure which ensured that British landowners got good prices for their corn whether their harvests were good or bad, and were therefore protected from competition from abroad. Townspeople began to notice middlemen buying in grain in the autumn in order to warehouse it until prices soared, and were growing resentful with an anger which was soon to start bursting out into organized demonstrations and protests against the Corn Laws.

Basset Down farmworkers were probably scarcely aware of the influence of the Corn Laws on their own low standard of living, but all over south western Britain the labourers' earnings from the land were very poor by comparison with the squires'. Flour at Basset Down cost twopence halfpenny a pound,

and meat almost a shilling a pound so, on a daily wage of one shilling and twopence, meat was a real luxury, and there was every incentive for poaching rabbits, pigeons and rooks from the woods. Anthony Story had felt obliged to take on a gamekeeper to protect the wildfowl on his two ponds and the game in his recently planted woodlands from the forays of increasingly hungry farm workers. To make sure that the gamekeeper did not turn a blind eye to poaching, he was paid two shillings a day – far more than the farmworkers.

At Basset Down House itself, the Story family and their household of servants consumed over £13 worth of farm produce and other food every week, and went to some lengths to vary their meals by using oranges and lemons, wine, raisins, cranberries, treacle, spices and maraschino, and they set jellies in fancy moulds, preserved mushrooms and nuts and dried their garden flowers for scented pot pourri. Although Basset Down was still lit by rush lights and candles, it was heated through the winter by £28-worth of coal which arrived in a 22-ton load by canal barge at Hay Lane wharf a mile away. Little Nevil was therefore born with a silver spoon in his mouth by comparison with most of the other children of Basset Down hamlet.

Anthony Story, like other landowners of his day, saw nothing disturbing in the wide differences between his own living conditions and those of his farm workers, but his efforts to increase farm production did not so far include the kind of machinery which replaced jobs on the land. Anthony Story was an intelligent and painstaking manager of his farmlands – considering carefully whether to feed oil cake or bean flour to the sheep, to make them produce the best manure for improving their own pastures. He had calculated that he could keep eight sheep to the acre, and that 20 acres of turnips would feed 300 sheep from November to April. On the lower farms, where rich greensand soil produced lush grass, he allowed 15 of his brown and white cows to every 27 acres, with three sheep to the acre as well. Oxen were still used at Basset Down for tilling the arable land and, although Anthony Story was selling well over £1,000-worth of grain a year by the time Nevil was six, it was still being extracted from the husk by winnowing fan.

The high marketing points of the agricultural year were celebrated by festivals of eating and drinking, especially at Harvest Home in October and at

Farm people round the pond

Sheep Shearing in June. For each of these occasions Anthony Story would provide 25 pounds of beef, eight pounds of mutton, vegetables and the ingredients for a mighty plum pudding, together with ten gallons of beer from the Basset Down brewhouse, to boost the song and dance side of the occasion. As Nevil grew into early childhood, he could take to the farm path with his nursemaid, in his little clogs, hat and holland dress, to see the busy working dairy at the Home Farm, where cheese stood in vats ready for pressing and cream was skimmed from the milk for churning into butter. He could watch the fat porkers, turkeys, geese, ducks and pigeons – all of which went off to market in their turn.

The Storys' was a community life, somewhat cut off, especially in winter, by the difficulties of travelling in heavy horse-drawn vehicles along narrow rutted earth roads. Hay Lane, which ran from Basset Down to the parish church at Lydiard Tregoz, was totally impassible by family coach for much of the year, so the young Storys were baptized in the dining room at Basset Down House, with water from a magnificent blue and white delft bowl – reputed to have been a gift from King William III to the Earl of Warrington. Perhaps it was this socially pretentious side of the Storys which irritated their nearest middle class neighbour, Mrs Benet, who suddenly took it into her head to cut off Hay Lane half way up Basset Down hill, so that the Storys could no longer use it. Mrs Benet lived in Salthrop House across the lane, half a mile from Basset Down. Anthony Story ordered his man Rawlings to remove the barricade, but the affair lingered on, and the Storys had to build themselves a new road parallel to Hay Lane for a quarter of a mile or so.

Despite the isolated position of Basset Down in winter, the Story children were never short of interest, and spent much time playing cheerful childish games – in fact there were times when their exuberance had to be checked, like the occasion when Nevil was caught jumping from one Hepplewhite chair to another around the room. 'Nevil', said his father, 'those chairs may be old but they have life in them yet.' This episode, recounted later by Mary Arnold-Forster, was not to be Nevil's last brush with authority for failing to show respect where respect was considered due. The children tended their pet dormice and canaries, and Nevil was given an elaborate cage for keeping

Margaret Maskelyne aged about 12, with (top left) Greenwich Observatory (from a painting by William Owen)

dormice. They discovered the habits of the the badgers, foxes and owls in the Basset Down woods, and Nevil became interested in the abundant varieties of wild plants, including a number of rare orchids, which grew around their home on the chalky hillsides. His eyes were opened to the starry night skies by his mother, Margaret, who had been the only daughter of Nevil Maskelyne, lately Astronomer Royal. As a child, Margaret had been given a little brass orrery by her astronomer father, who helped her to use it to understand the movements of the planets. Now, gazing up through the cold crisp air of the north downlands, Nevil in his turn learned the basic calculations of astronomy from his mother. Margaret had been brought up at the Greenwich Royal Observatory, perched on top of a hill overlooking Greenwich Park and the river Thames, busy with sailing vessels. Young Margaret had met many foreign scientists, who had fled to England at the time of the French Revolution and had been befriended by the Maskelynes, and she had learned to speak and write fluent French. She had also learned to draw well in pencil, ink and water colours, and occasional sketches by her son Nevil as a boy show that he was no mean hand with a pencil himself. Margaret had been 24 when, in 1811, her father had died and she and her mother had been obliged to leave their comfortable quarters at the Royal Observatory for the old country house at Basset Down. The house and estate had originally been bought by Margaret's uncle Edmund Maskelyne, brother of the astronomer, on the proceeds of his own East India Company exploits. He lived there only four years before he died, leaving the place to the astronomer, from whom Margaret herself had inherited it. She and her mother had moved their Hepplewhite chairs, their grandfather clock and other possessions from Greenwich to Wiltshire and had started busying themselves with making jams and preserves and quantities of cheese for Marlborough market. Margaret made sketches of the local cottages and farms, taking the occasional trip to London to stay with her devoted childhood friend, Peggy Tait, the daughter of the astronomer's friend and architect who had made many structural alterations at Basset Down, to make it more comfortable.

The marriage of Margaret Maskelyne and Anthony Story in 1819 had been a union of two only children. The Storys (equally often spelt Storey at this stage)

had their roots in Cumbrian sheep-farming country, but more recent genera-
tions had gone into the Anglican Church. Anthony's clergyman father had
died at his parish of Hinton Martell in Dorset when Anthony was only six, and
the child had received intensive private tuition from a clever but eccentric
neighbour found for him by his mother in the village. Anthony was intellec-
tually gifted and he studied extremely hard, sometimes visiting his uncle, Mr
Prower, vicar of Purton in Wiltshire, for extra coaching in theological studies.
Anthony's immense efforts were rewarded with a place as a Commoner at
Oxford University at the age of 15. He emerged at the end of his four years
with a Double First in classics and mathematics, went on to study law at the
Inner Temple in London and was called to the Bar in 1810. During his time in
Oxford and London his intellectual brilliance had made an impression. He
had acquired influential friends, like the Talbots of Margam in South Wales
and Dr Buckland and the Wollastons from the scientific fraternity, and had
been elected a Fellow of the Royal Society in 1823, the year that Nevil was
born. He also attracted the interest of leading Whig politicians, whose cause
he supported, and who saw in him a brilliant young legal adviser and even a
potential parliamentary candidate. He was offered the personal help of Lord
Brougham to stand for election, an opportunity which many a young man
might have seized for its power and wealth potential. Lord Brougham's
declared aims were to fight slavery, reform the law courts and give the vote to
more people – all causes which appealed to Anthony Story, in theory at least –
but Anthony was still hesitant about treading the dangerous path of party
politics and committing himself to the leadership of the volatile Lord
Brougham. He wanted to go on being able to discuss legal questions with Lord
Brougham, but not to face the hustings himself. Meanwhile he practised as a
barrister when he could pick up jobs, and he used to spend some time visiting
his uncle, the vicar of Purton. His uncle's parish was not far from Basset
Down, which was how Anthony Story had first met Margaret Maskelyne. As
his invitations to Basset Down grew more frequent, Anthony and Margaret
took to meeting by the 'trysting tree', close to the old house, and plans were
made for their marriage.

On his marriage, Anthony Story largely gave up his promising legal career

5

The church at
Purton

and his political involvements. Although he kept up his Whig friends for
some time, and always detested 'Tory squires', he now felt free to escape from
the scheming, pushing world of top legal and parliamentary circles and – after
a childhood spent in fierce academic competition with himself – who can
blame him? In his early years of married life, Anthony would take circuit work
as a barrister for a week or two a year, travelling to Chester or Salisbury on
assignments arranged for him by a London agent. On one of these journeys
through Welsh border country, he had travelled on the top of a coach with
William Peel, a local landowner, with whom he became firm friends. After
this Anthony often stayed with Mr Peel at Taliaris, his fine old Brecknockshire
house, and resolved to buy some property in the area for himself. Mr Peel
soon found him a house with some land, called Glanwysk, in nearby spectacular hill country at Sennybridge near Brecon – a sentimental but unprofitable

Taliaris

purchase which was to give him a lifelong excuse for revisiting the Welsh hills. In the summer of 1828, when Nevil was four, Margaret Story took her children and a nursemaid on holiday to the Welsh seaside, and sketched the whole party on Barmouth sands, Anthony presumably having stopped off to cast an eye over his new property at Sennybridge. We English do like to be beside the seaside, but it must have been a formidable even though beautiful horse-drawn journey from the Wiltshire downland to the coast of central Wales.

Anthony Story still travelled up to London at intervals and, at the age of six, Nevil accompanied him on one of his habitual visits to the Lord Chancellor, Lord Brougham, at his house on Highgate Hill. Nevil found it hard climbing the hill at his father's side, but he was diverted on the way by the sight of his first railway train, which was being hauled up the slope at Chalk Farm with the aid of ropes – the power of the locomotive not being quite up to the strain. The political conversation with Lord Brougham passed over Nevil's head, but Anthony Story was just beginning to visualize some kind of future career for the child, and was glad to give him a foretaste of the exalted spheres of London life – the very spheres which Anthony had himself renounced.

By 1829 Nevil already had three sisters, Charlotte, Antonia and Mervinia, and a baby brother Edmund, but Anthony's ambitions remained fixed upon his eldest son, and he sent Nevil off the following summer to spend some months sampling London life at 89 Jermyn Street, the home of Margaret Story's lifelong friend, Peggy Tait. Anthony Story was proud to learn that Nevil was managing to cope with life away from home in Peggy Tait's kindly care, so he wrote off to one of his old fellow-students from Wadham College, Oxford, who now ran a boys' boarding school at Bruton in Somerset. This man, the Reverend Hoskyns Abrahall, took in the sons of west-country squires, and was delighted to enter young Master Nevil Story to start his education at Bruton School (now called King's School, Bruton) the following year. The school fees were going to cost the family £52.10s a year, with stationery and books a further £2, but Anthony Story was convinced that education would reap its own rewards. In addition to his everyday 'trowsers', Nevil had two new suits bought for school, and a fine 14-shilling top hat, and his mother had to spend yet another 14 shillings on getting his existing clothes mended before he went away, for Nevil was not a careful child with his clothes at home.

To reach his school, Nevil had to catch the stage coach to Bath, where he would change to another one on down into Somerset. From Basset Down, the coach could be picked up at Beckhampton on the windswept downs, and in winter the wind could be very harsh indeed, especially for boys, who were expected to travel on the outside of the coach, sitting still for miles and miles in their uncomfortable tight-fitting trousers, wrapped in a great-coat and comforter.

Soon after he arrived at Bruton School, Nevil received a letter from home – unstamped because it was before the days of Penny Postage. In it his mother wrote in a warm and comforting style, sending affectionate messages from his younger brother and his four sisters, the youngest of whom – Agnes – had been born only the previous summer. It must have been a wrench for Nevil to be parted from a big household full of well-loved children, adults and animals, to spend most of the year among a community of men and boys whom he had not met before, for he had only two annual holidays, one at Christmas and one in the summer. His mother tried to cheer him by writing about domestic details like the arrival of the beautiful new tortoiseshell kitten – 'the pet of the whole house. We think it will have long hair' – and she added, 'I am writing this with a quill from one of our own geese and it makes a good hard pen'.

In sharp contrast to this homely message was the one from Nevil's father on the reverse side of the sheet of writing paper, in which he discussed his son's Latin verse and prose compositions, urging him not to flag at his studies if his companions started jeering at him for working. 'One of the chief distractions of your life', he told his nine-year-old son, 'must be that of writing and speaking well, without it you will be fit for no great employment; possessing the facility you will always find yourself courted and sought after. Above all, work the *imagination*.' Anthony had of course been an exceptional scholar himself, and the restless energy which had once driven him to success was now being chanelled towards his eldest son, as the child's potential began to fire his mind.

When Nevil came home for Christmas, he was taken out exploring the new romantic glades and paths being constructed up the hill behind the house, where Anthony Story was employing out of work farm labourers at sixpence a day. It was a paternalistic act on his part to take on digging labour like this in the dead season when no casual farm work was available, for it saved the men from spending the winter in the despised workhouse at Lydiard Millicent – but it was not all philanthropy, because Anthony Story did in turn receive rebate from the Poor Rate for giving them the employment. Nevil's sisters showed him their Little Fanny paper dolls with their paper cut-out clothes, and they turned the pages of their big cloth scrapbook into which they had pasted new pictures of locomotives, cameleopards, flags and other cheerful subjects. They arranged him small-scale events in their stuffily-furnished doll's drawing room, peopled with miniature dolls in full dresses of checked gingham or purple satin with lace trimmings (a *lady* never wears imitation lace, the girls were told). The holidays were over all too soon, and it was time for the long journey back to school.

At the start of every school day, Nevil and his classmates rose by a quarter to seven and dressed before a large fire which had been prepared for them by servants in a nearby dressing room, before attending a 20-minute session of prayers. Breakfast was held in silence, wrote a young master at the school named Carpenter, with each boy reading a book or one of the seven periodicals which the school took in, whilst being waited on by the housekeeper and two footmen. While he was still in the junior school, Nevil's morning lessons began with portions of the Greek Testament and the Gospels, advancing, as he rose through the school, to the Acts of the Apostles and the Epistles. There was a half-hour mid-morning break for a run and, as the day advanced, Nevil would come to grips with Virgil, Horace, Cicero, Aristophanes, Sophocles, Juvenal, Herodotus or Tacitus. Straight after morning school the senior boys played games, for which they had good facilities – three fives courts, two skittle alleys, a pond for winter skating and a large cricket field. Cricket was to remain a favourite pastime with Nevil for some years after he left school, and it was gaining popularity in Britain as a whole. While the senior boys played games, the junior boys were taken for a one-and-a-half-hour walk, not returning until two for a robust dinner of regency proportions, which followed a weekly pattern. On Mondays there were pork and veal joints and cheese; on Tuesdays, roast shoulder and legs of mutton; on Wednesdays, savoury puddings or pies; on Thursdays, soup and rounds of roast beef; on Fridays, joints of boiled beef or pudding; on Saturdays, legs and shoulders of roast mutton – while on Sundays there were both cold boiled beef and a highly popular plum pudding. The boys were quite expected to take up to four helpings of the meat course as well as cheese and pudding, for not only were they all brought up to the west-country squire's well-laden board, but the masters who presided at each table were there to ply them with helping after helping of the hot food as it arrived steaming through a hatchway. In fact they took note of any boy who was unfortunate enough to take only one helping and he was 'visited with a medical mixture' the following morning. Nevil, like each of the other boys, was served a pint and a quarter of good beer – of a strength described as 'four bushels to the hogshead' – with every midday meal and, when the dinner had finished at three, he would return to his classroom studies, breaking once for a late afternoon run before working on until six, when he was dismissed formal school for the day. He was then expected to continue his private studies by dim gas light through until 20 past eight in the evening, at which point he received a 25-minute religious discourse, with prayers, before turning in for the night.

The whole emphasis was on religion, together with a sound knowledge of the classics but, while Nevil was to remain interested in Greek classical works and culture for the rest of his life, his rigorous schooldays seem to have left him less firmly convinced on the matter of religious belief. Mr Abrahall urged his pupils to apply themselves to winning prizes and scholarships for their classical studies but, after the death of his wife in 1837, the headmaster's penchant for using the cane – already well-known – grew stronger than ever, and he beat boys to an extent which would appear brutal now. He carried not one but two canes under his arm as he moved about the school; but education then was still an austere process aimed at producing god-fearing gentlemen, and the public schools at large were as yet unreformed. Only Dr Thomas Arnold, headmaster of Rugby School, was introducing such innovatory subjects as French and modern history, and using more stimulating teaching methods and a slightly more liberal school régime. Nevil's younger brother,

Edmund, was entered for Bruton School and started his schooling there, but was later removed and transferred to Rugby, while Nevil himself remained at Bruton until his eighteenth year.

Science had no place in the school curriculum, but Nevil's first prize as a small boy at Bruton was a copy of a book by Mary Somerville, scientific writer and founder of Somerville College, Oxford. In later life, writing to Mrs Somerville on another subject, Nevil mentioned that this book had turned him into 'what is called "a man of science"'. It opened his mind to the great foundation work of modern science which was being carried out at that time in the world beyond his school walls – Michael Faraday splitting molecules by means of an electric current, Charles Lyell and Roderick Murchison, British geologists, querying whether the world had really been created in six days, and the Swedish scientist Berzelius devising a system of atomic weights and drawing up a set of symbols for describing chemical elements.

All these momentous scientific leaps were being made by comparative amateurs, particularly in Britain, where the field was open to gentlemen enthusiasts who all knew each other and whose interests encompassed the entire scientific range – because the amount of knowledge so far accumulated was still not enough to demand a specialist in every scientific corner. Both Nevil's parents had a number of scientific friends, and his mother Margaret had been brought up to meet and respect the many distinguished European scientists who had come to the Royal Observatory at the time of the French Revolution. She passed on this respect for foreign scientists to her eldest son, so Nevil was never to share the disdain which many of his contemporaries felt for new scientific ideas from abroad. He was to leave school with no scientific teaching behind him, but with his alert mind open to all advances in that fast-moving field.

In the year 1840, as Nevil approached the end of his schooldays, young Queen Victoria married Prince Albert amid fanfares, street illuminations and general acclaim – even though one junior master at Bruton School referred to Victoria in a letter as 'our trumpery queen'. The winter of 1840 was very cold, as bread prices rose and the hunger and desperation of the farmworkers spread to the unemployed hordes in the few large towns. A few riots broke out, and some 250 rioters were charged and sent to Van Diemen's Land (now Tasmania). Members of the London Working Men's Association, together with some radical Members of Parliament, had drawn up a six-point charter to try and secure political reforms which would improve the position of working people. This charter asked for secret ballots, votes for all adult males, yearly elections, equal electoral districts, payment for Members of Parliament and abolition of the clause which said that candidates must own property to a certain considerable value. These points were not to be won for many years to come, but they became a good fighting basis for the Chartist movement which started up during Nevil's last years at school. News of the Chartist riots spread fast because 1840 also saw two far-reaching advances in communication – the introduction of Penny Postage and a feverish programme of railway building. This was the year that the Great Western Railway line from Paddington arrived at the bottom of Hay Lane, only a mile from Basset Down House. The weather that winter was so severe that railway excavations had to be halted at Hay Lane and the workers laid off. Anthony Story employed a few of the gangers till spring by setting them to digging a cutting for a cart track through the chalk cliff behind Basset Down Home Farm, and to excavating little flint-lined tunnels, in a rather Brunel manner, under some of his favourite woodland pathways.

Visitors to Basset Down were usually taken on a tour of the latest walks, and one such visitor was George Dollond, great-nephew and adoptive grandson of George Dollond the inventor of the achromatic lens. He came to stay at Basset Down, probably in the summer of 1840, for Nevil was at home at the time, and George Dollond showed Nevil, now aged 17, how to form simple photographic images – or 'photogenic drawings'.

Attempts to make permanent photographic pictures had been going on since about 1800, but had always been hampered by the difficulty of 'fixing' the image, which had a way of appearing in a magical manner on the chemically treated paper placed in the back of the camera, only to fade away again, or else spread until the paper was completely shaded. The problem was to find a chemical which would stop the process at the moment when the image was at its best, and keep it like that permanently. A really reliable method of fixing had not been discovered until 1839 – by Sir John Herschel, an outstanding gentleman scientist friend of Talbot's – but Henry Fox Talbot had sometimes managed to hold his images four or five years earlier, as he was later to recall in a letter to his solicitor, J.H.Bolton. 'In 1834 I discovered, or rather rediscovered, the art of photography on paper, and after some difficulty I succeeded in fixing the images. Having done so, I proceeded to obtain positive images from these negative ones by transferring them to a second sheet of sensitive paper by the agency of light. This was of course impossible to do, so long as the first-obtained or negative images could not be fixed. I was thus the first discoverer of positive photographic images. In the next year 1835 I succeeded in obtaining satisfactory views of buildings and other distant objects with a Camera Obscura, which produced a degree of astonishment in my own mind, and in those of my friends to whom I showed it, which I shall never forget.'

The camera obscura (darkened box) was a box-like device with a lens and an angled prism which threw the image of any well-lit object or landscape onto a screen within. This screen was usually translucent, so that an artist, from outside, could trace the outline of the projected image, as an aid to drawing. Nevil's grandfather, the Astronomer Royal, had possessed a camera obscura through which he could observe solar eclipses and sun-spots without damaging his eyes, and this old mahogany instrument was still at Basset Down.

The year before George Dollond's visit to Basset Down, Henry Fox Talbot's first public announcement on photography had been read out at a meeting of the Royal Society in London. The discovery of photography had been running a neck and neck finish for publication, for only a few weeks before, the Frenchman, Louis Daguerre, had been reported in the papers for his discovery of a method of obtaining and fixing pictures in his camera obscura. The difference between Fox-Talbot's process and Daguerre's was basically that Daguerre produced positive pictures upon a highly polished surface of silvered copper, acted on by chemicals in vapour form; whereas Fox Talbot produced paper negatives called 'calotypes' by applying a liquid solution of light-sensitive chemicals to the paper. Daguerre's polished metal surface gave a more finely detailed picture, the correct way round from the start, but it could not be reproduced. The ultimate advantage of Fox Talbot's calotype process was therefore to lie in the fact that many positive prints could be made from one original paper negative.

Nevil's
early
photograms

Fox Talbot was making very beautiful 'sun pictures' or 'photogenic drawings' by his calotype method, though at first he concentrated mainly on making negative silhouettes of objects by laying them on the sensitized paper and leaving them in the sun for a quarter to half an hour. Public imagination was swept up by the whole exciting concept of photography, but so many of the enthusiasts who bought light-sensitized papers or prepared chemicals themselves, were disappointed with their photographic results because they were still working to Fox Talbot's first published formula which was none too reliable for a complete amateur to apply.

It was this 'primitive form of the art', as Nevil described it, which George Dollond demonstrated at Basset Down. After Dollond had left, Nevil experimented further, trying out various papers, exposure times and strengths of chemicals. He gathered feathers dropped by the local chickens and owls, leaves from the garden and lace trimmings from his mother and sisters, and he placed them carefully on sensitized paper, under glass, fixing them afterwards with Fox Talbot's potassium bromide fixer. He managed to record the shadows of these delicate objects, which still stand out from their backgrounds of varying shades of sepia, showing subtle tone gradations within the mottled plumes and veins.

On 19 November 1840, during his last year at school, Nevil matriculated as a commoner to Wadham College, Oxford, the establishment where his paternal grandfather, his father and his headmaster had all been educated, but it then became a case of waiting until suitable residential accommodation came vacant at the college, so Nevil could not take up his Wadham place until 1842. Meanwhile, he dabbled a little more in photography, converting his grandfather's old camera obscura for the purpose, and creating a second, smaller camera from an old cigar box; but he kept being frustrated by his inability to get consistent results in his attempts at 'sun pictures'. However, his problems with photography were awakening his curiosity over chemical reactions and the physical properties of light, and his lively mind was unlikely to leave the matter there.

Wadham Infidels

As there were to be many months of waiting between leaving school and going to university, Nevil implored his father to let him travel abroad and see the world, asking him not to treat this request with harshness or irony, as he knew he easily might. 'My beloved boy,' replied Anthony paternalistically, 'I am always grateful to you for your letters, they show a manliness and a worth which I trust your coming years will prove to be not your assumed but real character. I am pleased at the very discursiveness of your imagination, which carries you over the globe on its wings . . . I am only afraid that you must wait for three years before we may hope to put your ideas into practice . . . Nor have I neither time nor money, nor could think of sanctioning your travel at your early age with anyone but myself!' Anthony did admit, though, that his own European tour, as a young man, had made him realize the extent of his own ignorance, prejudice and lack of understanding of political rights and religious questions. That tour, he told Nevil, had made him grateful for what little he knew of these matters already 'but hourly to deplore my deficiencies in book-learning, in historical research, in extensive classical reading in those studies and theories which you have yet time to make yourself master of before you need wish to travel.' Anthony assured Nevil that by applying himself to learning at his age he could find 'not only the means of acting safely and honourably with regard to the most difficult problems, but of gaining friends and introductions to the best families'. Anthony still had it in mind that Nevil should move in higher social circles, and this was largely behind his pressure on his son to achieve academic success. 'Banish from your mind as much as you can of the thoughts which tend to give a restlessness to your disposition. To excel in anything we must concentrate our thoughts and address them all to that one object. The pleasures of mere idleness destroy the tone of the mind. Imagination becomes charioteer and runs away with the judgement.' Anthony was already growing suspicious that Nevil was showing undue interest in the physical sciences at the expense of his classical studies, so he exhorted him to concentrate on the classics for the time being and turn to 'scientific lore' later on. He thought that he and Nevil might perhaps visit the continent together some day, after his university years, but for the time being he would see if they couldn't visit some sea-bathing resort nearer home.

When Nevil finally came home to Basset Down from Bruton School in the summer of 1841, he found that the railway excavations which had reached the bottom of Hay Lane the previous Christmas, had now been continued towards Chippenham. The freshly dug railway cuttings and embankments attracted a very distinguished visitor to stay with the Storys at Basset Down – Dr William Buckland, Professor of Mineralogy and Geology at Oxford University and a most dynamic and delightful man. He had come in search of fossils in the chalk beds laid bare by the railway gangs. It was a form of hunting he knew well, for he had been all over Europe looking for fossil remains, and it was he who had described and named the bones of the giant pterodactyl found in fossil form in the Lyme Regis cliffs by a local girl, young Mary Anning.

While he was at Basset Down, Dr Buckland was impressed by the 18-year-old Nevil's grasp of scientific matters, and promised to introduce him to a select scientific club, the Ashmolean Society ('Ash' for short) as soon as Nevil arrived at the university. Science was something of a dirty word among the bulk of Oxford dons at the time, so the 'Ash' existed to keep research ideas circulating privately among the small dedicated fraternity of scientists. It was the current climate of fundamentalist religious feeling which had brought science into disrepute at Oxford. Whereas a century earlier science had taken its proper place at the university, pious religious feeling was now so strong as to stultify most attempts at creative scientific thinking. Neither the high-church nor the low-church faction would countenance any scientific theory which appeared to challenge the authority of the Bible or of the Church as an institution. Since most current scientific discovery was seen to be threatening this authority, the only answer was to make sure that scientists were deprived of power by any available means. William Buckland had received both ridicule and minor persecution for his outspoken stand in the cause of the natural sciences, despite the fact that he was himself ordained to the Anglican Church. Lectures in scientific subjects were attracting fewer and fewer students, so it was no wonder that Dr Buckland was glad to find a ready-made recruit at Basset Down. Nevil, for his part, felt privileged to have met this outstanding geologist and to have helped him find specimens for his bulging blue fossil bag. He looked forward with some excitement to attending the meetings of the Ashmolean Society, even though he may have realized he was treading onto dangerous ground.

Months ahead of his scheduled arrival, Nevil had had to make an appearance at his college to matriculate. From there he had been conducted across to the imposing Senate House to pay fees, swear loyalty to the institution and subscribe to the Thirty-Nine Articles of the Anglican faith – a document which was the object of intense interest, not to say raging controversy, at that moment in Oxford. In every common-room people were talking about the

Martyr's Memorial, with the new Taylor Institute to its left

religious question and professions of faith and, above all, about the Thirty-Nine Articles. Originally, these Articles had been set down in Elizabethan times as a set of beliefs which were common to both Catholics and Protestants – in an attempt to make the newly-constituted Church of England work more peaceably. This of course meant that there was still plenty in the Articles for both sides to seize upon nearly 400 years later.

The Anglican Church in Oxford at the time of Nevil's arrival was loosely divided into two main factions. On the one hand there were the Evangelicals, heirs to the puritan Protestant tradition, who placed their faith in the authoritative word of the Bible, the preaching of the Scriptures and the personal conversion of sinners. To them, the sacraments of the church, such as baptism and the Lord's Supper, were symbolic commemorative acts. The Evangelical faction identified itself closely with the Thirty-Nine Articles of Faith which furnished much material for evangelical preaching.

The second, large and growing, faction in Oxford was the Tractarian movement, whose members placed the Church itself in the position of supreme authority. The Tractarians too put faith in the Holy Scriptures, but only in so far as the they had been interpreted by the Church and its councils, for they saw the Church as a Catholic inheritance, and its priests and sacraments as ordained means of grace.

Religious differences had been fermenting between the two factions for a decade and more, but matters had come to a head recently when Dr John Henry Newman, a leading Oxford high-churchman, had published a controversial pamphlet – 'Tract Ninety' – one of a series of tracts put out by the high church movement and avidly read by student sympathisers. In his tract, Dr Newman claimed that the Thirty-Nine Articles, so dear to the Evangelicals, were consistent with the authority of the Roman Catholic Church – a very inflammatory claim in the existing climate of religious opinion. The Evangelical enthusiasts at Oxford, heirs to the low-church squire-parson era, were totally incensed at this bid by the Tractarians to take over for themselves the very body of doctrine which Evangelicals saw as exclusive support for their own religious beliefs and practices. The Evangelical movement, egged on by the Tract Ninety troubles, had just erected a monument to commemorate the sixteenth century Protestant martyrs, Cranmer, Latimer and Ridley. It was called the Martyrs' Memorial and was the latest interesting place to take one's visitors for a walk.

The author of Tract Ninety, Dr Newman, was quite a gregarious preacher at this time, and he liked to fill his college rooms with followers and to influence undergraduates by personal example, but the high-churchman who was now taking over the Tractarian leadership from Newman was Dr Edward Pusey, Professor of Hebrew and Canon of Christ Church, a mystic who rarely appeared in a trivial social context but who was capable of filling his great cathedral church to its walls. The receptive young men found an appeal in the sermons of this ascetic and, by now, unkempt figure, immensely clever and well-read, and with a penchant for the theologies of Rome. He would pass through Christ Church College with sad downcast eyes – some said from his belief that there was no hope for the post-baptismal sinner, and others that he was still sorrowing for his late beloved wife. Dr Pusey's influence upon Oxford was very strong, and his highly intelligent writings attracted many imaginative and emotionally impressionable young intellectuals to his cause.

Nevil, who entered Oxford at the height of the Tractarian controversies, fell

Wadham College
chapel

with his feet to the Evangelical side of the fence, by virtue of his choice of low-church Wadham College, but he was destined to be influenced even more by the liberals. Tract Ninety had alarmed the Evangelicals enough to persuade them to ally themselves with this third group of religious believers, the liberals – heirs to a more free-thinking religious heritage – who emphasised the importance of men developing their own talents, being self-sufficient and ordering their own affairs. Also known as 'Broad Churchmen', they preached a life dictated by individual good sense and high moral code, and Dr Arnold, who had become known as a liberal spokesman, argued the case for religious tolerance, hating to see petty division and quarrel within the religious community. Arnold had recently been appointed Regius Professor of Modern History at Oxford, and his first lectures had been immensely popular, both for their lively and varied content and for the way in which he could bring battles and political problems right before his audience. Dr Arnold's personal popularity might have made him a useful leader on the non-Tractarian side, but he suddenly died of a heart attack even before Nevil had started his first term. After their leader's death though, Arnold's pupil's and Rugby School staff came on to Oxford inspired by his personal charisma, and they spread his liberal views. Nevil was to get to know a number of Rugby men really well, and the strength of Arnold's personality and opinions was to reach him through them.

Wadham College itself was currently a hotbed of evangelical Protestantism under its head, the Warden, Ben Symons, whose powerful Sunday sermons in chapel treated the Thirty-Nine Articles from a strictly non-Tractarian point of view. The Warden of Wadham was a large, determined man with a hearty manner, and to nervous undergraduates called to his study he appeared distant and portentous. However at the time of Nevil's matriculation, Ben Symons had decided to promote good fellowship between dons and students by starting up a 'Beef Steak Society' to hold occasional social breakfasts. (An undergraduate would normally expect breakfast brought to him in his own rooms by his scout – a personal servant). Unfortunately the warden's social breakfasts of beefsteak and sausages were sometimes found more of a strain than a relaxation.

A college servant
with one of the
'young gentlemen'

College butlers, under-butlers and other servants were mostly very stout, owing to the amount of beer they brewed for the undergraduates, and slipped down on the side. The college porter sat omnipotent in his lodge at the entrance and noted down how late the young gentlemen came in at night (they had to be in by twelve), whilst keeping out stray dogs and tradesmen by day. All the students dined in hall at 5pm, dressed in cap and gown, and would listen to a Latin grace before consuming their meat course, followed by pudding, bread, butter, cheese and beer. In the first year, Nevil drank appreciably more beer at table than any of the 35 other new entrants, so perhaps the habits of Bruton School died hard. It may be that somebody noticed his beer consumption from his college bills, and had a quiet word with him about it, for he was drinking the same as the others by his second year.

Breakfasts, as meals, varied with the occasion. The most frugal college breakfast was bread and hot chocolate, stuffed down while the unfortunate scholar sweated over his books. A 'normal' breakfast consisted of buttered toast and eggs, broiled ham, bread, marmalade and maybe bitter ale to finish with. Hospitable people like Dr and Mrs Buckland at Christ Church College gave more sumptuous parties with, for example, turkey at the top of the table, two wild ducks at the bottom, piles of muffins in the centre, and two kinds of toast; while on the sideboard there were supplies of steaming sausages, cutlets and other hot meats, and tea, coffee and chocolate to drink. Over the years, the Bucklands, who had children of Nevil's age, were very hospitable to him.

Dr Buckland's university lectures were so graphically presented that he almost brought his fossil ichthyosauri and other monsters of the past to life in front of his class, so much so that Nevil saw the creatures 'tearing each other in their slime' before his eyes. The upper floor and attics of the weighty Clarendon Building at Oxford were given over to Dr Buckland and his collections – the geological department to the left of the entrance and the mineralogical to the right, for Buckland was professor of both. He would stand in his fine classical lecture-room, surrounded by ammonites and bones, addressing a few undergraduates but also a number of dons, for whom the appeal of his subject lay in its risky relationships with theology and the Bible. Although Dr

Dr William
Buckland

Buckland had been ordained in the Anglican Church, and had long attempted to reconcile his fossil findings with the Creation stories and Noah's Flood, he was now making daring assertions about prehistory which made even Dr Pusey admit in private that the world might not, after all, have been created in six days. All through the first part of the nineteenth century, scientists had still accepted the Diluvial Theory – the belief that a great deluge of rain had occurred at one particular time, causing Noah to build his ark, and that it had been the withdrawal of this flood water which had deposited all the salt and freshwater shells, bones and creatures which are to be found as fossils in layers of clay, sand and gravel.

It was in the year before his visit to the railway cuttings near Basset Down, that Dr Buckland had been to the Jura mountains to visit a young Swiss-born scientist named Agassiz, who had been coming to the view that the flood deposits might have been formed at different dates, within geologically recent time, by the melting of gigantic glaciers. This was the Ice Age Theory in its earliest form. In the year he had come to Basset Down, Buckland had examined glacial effects in Switzerland with Agassiz, and had realized that upland boulders in Scotland showed the same effects of loosening, scratching and polishing by water – even though no glaciers had existed in Scotland for centuries. He could see that such terrain had been formed by vast shifting masses of ice and melting water. Dr Buckland, in fact, became convinced of the truth of the early Ice Age Theory, but anyone who seemed to be 'going against the Bible' in this way, by discrediting the mainstream belief in the after-effects of Noah's Flood, was of course unpopular in those pre-Darwin days, and his Oxford colleagues refused to understand Buckland's researches.

Only the scientific few were deeply interested, and they included Dr Charles Giles Daubeny, whom Buckland had mentioned to Nevil when he had been at Basset Down. Dr Daubeny was now Nevil's chemistry lecturer and he was, like Buckland, a behind-the-scenes fighter for the acceptance of the natural sciences in Oxford, where they formed no part of the university examination curriculum. Like Buckland too, Dr Daubeny had made frequent research trips in Europe, especially to the Auvergne, for he was interested in the study of ancient volcanoes, for the clues they might give about the formation of the earth. Dr Daubeny, being a true man of his time, did not stop at the chemistry of volcanoes. In addition to being Professor of Chemistry, he was Professor of Rural Economy, Professor of Botany and a Doctor of Medicine – a profession which he had practised for many years too. He lived in a magnificently placed house in the riverside botanical gardens at Oxford, where he had rearranged the garden specimens, partly after the traditional classification of Linnaeus and partly after that of his own Swiss contemporary, the botanist Augustin de Candolle. These botanical gardens held extensive hot-houses, largely donated by Dr Daubeny himself, in which grew exotic plants, including the giant Victoria water-lily.

Dr Daubeny was a small man who always wore spectacles, and one rather earlier description mentions him wearing a blue tailcoat with gilt buttons, a velvet waistcoat, satin scarf, outsize kid gloves and an excess of trailing coloured bandana handkerchief. He had even affected a collection of monkeys, but these had been let loose the year before Nevil arrived, by a roistering duck-shooting party which had passed close by along the River Cherwell. In his first year at Oxford, Nevil attended several Ashmolean Society talks given by Dr Daubeny, and heard him explain the experiments of the botanist de Candolle, who had studied the effects of light on plants, noticing that plants which were white when they grew without light in a cellar, could be turned green by shining light on them for a sufficient time. Nevil was becoming deeply interested in the chemical effects of light, but Dr Daubeny's other lectures – on the plant and animal life of glaciers and on an institution for cretins – must have been mind-broadening too. As a lecturer to undergraduates, Dr Daubeny had passed his prime, for he lacked his earlier enthusiasm of manner, and Nevil later recalled that while Dr Daubeny's lectures gave a fair amount of interesting instruction, they were well-attended more for the shortness of his courses than for their content – 'conscientious but hardly inspiring'.

Dr Daubeny's glasshouses with Magdalen College beyond

No undergraduate at that date was ever expected or allowed to touch chemicals or apparatus himself, but the lecturer would sometimes stage an experiment to demonstrate a point. The old professor's assistant was well aware that Dr Daubeny's experiments rarely went right during lectures. One week the professor held up a glass vessel and explained that it held a liquified gas, which, if he should accidentally drop the vessel, would vapourize and asphyxiate them all on the spot. The vessel at this point slipped and crashed to the ground, but nobody collapsed. 'Why aren't we all suffocated?' asked Dr Daubeny, surprised, so John Harris had to confess that just before the lecture he had substituted distilled water for the toxic gas. Nevil's own hands were burning to start handling chemical retorts and jars, and even at this early stage he was paying too much attention to science for the good of his exam results. Since the natural sciences had no place in the university curriculum, it was generally considered a waste of undergraduate time to study them at Oxford – in fact college tutors actively discouraged undergraduates from attending lectures given by science professors.

At that time, professors were employed by the university, and it should be emphasized that the university, as an authoritative body, was as nothing when compared with the colleges. The examination system, which awarded degrees, had been initiated earlier that century by a college head. Undergraduates could read for a pass degree or for an honours degree and if, like Nevil, they read for an honours degree,they were limited to reading for classical or for mathematical honours, or (like Nevil's father) for both. Mathematics was purely of the ancient philosophical kind, and instruction for these subjects was the prerogative of the colleges. Teaching was given within each college by the college's own tutors, who provided all the knowledge necessary to pass the degree examinations. Since this system placed all the power in the hands of individual colleges and college tutors, only the college tutors' lectures were well-attended. The professors were giving inter-collegiate lectures, following a system of university lecturing which had held good before the examination syllabus had first been introduced half a century before, but the college tutors actively discouraged undergraduates from attending professors' lectures. Clinical medicine, chemistry, mineralogy, geology, physics, modern languages, modern history and law all took a back seat, because they were covered in the lectures of professors only.

In 1841 Dr Ogle, the Clinical Professor of Medicine, had written a letter to Dr Symons, the Warden of Wadham, suggesting that the natural sciences should be an examinable subject for the Final Honours School at Oxford, offering a scientific syllabus which students could study openly, to the benefit of themselves and of everyone else. It was a dual power- struggle, partly between the university and the much more powerful individual colleges, but partly between the authoritarian religious Establishment and the fast-moving creative thinking of contemporary scientists, which could, it was felt, threaten the authority of the Scriptures. There were long and painful years of struggle ahead before the science and educational aims of Dr Buckland and Dr Daubeny could be achieved, and in the meantime Nevil, as a Wadham man, received all his syllabus teaching from the tutors – the elected Fellows – of Wadham College.

Although college tutors were the main teachers, they were not always able men, nor even specialized, and no Fellowships had ever been awarded to men whose attainments were primarily in mathematics or the natural sciences. In fact most college Fellowships at Oxford were open only to theologians, who had little interest in working up lay subjects like classics or mathematics, to teach to undergraduates, because they were more or less marking time until a college clergy living fell vacant, for each college was patron of certain parishes, where it could install its own men as curates and vicars. As soon as such a parish fell vacant, the tutor would thankfully relinquish his college Fellowship and teaching, to take it up, not least because it left him free to marry. College Fellows had to remain celibate. There were occasional tutors who became enthused with teaching a particular subject and did not wish to leave the university, but they usually left their colleges and took to tutoring privately. Private tutors, in fact, were so powerful a force in the exam curriculum that they almost dictated it, and practically every undergraduate relied on private tutoring to prepare him for his examinations. Tutors, both college and private, taught classics, with mathematics taking second place, but excellence in classics was the only way for an undergraduate to win any of the available university academic prizes. Nevil received about twelve hours of morning lectures a week from his college tutors – covering classics and mathematics, which included parts of Herodotus, the Aeniad and Euclid, but this teaching was all over by midday. Professors' lectures, being optional, were largely relegated to the afternoon, and some professors never lectured at all.

After lunch there was a great flow of students and dons out from the city towards the countryside close by. They set forth on foot in twos and threes at two o'clock, heading in the direction of Cowley Marsh, the Cumnor cowslip meadows, Woodstock, Applecot or Iffley lock, walking perhaps six or eight miles in an afternoon. It was important to carry on intellectual conversation whilst walking, and the botanists also profited from the outings by hunting for specimens, and generally botanizing, in Bagley Wood. There were no less than 47 well-loved footpaths over Cowley Marsh in those days, and the innumerable streams and ponds near Oxford were used for summer bathing, while a small number of enthusiasts, including Nevil, enjoyed playing cricket on Bullingdon Common. Although official athletics were unknown at Oxford,

Oxford walkers
resting,
probably in
Bagley Wood

one major high-jump feat (remembered and talked about for years by the locals) was achieved by Matthew Arnold, who leapt the Wadham College railings. An undergraduate at Balliol, Matthew Arnold was already a rising young poet and a liberal after the style of his father, Dr Arnold of Rugby. He and Nevil were two free-thinking and somewhat studious undergraduates who became friends and remained in touch with one another on and off for the rest of Matthew Arnold's life.

By no means all the undergraduates at Oxford were studious, in fact many rich young men came there with no intention of studying, and were said to use their college as 'a tavern and a shooting box'. They might or might not bother to take their degrees, but then there was always the option of aiming at a pass degree, rather than an honours degree, and following a lower level of tuition so that they were free to enjoy themselves. These members of the 'fast set' (as opposed to the more studious 'reading men') were very much part of the total Oxford scene, and Anthony Story was naturally in a constant state of worry lest Nevil should stray in the direction of the fast set. Indeed, he was growing concerned over the size of Nevil's wine bills, which were additional to the £250 paid out each year for his tuition and living at Oxford. Nevil's sisters, Charlotte and Mervinia, donated £4 and £7 respectively from their own allowances, to help their brother out, and Anthony Story arranged with an emigré friend, Freznoy, living in Oxford, to supply Nevil with good, reasonably-priced port. All undergraduates were inclined to give evening wine-parties from time to time, but those of the fast set were on an extremely lavish scale, and the tables were loaded with dishes of almonds, raisins, oranges and sweet cakes. As the students were too busy drinking to eat many of these desserts, the college servants could slip them out again, to be sold at a profit to the next wine-party host at a nearby college. Drunkenness was common, and Wadham students still remembered the night when some undergraduates returned to the college too late (after midnight), smashed the lantern to avoid being seen and identified, and all ran down the unfortunate porter in a body. Dinners of the cricket, archery and boat clubs grew very wild, and many supper-parties carried on into the bawdy song phase.

A hurdling mishap

Steeple-chasing, hurdling and horse-racing generally were heavily frowned upon at Oxford. Hurdling took place at Bullingdon Common and steeple-chasing at Abingdon and Woodstock. One of Nevil's more studious friends, George Butler of Exeter College, owned a steeplechase mare called Maria, which he was riding on Bullingdon Common one day, when he saw a tempting fence, a thickset hedge and ditch, and left the path to set his mare at it. Just as they had cleared the fence, a tenant farmer and his labourer rushed forward with pitchforks, to claim a trespass fine from George, who hastily leapt the mare over a second broad hedge and ditch, to escape, but the mare caught her foot in a wire, and George fell, dislocating his shoulder. Perhaps it was no wonder that the sport was discouraged.

Nevil had another acquaintance, Robert Mansfield, who in his first term staked £1 on a friend's horse in a raffle, and won the horse. He hunted it that season, and used to boast at wine-parties that his steed was so steady a jumper that he would cheerfully ride it over a fence seated backwards, facing its tail. A 20 to 1 bet was launched, and the next day Robert Mansfield took his friends and his horse into a field behind a nearby stable yard, smacked the horse with his hand, leant well over its tail and flew over a double hurdle. Robert used to take this horse out with the Heythrop hunt, and it shows how small and rural Oxford was, that on one of Robert's days out with them, hounds picked up the scent of the fox at Blenheim, chased it down the upper Thames valley and ran through Port Meadow to Oxford, where Jack Goddard, the huntsman, whipped off hounds close to Wadham College in the Parks. Almost the whole of that run would be through heavy urban sprawl these days.

Another popular sport with the fast set was tandem driving, which sounds harmless enough, but was considered highly dangerous by the proctors, who were (and still are) the university disciplinary officials, aided by a band of heavies known as 'bulldogs'. Tandem-driving consisted in driving two horses, one before the other, from a light dog-cart. The undergraduate left the livery stable driving only one horse, but a second horse was sent on ahead to wait out of sight, just past the turnpike out of town. As soon as the horse was harnessed on in front, the young driver blew his long straight horn, applied the tandem whip, tied in a double thong, and away they galloped, capable of hair-raising speeds. They could easily reach places like Bicester, out of bounds to Oxford students because tradesmen there had not signed agreements with the university to protect undergraduates from their own immoral and debt-accumulating habits. Fear of accidents to villagers, let alone to the reckless tandem-drivers themselves, caused the bulldogs to lie in wait near Oxford to catch any tandem as it returned at night. Robert Mansfield and his friends, however, grew wise to this, and unhitched the front horse three miles outside town.

One junior proctor was becoming exceptionally unpopular during Nevil's first year at Oxford – perhaps the most unpopular proctor ever – on account of his fury over lax undergraduate morals, houses of ill-fame, and the dangers of tandem-driving and steeple-chasing. This man was the Reverend Doctor W.E.Jelf of Christ Church College, who would accost and stop any under-graduate he suspected, on the street. The rumblings of ill-feeling generated against Dr Jelf broke out at last in a storm of abuse in that elegant building, the Sheldonian Theatre. It happened in the summer, whilst an American Unitarian minister was being given an honorary degree, after which Jelf was

Inside the Sheldonian Theatre

to be promoted to senior proctor. A small high-church faction of undergraduates swore they would halt the proceedings – first they would get the hated Jelf out of the way, by driving him from the Theatre, then they would proceed to their main target and stop the degree from being presented to that dissenting heretic, the Unitarian minister. The random mob of undergraduates outside was interested only in the first half of the plan. Once aroused against Jelf, they roared, hissed, yelled and hooted at him – while the honorary degree-giving continued in dumb-show, the long Latin oration unheard. Robert Mansfield, who had joined Nevil's cricketing set on Bullingdon Common that afternoon, leapt to his horse on hearing the distant uproar, raced to the Sheldonian Theatre, climbed up to a window and dropped down into the ladies' gallery to witness the last of the confusion.

At the end of his first academic year, summer 1843, Nevil sat his first university exams, known as 'Little-go' or, more formally, as 'Responsions'. These rituals were held in the Examination Schools, in the ancient complex of buildings which lie between the Clarendon Building and the Radcliffe Camera. After a week of written exams, Nevil had to face the *viva voce*. Four candidates a day entered the Schools for this spoken ordeal, wearing white tie and bands. Supported by friends and private tutor, each candidate in turn stood before a row of quiet fully-robed examiners, seated behind a table. The curious public, too, came in numbers to witness this free torture show, as the examiners posed cunning questions and tried to catch their victims out on points of classical criticism or theology. Private tutors usually sat in the front row of the public enclosure, keeping an ear out for the way the stern questions were falling, while young relations and friends slipped in and out of the back

Agnes Story, aged about 12

rows, lending distant moral support to the lonely undergraduate out at the front.

Nevil came out of the ordeal triumphant, for he passed his 'Little-go' and his family congratulated him – even his father was pleased. Commemoration week, in which the university celebrated the close of its academic year, followed the exams, and the Story family turned out for the event. Nevil's mother wrote at the end of May, to tell him that she and Anthony would be arriving in Oxford next Friday, together with some friends called the Simpsons, Anne the maid and Nevil's youngest sister Agnes (who was only twelve, so her head would not be turned by the presence of so many young men in Oxford). 'Do not be extravagant, dear Nevil', wrote his mother, who tended to be on Nevil's side over money and did not want him to spend out large sums of his allowance from Anthony on grand breakfasts and dinners for themselves. She told him that she was quietly bringing with her 'plenty of Vegetables, a Tongue and a Ham, a Veal Pye and a piece of Stewed Beef, all ready cooked, and some of our fresh butter . . . It is a secret between ourselves that I bring what I have mentioned, which I do to lessen your bills.' Margaret knew how tight Anthony was over money, and how easily upset over the details of Nevil's spending of his allowance, so this was her conspiracy to get Anthony to pay for the feasting from another pocket without noticing.

Commemoration week celebrations were lavish – though even Oxford University had drawn the line, a few years earlier, at paying Paganini his asking fee of five hundred guineas to 'scrape a single string' at the Commemoration week Grand Concert. The Story family had a good selection of entertainments before them – they were expected to attend chapel and to parade up and down Christ Church Meadows on 'Show Sunday', escorted by Nevil in his cap and gown, while they took note of what everyone else was wearing down the Long Walk. They could admire the flower show in Worcester College, inspect the Martyrs' Memorial, picnic at Nuneham, listen to concerts, dance at the college balls or take tea in Nevil's rooms. Nevil had paid his membership to the college boat club, which entitled him to take his family to watch the rowing eights from the ornate Wadham College barge. Robert

Eights Week

Mansfield was rowing for University College in the Eights that year, and he ate a large supper of underdone steaks and plenty of porter after every one of the eight races. On this diet it was perhaps no real wonder that he collapsed the following year during a practice for the Oxford and Cambridge boat race. The race had, incidentally, been won this year at Henley by an Oxford crew of seven against a Cambridge crew of eight, but nobody took much notice.

On a quieter note, Henry Fox Talbot paid a three-day lone visit to Oxford that summer, to photograph streets and buildings. It was a long patient task, for each shot had to be left exposed in the camera so long that although the tranquil streets were nearly empty, it didn't make much difference if anyone passed by, because they would be unlikely to remain long enough to show up on the negative. Oxford was still a backwater, with no railway station and a very small permanent population, so it only occupied what is now the central university area, surrounded by meadows and marshland.

Nevil was very interested when he saw Fox Talbot's Oxford views published that year in an album called 'Pencil of Nature', and he particularly admired the finer detail, compared to some earlier calotypes he had seen in London two or three years before. Nevil, whose enthusiasm for photography was increasing fast by 1843, had started accumulating materials and equipment for himself. By mid-January 1844 he was running up considerable bills with an Oxford chemist, for equipment which included spirit lamps, blowpipes, scales, crucibles, evaporating dishes and a large Liebig condenser, as well as a large variety of raw chemicals, amongst which were a few which he must have been using for photography – like gallic acid, acetic acid and potassium bromide. He was also buying chemicals and photographic sundries from another chemist, Edward Palmer of 103 Newgate Street, London, from whom he acquired a booklet on 'photogenic manipulation' on 15 February 1844. Mr Palmer was already sailing rather close to the wind, for Henry Fox Talbot had taken out a patent on his photographic process exactly two

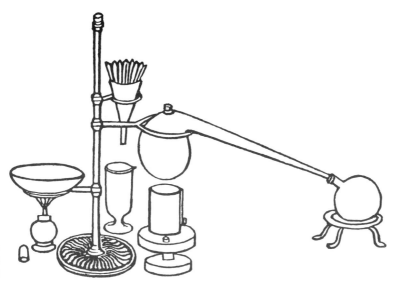

Some items from
Mr Palmer's
catalogue

years before, and was battling to ensure that everyone who used his process paid him fees. Here was Mr Palmer using the process without licence, instructing his customers in its use and selling papers prepared to the Talbot formula – as Talbot was to discover to his great irritation some time later. Nevil, however, found Mr Palmer's booklet extremely helpful in explaining how to achieve more success with his photographic prints. In September 1844, he read an article by George Cundell, in the *Philosophical Magazine*, suggesting a way of improving the camera obscura for photography, by using two symmetrically placed lenses, instead of one. Cundell was highlighting

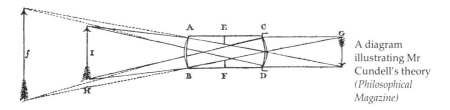

A diagram
illustrating Mr
Cundell's theory
(*Philosophical
Magazine*)

the problem found with the early saucer-shaped (meniscus) lens used in the camera obscura, which was that, while it gave a good flat appearance to the picture, it produced a blurring at the edges of the photograph and a slight distortion to shapes, because not only did the edges of the lens focus in a different plane to the middle of the lens, but each coloured wavelength of the light spectrum was also – after passing through the curved lens – focusing at a different point. Cundell's article further suggested that the distance between the two lenses could be varied, for focusing purposes, and that a blue filter medium could be used to fill up the space between the two lenses – for shortening the focal length and for absorbing the red and yellow wavelengths from the light spectrum, so that they could not distort the picture. Cundell's article was theoretical, but Nevil resolved to attempt to put the ideas into practice. Anthony Story, meanwhile, can hardly have welcomed the news that Nevil owed the chemists over £20 by the end of February. According to family lore, Nevil carried out his experiments in his college rooms at Wadham but, since most colleges specifically disapproved of such chemical activities, on safety grounds, he had either done some fast talking to the college authorities or he had greased the palm of his scout. He also opened up a laboratory for himself in a small room in Basset Down farmhouse – perhaps even more of a fire risk, because it had a thickly thatched roof.

In his second year at Oxford, Nevil was invited by Robert Walker, a Fellow of Wadham and an able mathematician, to attend his lectures on optics. Nevil wrote an enthusiastic letter to his father (who would have to foot the bill for the lectures), telling him of the invitation. Anthony Story seemed pleased to hear about it and commented that the new subjects Nevil would be tackling would complement one another and that he was glad Nevil was already familiar with some of them – 'even with Optics you have coquetted not unsuccessfully'. Anthony began to hope that Nevil was becoming less of a 'thoughtless idler' and might even be throwing off his boyish habits of 'inattention and wanton carelessness'. Even so, he could not resist exhorting Nevil to read up the subject before listening to Mr Walker's lectures, and 'I entreat you to take the most copious notes at the time he delivers them, and not to suffer your attention to be diverted for a moment from the professor.'

Anthony recalled the 'hair-brained fools' of his own young day, who failed to pay attention to lectures and whose fate it was to leave university 'as ignorant as when they came up, and more conceited'. Anthony hoped that by writing firmly enough, he might keep Nevil from such a disastrous end. In the case of Robert Walker's lectures he need not have bothered, for this cheerful speaker could attract whole roomfuls of students to his lectures on experimental philosophy and hold their attention without difficulty. In his lecture room in the Clarendon Building, he would form gases and then explode them in front of the class; he showed the inner workings of pumps and steam engines, forced mercury through wooden blocks in a vacuum, and operated galvanic batteries, magic lanterns and airguns before his students' astonished eyes. Robert Walker was a professor and he was, like most professors, also a member of the clergy, an Evangelical preacher of standing, but his energetic and capable science teaching must have given Wadham College a certain advantage in this field.

Another very able Wadham tutor, who arrived in Nevil's second year, was Richard Congreve who had been a master, and before that a pupil, at Rugby School under Dr Arnold. He was brimming over with liberalism and with enthusiasm for broad-based study. Congreve had travelled widely and was widely read in the European literature of the day, interested in foreign politics and involved in French intellectual circles. This was a rare set of interests for an Oxford academic, for continental points of view, if understood at all, were usually frowned upon at that time. Most tutors concentrated solely on the examination syllabus, but Congreve – himself a most industrious man from morn till night – urged his students to increased activity on a much broader front. He encouraged them to read, to assess what they read and to form judgements on people and on the political events of the day. His attitude was that nobody should work simply for the sake of an examination. 'What a bore examinations are', he wrote to his wife, 'when as up here a man's whole future seems to depend entirely, and undeniably does in a great degree depend on the result of them'. Rather than cramming students with examinable facts, Richard Congreve aimed to get the students to train themselves to

Richard Congreve

ask the right questions and to get into the habit of expressing themselves in a straightforward way. His own teaching methods consisted mainly in questioning, suggesting and stimulating further enquiry among the undergraduates. He taught a Thucidides class that year, amongst other classical studies, but he avoided theological matters. Congreve was a thinking Christian himself but, like so many of Dr Arnold's disciples, he thought so liberally that he was already veering towards his own brand of humanism. Nevil found a good deal of sympathy with Congreve and his ideals, and he and most of the rest of the Wadham undergraduate population were swayed by the fervour of this dignified but compelling young tutor. That year, reports W.R.Ward, the studious undergraduates at Oxford – the 'reading men' – were described as belonging to either 'the classical set', 'the religious set' or 'the infidels'. This last category, the infidels, were further subdivided into 'Rugby men' and 'Wadham men'. It is clear that the influence of Richard Congreve was behind the inclusion of Wadham men among the infidels, and Nevil was a willing infidel. Congreve encouraged his students to look around them and take in the difference between their own position and that of the thousands of unemployed people who existed all over Europe in those days of widespread depression. Improvement in the social and working conditions of these deprived people had been among Dr Arnold's ideals, but Nevil and his Wadham contemporaries were probably being faced with such socially-conscious thoughts for the first time. It was also growing easier for them to grasp the extent of the poverty and deprivation in remoter parts of the country now that the railway network covered most of Britain.

In 1844, even Oxford was at last connected with London by rail, and a distinguished academic from Europe took this opportunity of travelling to Oxford to see the scientific work of the university. Dr Carl Gustav Carus, professor to the medical college at Dresden and physician to the Court of Saxony, was appalled at what he saw. *Jackson's Oxford Journal* reported his visit to the Old Ashmolean Museum, where Dr Daubeny's lectures were held, and also the Anatomical Theatre at Christ Church College, which, wrote Vernon, he declared to be so hopelessly primitive as to be reminiscent of the time of

Vesalius – the early sixteenth century 'father of modern anatomy'. Dr Carus' condemnation of the science facilities at Oxford (which had only produced about two successful medical students a year for over a decade) was rather a shock in several quarters. Whereas Edinburgh, Aberdeen and London universities were pulling out ahead on the science front, progress in Oxford had been stultified for years by the political power of the high church movement – ever fearful of the consequences of the overthrow of church authority on interpreting Holy Scriptures. It was not only the high church movement either, for the ultimate power at Oxford lay with the voting members of the university governing body, the Convocation, who were past members of the university and also mainly dyed-in-the-wool low church country parsons. They would flock back to Oxford in vast numbers once every few years, to vote in Convocation against some particular motion which had been rumoured to smack of change or reform, and they were certainly suspicious of any move to establish science on a firmer footing at the university, because of the view that science threatened the authority of the Bible itself.

At the outset of Nevil's final year at Wadham, there was excitement over the election of a new university Vice-Chancellor. On hearing that Ben Symons, Warden of Wadham, intended putting himself forward as a candidate, the Chancellor himself – none other than the noble Duke of Wellington – entered the lists straight away in Symons' support. Indeed the duke, who thoroughly approved of Symons, said that he would resign his own post as Chancellor if Symons' name were not approved for the list of candidates. It would have been interesting for university politics if the duke had resigned, but it did not prove necessary. The reason the affair loomed so large was that it had become, as usual, a high church versus low church issue. Dr Symons was effectively the leader of the Evangelicals in Oxford, an obvious choice from the point of view of his standing, his reputation for fair-mindedness and his seniority, but he was a real red rag to the Tractarians, who had not forgotten last year, when Symons had been a member of a committee of Doctors of Divinity called to judge the content of one of Dr Pusey's sermons. Pusey had been accused of romishly teaching 'the Real Corporeal Presence of Christ' in the sacraments, and the committee found this to have been, indeed, the case. As a result, Pusey had been suspended from preaching to the university for two years and had accused Ben Symons of trying to throw him out of the Anglican Church (all of which Symons stoutly denied). It is not surprising that the Tractarians, led by Pusey, Keble and Newman, now threatened strong action against Ben Symons' election, but the Wadham tutors, catching wind of the Tractarians' intentions, put out notices 'to Wadham men and others', rallying support for Symons on 8 October. In the event, 'Big Ben' gained a 669 majority, became Vice Chancellor, and caused Wadham College to start its academic year with celebrations. A few months later, Dr Newman 'went over to Rome' and the religious controversy, which had almost burned itself out, gradually took a less prominent place in university politics.

Nevil started his own academic year under the shadow of the imminent final Honours Schools, for which he would be sitting examinations in April. Although Richard Congreve spread the philosophy at Wadham that study was for learning, understanding and evaluating, rather than for examinations, Anthony Story took the opposite view, particularly as the final day approached. He kept writing to Nevil, to urge him to his books and, as soon as the first examinations were over, he exhorted his son to make the most of his

Anthony Story
Maskelyne

last few days and hours before the next ones. He even recalled his own Oxford finals, 'I had but 38 hours between my first and second examinations, those in mathematics. Everybody said "Refresh yourself" but I worked 22 hours out of the number, going through every formula and puzzling myself in all the diagrams in the books as much as possible. I was describing the last of the trajectories of Sir I.Newton's Principia as I was passing under the gateway into the schools', and Anthony added, 'I beseech you, let not an hour be lost, nor imagine that any more precious time can be yours . . . Pray, pray, lose not a minute in the idle courtesies of life.' It must have been daunting facing those last few days under such parental pressure, but Anthony could not resist the final words – 'I need not say that I shall be on the rack till I hear of the issues of your examination.' Quite what he felt when he heard that Nevil had gained a second class degree in mathematics, we shall never know.

After sitting the examination in April 1845, Nevil returned to Oxford for the summer term, in order to finish serving out his residence in college and so qualify for the degree of Bachelor of Arts. Nevil's horsey friend Robert Mansfield had his mother and elder brother Charles staying in Oxford that summer. This elder brother, Charles Mansfield, had gone to university late and was in his final year at Clare College, Cambridge. It was in Charles Mansfield that Nevil was to find a true kindred spirit and a lasting friend, for Charles too was thoroughly given to chemistry and chemical experiment. He was soon to start a course at the recently opened Royal College of Chemistry in London – an opportunity which Nevil would dearly have liked for himself, and no doubt discussed with his father. Anthony Story had however already decided that Nevil should become a successful barrister and that he should study law in London, by reading for the Bar at the Inner Temple. Robert Mansfield had just been enrolled to read law at Lincoln's Inn, nearby, and Charles would be at the Royal College of Chemistry, so Nevil was to see much more of the Mansfield brothers over the next few years.

Creative Thoughts

Even before Nevil had taken his degree, Anthony wrote to him to announce that from now on the whole family were to add Maskelyne to their surname and be known as the Story Maskelynes. Anthony expressed himself sad that his own name was to be 'spunged from the record', but he had signed an undertaking when he had married Margaret Maskelyne, saying that he and his heirs would take on his wife's family name when their eldest son came of age. This was because the estate was in Margaret's name and it had been felt right that the name Maskelyne should remain with the heirs of the estate. Nevil was now 21, so he became known as Story Maskelyne, or just Maskelyne to his friends. Double-barrelled surnames were rarely hyphenated until late in the nineteenth century, by which time the family started being addressed as the Story-Maskelynes.

It is not very likely that Nevil was given his continental tour with his father when he left university in 1845, however he spent a good deal of time on photographic experiments in his little laboratory room in the thatched farmhouse at Basset Down. It was only a hundred yards from the big house, just along the hill to the west, close to the chalk-walled farmyards, the cowsheds and byres and the great thatched barn. It was only one of a number of farms owned by the Story Maskelynes in north Wiltshire, where the Maskelyne family had farmed since the Middle Ages, and Nevil went about with his camera, making calotype photographs of local scenes.

Nevil's pictures of life on the farm in the mid-1840s give a somewhat idyllic glimpse – not the whole picture, it could be argued – for the pay of farmworkers had been especially poor in the south-west over the past decade and the labourers were still deeply embittered at the attitudes of the free-spending

Basset Down
farmhouse, home
of Nevil's
laboratory

sporting squires, with their business-like sons who had been introducing machinery to replace men. In protest, labourers in some areas had sometimes been known to creep out at night to wreck a threshing machine or winnowing machine, or burn a hay rick, but they had no power to do more.

Indignant town workers, incensed at the price of bread, had been holding anti-Corn Law meetings throughout the 1830s. A Wadham College undergraduate named Maclaine who had slipped into one of these meetings in Oxford Town Hall shortly before Nevil had come up to the university, had reported that he had found himself among 'numerous highly respectable but very dirty individuals' and that a Town and Gown brawl had broken out after the meeting. This was certainly not the only riotous scene which had flared up around the Corn Law issue, and it was all leading towards a genuine people's movement of protest against a wider spectrum of grievances – the movement which manifested itself in 1838 as Chartism.

The Chartists began to attract a large following from the crowds of north-country working men who were dissatisfied with the way they were being exploited by their middle-class employers, and these Chartists were in turn joined by anti-Corn Law rioters and by the destitute unemployed men from the bigger towns, who were angry at the Poor Law system which forced them to take to the workhouse as the only means of assistance available. Disgruntled early trades unionists also supported the movement, and the flames of protest were fanned by extremist articles in a popular paper, the *Northern Star*, edited by Feargus O'Connor, a self-promoted campaigner for the Chartists. Although the agricultural workers of the south-west of England were among the poorest paid of all, this urban industrial movement had little impact among them. Basset Down farm workers were little better off than they had been for 15 years and still found it hard to rise to a loaf of bread every day, but Anthony Story Maskelyne was giving his own three daughters a monthly allowance of £5 each by this time, as well as providing them with their silk dresses and bonnets, and with all the accessories to the life of a young lady – the harp, violin and piano, the drawing paper, paints, embroidery materials and the visiting cards for their social calls.

Anthony Story Maskelyne had not joined the squire fraternity of north Wiltshire, being no sportsman, but despite his liberal and anti-slavery background he was as paternalistic towards his labourers and tenants as the rest of them. While he was interested in improving his farming methods, by trying out fertilisers like 'bones mixed with sulphuric acid', and was installing a good rotary butter churn, his view towards the farm people seemed to be that they were there and always would be, blending into the landscape in their picturesque smocks, bonnets and straw hats, just as Nevil photographed them.

Nevil was wishing that these photographs of his would come out clearer and with more detail, so in December 1845 he took the bold step of writing to Henry Fox Talbot himself, to beg for personal advice from the inventor of the calotype process. The letter was written in tones of abject politeness, for Fox Talbot had patented his photographic process only two years before, and was known to guard his patent rights most jealously. Nevil put himself over as a young gentleman amateur, 'dedicated to photography' but unable to achieve the results he knew he should be getting from Mr Talbot's great invention. By way of gentlemanly credentials, he added that he was grandson of Maskelyne, the Astronomer Royal. The tone of the letter had been correctly pitched, for Henry Fox Talbot encouraged him to ride over to his home at Lacock Abbey, to share photographic knowledge. It was a 20-mile ride from Basset Down to Lacock, over exposed downland, but once he had clattered into the Lacock Abbey stable yard Nevil was in sheltered and civilized surroundings. The Fox Talbot's family home was a vast rambling stone house built over the cloisters of a mediaeval nunnery. The windows of the galleries looked out over damp lush meadows, laced with streams, and the inner windows looked down onto the cloister lawn.

Henry Fox Talbot was a careful man who held himself slightly aloof, and though he doubtless showed Nevil a number of interesting things, he does not seem to have given him much practical help with his photography, for Nevil later recalled that the one person who helped him at that stage was Nicolaas Henneman, the Dutch manager of Fox Talbot's new photographic establishment at Reading. Henneman had been a servant at Lacock Abbey before starting up at Reading, and he had learned all the tricks of the art from his master, together with some more from his own experience. When Nevil visited Henneman in Reading, he was shown some of the refinements which could be made to the calotype process and his technique was greatly improved. He also bought a new camera from Henneman, one of a consignment just arrived from the French lens-maker, Chevalier, and he was still using it ten years later.

Today, as we lift some little micro-chip marvel of a camera to our eye, press a button and send the film off for processing, we might well spare an occasional thought for those toiling pioneers of the 1840s. Nevil's own account of the current method of producing a photograph, written out in his 1847 manuscript scientific paper, illustrates what a struggle it was, but anyone unable to face suffering the experience with him should skip the next five paragraphs. He used the calotype process because it was still the only practicable way to take pictures, apart from the daguerreotype which, although popular with professional studio photographers, was out of Nevil's reach financially since it needed special silver plates and major machinery to polish them. To make a calotype paper negative he took a sheet of writing paper, washed it over with 30 grains of silver nitrate to one ounce of water (twice as strong a solution as Fox Talbot's), dried it and then drew it through a solution of potassium iodide – one ounce to a pint of water – working by weak daylight, until the paper was a pale yellow. He then dried the paper with blotting-paper, soaked it in clean waters and dried it again, ready to be kept until needed.

Shortly before putting the paper into use as a negative he would sensitize it with silver nitrate (50 grains to one ounce), a saturated solution of gallic acid and some pure acetic acid. The amounts of the acetic acid varied according to the temperature of the weather and the sensitivity of the paper he wanted – 'for portraits and most sensitive purposes – half part acetic acid – one part Nitr. Silv. plus one part Gallic acid.' That preparation had to be used soon after application to the paper. A less sensitive preparation, which allowed the paper to be kept for some hours and taken out on forays to photograph landscapes, involved 'six to ten parts of gallic acid, plus one part of silver nitrate, plus one to three parts of acetic acid (more in hot weather)'. The light-sensitive liquid was left on for half a minute, or less if there was less acetic acid in it, and then dried with blotting paper and a roller.

The first stage completed, the great moment had arrived for the paper to be transported to the scene of the photograph, lifted from the darkness of its carrying-box and placed in the back of the simple box-like camera, for exposure to the subject. When the paper was lifted out of the camera, after many minutes of exposure, there was the exciting prospect that it might already carry a very apparent image of the subject it had been aimed at. In this case Nevil would develop it in one part of silver nitrate to three parts of gallic acid. When it was at 'maximum effect' Nevil plunged the paper into water, left it there for a quarter of an hour and then washed it over with a solution of potassium bromide (20 or 30 grains to one ounce of water). He then soaked it yet again in water, where it was necessary to 'keep it so half fixed till ready'. Finally it was fixed by soaking it in a nearly boiling solution of hyposulphate of soda (four ounces to one quart of water), 'to remove the yellow tint that still remains in the highlights of the picture'. Nevil did achieve very good high-lights, but the time and energy involved in all this must have been daunting at times, especially when one realizes that he had so far made only the negative.

For producing positive prints from it, it was perfectly possible to prepare papers in exactly the same way as for negatives, Nevil however recommended a less sensitive and therefore more manageable process, which he called the 'Nitro Chloride of Silver process'. For this he used a paper called 'Common blue wove', because it was coated with a size which became involved in the breakdown of the chemical compounds. He first soaked the paper for a few minutes, until thoroughly wetted, with a solution of sodium chloride (about 50 grains in a quart of water) – a preparation which gave this type of paper positive the name 'salted print'. Once the salted papers were dry they would keep indefinitely, but when shortly to be required for use, they were washed again with a silver nitrate solution of about 70 grains to the ounce. After this second wash the papers would keep for up to three days, or longer in cold weather. Nevil himself favoured 'a pretty modification of this second wash', whereby, instead of plain silver nitrate, he prepared 'ammonio-nitrate of silver, i.e. a solution of Nitr. Silv. to which ammonia is added until it just redissolves the precipitate which it at first throws down. By this means we get a darker picture and a more speedily formed one.'

The prepared picture was set in a frame in the sunshine, with the negative laid face down on top of it, and left there for from 20 to 25 minutes. The image, explained Nevil, should be fixed by being 'soaked in nearly boiling water for a quarter of an hour or so and this repeated four times, the last containing a very few grains of salt. Then plunge it into hyposulphate of soda of strength about three ounces in three pints of water, until it turns of a yellow tint and seems more or less fading. Then it should be removed and soaked in about three more waters in which it cannot lie too long.' All this near-boiling water and plunging sounds a bit drastic, but his results show that he knew what he was doing, for Nevil was undoubtedly producing better quality calotype prints

A successful calotype made in the mid 1840s

than most of his contemporaries, and his chemical knowledge must have been the key to his success. He was using more acetic acid than required by the standard Fox Talbot process, both to sensitize the papers and to develop the image, and his ratios of gallic acid to nitric acid were higher too – giving a more sensitive paper, which led to a blacker picture and a faster development time. These qualities were particularly useful in portraiture, as Nevil pointed out, because the chemicals needed less light to start them reacting, so the sitter had to hold the pose for less time in front of the camera. This must have been a great encouragement to a lively and gregarious young photographer like Nevil, who enjoyed making portraits.

He was also trying out the idea of printing up copies of pictures in startling blues and purples, using copper sulphate and other chemicals, but the problem which taxed him during the early summer of 1846 was that nobody's contemporary tree photographs really showed up the details of foliage. Nevil was irritated by this, because it meant that trees had to be photographed when bare of leaves. When covered in foliage, thay came out virtually black on his paper negatives, and virtually white on the positive paper prints. He knew well that his chemicals would only blacken under blue-violet light from the short-wave end of the spectrum, so he realized that trees were giving off excessive amounts of short-wave light, which he put down at that stage to the green colour in trees, since it was not then understood that trees in sunlight gave off heavy amounts of ultra-violet, which blackened his chemicals most of all. Nevil knew about ultra-violet but he had just not connected it with his problem, however he was well aware that the foliage of trees gave off large amounts of infra-red, which he called 'the extreme red'; though he could have had no idea that this was due to the chlorophyll in growing foliage. He decided to try to cancel out the blackening effect of the blue-violet short-wave radiation, by means of the 'extreme red', by using the 'Herschel effect'. This was the recently discovered quenching effect of longer-wavelength light on a photosensitive surface which was afterwards exposed to shorter-wavelength light. Nevil realized that out of the three salts of silver available for photography, only silver bromide was at all sensitive to radiation from the red end of the spectrum – the longer wavelengths – and by experiment he believed he had found it to be faintly sensitive to even the 'extreme red' beyond visible light. He therefore sensitized his paper with silver bromide, exposed it to sunlight (pure white light) for a short time, exposed it to the subject for rather longer and then developed it in the dark, to bring out the latent image – the continued blackening of the silver bromide due to radiation effects which continue in darkness. When the tree image was fully black the Herschel effect took over, and the 'extreme red' radiation actually reversed the process, until the darkest part of the picture started to lighten again, showing up the mid-tones of the leaves. At this point Nevil would stop the process by fixing the paper negative. The positive print he made from it showed up the mid-tones of foliage, instead of leaving the tree a white blank on the print. Nevil was also experimenting with colour filters, following Mr Cundell's article which he had read in the Philosophical Magazine some time before, and he found that a green liquid medium behind the lens prevented the solarization – or sun-dazzle effect – of bright objects; also it seems that he may have been applying a green or yellow filter half way through his tree exposures, to exploit the Herschel effect more efficiently. That summer he took quantities of experimental tree photographs at Basset Down, including several studies of the avenue of elms along the Roman Walk – a footpath which led from the farmhouse to the back of Basset Down House.

Nevil moved to rooms in London that autumn of 1846, but this did not mean that he had been paying very much attention to his legal studies, and nor had Robert Mansfield. Robert had attended his compulsory weekly dinners at Lincoln's Inn regularly enough during his last term at Oxford, but had since been off on a six-month continental tour with friends; while Nevil had spent the time reading up the latest in scientific developments. In early October 1846 Nevil managed to get down to Southampton to attend the great scientific get-together of the year – the annual meetings of the British Association for the Advancement of Science, and he received favourable comments from the few people there to whom he showed his tree photographs. A prominent speaker

PROFESSOR SCHÖNBEIN.   DR. DAUBENY, F.R.S.   DR. FARADAY.

Personalities drawn at the 1846 British Association meetings

at these meetings was Professor C.F.Schönbein from Basle, who introduced a new substance he had just discovered, called guncotton because of its explosive nature. It was formed from cotton – wrote Thomas Graham, a contemporary chemist – reacting with nitric acid 'in the presence of sulphuric acid'. Professor Schönbein had sent a cup made from his guncotton to Michael Faraday's laboratory in London. The guncotton had been dissolved in ether solution, poured around the inside of a cup, to coat it, and left till the ether evaporated. The explosive cotton material had now been formed into what was in fact the first-ever plastic cup. The following year the dissolved guncotton was to be used in America for sticking wounds together, as an adhesive film named 'collodion', and it was to have even wider implications in a few years time in the field of photography. Nevil saw the plastic cup when it arrived at Faraday's laboratory, and described it as 'transparent as glass and of the texture of goldbeater's skin'.

That autumn and winter, 1846-7, Nevil haunted Michael Faraday's basement laboratory at the Royal Institution when he could. Faraday was a sensitive person, who had been seriously ill with a mental stress condition

Michael Faraday
(photographer unknown)

ever since Nevil had left Bruton School, but he emerged from his illness at intervals to carry on his brilliant individual experimental work on light, magnetism and electricity. The previous summer, Faraday had at last managed to get back to some serious research on polarized light – light which has been reflected off a surface such as glass, at a certain angle. He wanted to show that polarized light would show stresses and strains if placed within a strong magnetic field, so he passed a light beam through a piece of heavy glass placed between the two activated poles of an electro-magnet. Sure enough, the plane of polarization of the beam of light was rotated when the beam of light travelled through the glass parallel to the lines of force of the electro-magnetic field, and it rotated more and more, the stronger the magnetic force. From this he concluded that magnetism and light were indirectly related, but he did not believe that magnetic forces acted on light directly – only through the medium of a material such as glass.

Faraday had also discovered late in 1845 the general principle that all matter responds to magnetism either by setting itself along the direction of the magnetic field of force, or at right angles to it. The attracting and repelling effects of magnetism were well known, but to demonstrate 'diamagnetism' – as he called the acrosswise alignment – Faraday suspended a bar of specially made optical glass on a six-foot-long thread, between opposite poles of a powerful electro-magnet. When the current came on, the bar set itself *across* the magnetic field, not in line with the two magnetic poles, as ordinary magnetic substances did – 'paramagnetism'. Although he was never to discover it himself, Faraday was hot on the trail of the electro-magnetic theory of light, particularly in his 'Thoughts on Ray-Vibrations' of 1846, in which he boldly suggested that radiation – the effect of rays – was 'a high species of vibration in the lines of force which are known to connect particles and also masses of matter together'. Faraday did not share his discoveries with others until he was sure of them himself, and he had first shown his magnetism of light experiment quietly to a few friends, in his cellar laboratory, a few months before Nevil came to live in London.

Anthony Story had hoped that by separating Nevil from his scientific

Oxford friends he had placed him in an atmosphere of single-minded devotion to the law. Nevil had found rooms at 2 Elm Court, right at the heart of barrister country, and under the shadow of the Inner Temple itself. Nevil was the dutiful early Victorian son, and he studied law, but at the same time he was reading up the latest theories of French, German, Italian and Swiss scientists, who were thinking fast and receiving more encouragement from their universities and governments than British scientists. Nevil followed their work when he could find out about it – not always easy, because their continental upstart notions were often disdained by British academics and did not always reach British journals.

Living in Elm Court, Nevil was within easy walking distance of central London and could visit both Faraday and Charles Mansfield without difficulty. Charles Mansfield had been studying at the Royal College of Chemistry under Professor Hofmann – himself a pupil of Liebig – since the spring, and was already applying his inventive genius to his experimental course work. Charles was a very intense and compelling person, full of childlike charm and a brilliant talker, but with a deep and passionate intention towards life by comparison with his younger brother Robert, of the horse and hound exploits. Although slightly built, Charles Mansfield was athletic and very active, always planning and working out problems, and alert to new ideas on any front – mediaeval science interested him, and birdwatching, religion, magic – in fact some subject was always playing in his mind. Everyone who met him noticed his high brow, his particularly bright eyes and his immense powers of concentration, and Nevil, like all Charles Mansfield's friends, was immensely attracted to this gentle but eccentric young scientist. They used to discuss chemistry together, and Charles was able to refer Nevil to a number of useful journal articles which he had come across during his studies at the Royal College of Chemistry.

London was a much smaller place to live in then, recalled Robert Mansfield, and the ride from Kensington to Putney, for example, was through leafy country lanes. A turnpike gate stood across the road from where the Albert Hall now stands, and you paid your toll before riding on past the few big houses and the fields of hay, in the direction of Kensington. Robert Mansfield, riding back from a ball at three one morning, found this turnpike gate shut, and earned ten shillings in stakes from his companion, young Baron Huddlestone, who had foolishly bet Robert that he would not jump it. Parties and balls were popular, the polka having come in as a dance only two years before, and Nevil was sociable enough to join in when he could. Grand dinner-parties were thrown by the London rich, and Nevil's most socially acceptable hostess must surely have been his godmother, the Duchess of Northumberland, who at the time of Nevil's birth had still been governess to the young Princess Victoria, now queen. The duchess was a distant cousin on the Maskelyne side, being a grandaughter of the Astronomer Royal's sister. Her husband, the Duke of Northumberland, was currently Chancellor of Cambridge University and a Trustee of the British Museum, so he would have been a very useful contact, had he not died the following February! With his godmother, however, Nevil remained a favourite. The keynote to the really successful London dinner-party at that time was a mahogany dining-table polished to a mirror-like finish by footmen, who whisked off the tablecloths at the end of the meal but before the dessert stage, to reveal the result of their hours of polishing, radiant under the candlelight.

Westminster Abbey

One of the most hospitable of London households was that of the Bucklands, who had moved to Westminster from Oxford that autumn of 1846. Dr Buckland had recently been appointed Dean of Westminster by Sir Robert Peel, but he still travelled back and forth to Oxford to deliver lectures in geology and mineralogy, because he was still professor of both subjects. He and his family lived in the deanery, a spacious house opening into Westminster Abbey. One of the sons, Frank Buckland, was a friend and contemporary of Nevil's and had just started a training in surgery at St George's Hospital. He used to enjoy taking his old Oxford friends along to watch surgical operations being performed at St George's – in fact this seems to have been a favourite London spectacle for those in the know. Robert Mansfield rather fancied he spotted Louis Napoleon among the spectators, on one of their operating-table visits with Frank. The deanery was open house to the scientific fraternity in London, who used to frequent it in numbers to discuss their new ideas or demonstrate findings to one another. The Bucklands still gave numerous breakfast parties, as they had at Oxford, and on Sunday they threw large luncheons, when Dr Buckland would entertain the whole company with amusing stories and forward-thinking imaginative ideas. Nevil, who was often at the deanery, later wrote of him that 'Dr Buckland's wonderful conversational powers were as incommunicable as the bouquet of a bottle of champagne, but no one who remembers them, as I do, can ever forget them.'

Faraday used to frequent the deanery too, and the young Bucklands used to bring out their pets, to the amusement of the assembled company. Frank kept an eagle on the abbey roof, where a number of their managerie animals were caged, and there were tanks of fish, lizards and snakes in various parts of the house. William Harcourt, founder of the British Association for the Advancement of Science, who had been experimenting with the use of chloroform as an anaesthetic, came to demonstrate its effect on the Buckland pets, 'Bird, Beast, Reptile and Fish', before his fellow luncheon guests, which must have been an unusual mealtime entertainment, even for the Bucklands, who liked to have their pets about them. Despite its high-powered social life, the deanery had no connected water supply because there was no water laid on in

41

London homes at that period. Looking down from their windows onto Dean's Yard below, the Bucklands could watch crowds of water-carriers arriving all day to draw water from the well which was supplied from a spring arising in Hyde Park. The men, women and children fetched water in pitchers or in two buckets slung on chains from a wooden yoke across their shoulders.

For Nevil, visits to the Bucklands were interludes of light relief from the study of conveyancing in his tutor's chambers. Robert Mansfield too, complained that he spent many weary hours in the cellar chambers of his first law tutor, without much profit. However some of their other Oxford contemporaries were reading for the Bar with rather more relish – among them Thomas Hughes, author of 'Tom Brown's Schooldays' and a good friend of Matthew Arnold's. Anthony Story Maskelyne, discerning Nevil's restlessness, had suggested he might satisfy his scientific cravings by collecting material for a biography of his grandfather, the Astronomer Royal. With this partly in mind, Nevil decided to buy a large camera, photographic chemicals and six sensitized-paper holders, from a London supplier, so as to try and photograph the moon, which would be in a favourable phase just after Christmas. A moon photograph would be a useful illustration to his account, because a mountain of the moon was actually named 'Maskelyne' after his grandfather – who had first described it. The Astronomer Royal had spent many years in the observatory perched up on the hill at Greenwich, puzzling away at mathematics, and observing the movements of planets. Over the years he had compiled the Nautical Almanac, a manual which had at last given sailors an accurate means of navigation. In those days, shipwrecks had taken an appalling toll of lives and vessels, and the almanac was to make a huge improvement in safety at sea. The astronomer's mathematics had also enabled him to rig up a neat little experiment for weighing the earth, which had involved hanging plumb-lines one on each side of a Scottish mountain.

Photographing the moon required a good telescope, and Nevil was put in touch with what sounded like the right instrument, in Bath. Just after Christmas 1846, he took the train from Wootton Basset to Bath, where he was to stay with Mr and Mrs Lawson at 7 Lansdowne Crescent. This elegant façade was to set the scene for what was presumably the first attempt at moon photography. Nevil had to scale the roof, in order to set up Mr Lawson's huge telescope and locate his grandfather's mountain, which was hard to see anyway, being rather an insignificant excrescence by comparison with earthly mountains. Nevil drank mulled wine with Mr and Mrs Lawson before going up to start his moon watch on the roof. 'I am very snug here waiting for the breeze,' he wrote home. 'Three o'clock New Year's morning. There I was taking the diameter of the moon whenever I could get a squint at her, and the first minute and a half I can get a clear view of her Majesty I shall have her picture of the size of an inch and a quarter in diameter. Eventually I hope to have it four times the size with this noble telescope – only my good friend Mr Lawson knows nothing of mathematics and I know nothing of his lenses, so I have to take practical measures of the focal lengths, and to do this I must have either sun or moon. Precious little of either have I had yet. However tonight or tomorrow the atmosphere must clear, as the Barometer goes down so fast and the Thermometer remains up, and then I hope to have got the apparatus ready and to work. We must construct a paste-board cone and apply it to the concave lens that fits into the telescope, but as yet I have not got the proportions of the curves of the lens and am in rather a fix about it. However I will not despair of

Lansdowne Crescent, Bath, with the telescope showing above the roof of No.7

getting it up in readiness, but the old gentleman is very touchy about his apparatus and I can scarcely do anything with it but through his fingers, which are not very handy now. I hope to be home on Thursday and shall be much disappointed if I do not bring the moon with me.' This, however, was not to be, for the moon photographs were a complete failure, and Nevil was afraid of what his father would think. He wrote to his mother, saying, 'I do not write to the Govenor 'cause I suppose he is very indignant at my bad luck. Tell him however with my love, that he need not be angry on account of expense for my whole expense will be covered by 15s, and I have saved him more than that in *grub*.' Nevil asked for the chestnut horse to be sent to Wootton Basset station to meet him on his ignominious return on Thursday.

After that vacation he returned to London determined to write just one scientific paper himself – setting out the position of photography in relation to what was currently known in chemistry and physics. He scrawled down ideas on sheets of paper and every now and again he would slip along to Regent Street and leave some sheets with his friend Charles Mansfield, who would scribble suggestions or arguments in even worse writing alongside. Nevil wrote his 1847 manuscript paper – which still exists in private hands – at the time when the foundations of modern science were just being laid, but when there were still many concepts which had not been sorted out, so they were exciting and puzzling times for anyone interested in the frontiers of chemistry and physics.

Chemical symbols as we know them had first been used in England almost 15 years before Nevil's paper was written, but they had been adopted slowly. Formulae could show the type of a compound but not the way the atoms were arranged, since it was not thought possible to find this out, nor were the relative numbers of atoms in a particular compound known. So in written formulae, any one compound could be expressed in several ways. One of Nevil's favourite developers was diammine silver hydroxide which is now written $Ag(NH_3)_2{}^+OH^-$, which he expressed as $HNO+Ag\ NH\ Cl+HO$, which may have meant that he prepared it by adding an excess of ammonia to silver nitrate solution. Nevil was writing at a time when momentous discoveries were continually being made in chemistry, but the rules of the game, as it were, had not yet been drawn up. To begin with, there was confusion between atomic and molecular weights, for although Avogadro's law of 1811 had provided a basis for measuring both, it was little used until much later, when in 1860 a national congress decided to bring order out of chaos. Nevil who was still only 23, was writing his paper in the early spring of 1847, when there was still no conception of the structure of organic compounds. It was not until seven years later, in 1854, that August Kekulé, sitting on a London bus, was to imagine carbon atoms joining up in chains, and was to put his daydreams onto paper that night in his journal – the 'atoms all whirling in a giddy dance and the larger ones forming a chain, dragging the smaller ones after them'.

When Nevil was writing, the relative weights of atoms had been calculated but not proved, and it had been established that a fixed weight of one chemical was needed to react with another. However, nobody yet understood the relationship between the weight of one type of atom and the space which that atom took up, which made life very confusing for scientists, since atoms of similar weights have very different volumes. Nevil was also writing six years before anyone had arrived at the concept of valence – the idea that each atom will only combine with a fixed number of any other type of atom. All these limitations in their working knowledge made it hard for scientists to see the need for balanced equations, and certainly some of Nevil's assumptions were inaccurate for this reason. For example, he followed a popular scientific misconception in thinking that water could be expressed by the formula HO (rather than H_2O) and he thought that water could be broken down by light into single oxygen and hydrogen atoms, but that the single hydrogen atoms so formed were more reactive than normal hydrogen.

Nevil was familiar with the experiments of Sir John Herschel and of Mary Somerville, made in the previous two years, which showed that certain vegetable juices and chemical compounds were more readily decomposed, or broken down, under the influence of particular rays of the light spectrum. These coloured rays, corresponding with the hues of the rainbow, could be isolated from sunlight by shining that white sunlight onto a glass prism, through which each different colour-wavelength was bent at a different angle. Nevil had of course been experimenting with photographic chemicals the previous summer, trying out the silver iodides and bromides to see which reacted more to the red end of the spectrum and to what is now known as infra-red. Since the beginning of the nineteenth century it had been known that radiant heat came in wavelengths shorter than visible violet light. Nevil suggested that some animals might even be able to see this light beyond the visible spectrum – an interesting idea that was later shown to be correct. He used the analogy that certain animals are sensitive to sounds outside the range of the human ear.

Nevil pointed out that although all the rays of the spectrum, both light and 'heat-power', might be uniformly directed at a chemical substance, some of the wavelengths would be absorbed and others transmitted by (reflected off) the substance. He considered that this meant that only a narrow waveband of heat or light energy effected a reaction in the molecules of the substance, causing them to decompose. Since the chemical decomposition varied in different substances, under a uniform energy source, Nevil argued that there was no reason why the energy source should not be causing 'diverse mechanical action' too – 'exciting the molecules to regroup themselves in various ways', as they did during the formation of crystals. He felt that the property of chemicals to react in a particular way to certain wavebands of light must be 'caused by the molecular form of that matter and in many cases, probably, the character of its atomic constitution'. He also believed the action of the various light rays to be different in degree only – 'producing very similar effects to those of a current of galvanism of very feeble intensity and of small quantity'. Remembering the limited knowledge at that time, it is surprising how near to the truth his ideas were.

Nevil was sure that it would one day be proved that infra-red wavelengths were affecting the chemical changes which took place in the dark during the 'latent development' of the photographic image. He also noticed an analogy between phosphorescence (the after-glow started up in certain crystals by light but continued in the dark) and the glow between two electrically-charged charcoal points, which shine on in the dark after the electrical charge has been removed. The similarity which he observed was that the energy could 'alter the molecular structure' by, for example, 'imparting a more or less crystalline structure', but it was not causing chemical change in the sense of breaking down the molecules. Nevil, like his old chemistry lecturer, Dr Daubeny, went against the main stream of English scientific thought of the day, by following Dalton's atomic theory. Nevil considered that chemical changes took place within the molecule when some condition conferred 'a more or less polar character, and so a state of unstable equilibrium to the atoms', making it easier for them to part, at which point 'a considerable accumulation, so to speak, of Actinic force' was required to complete the decomposition.

In his 1847 paper Nevil used the word 'actinic' to describe the mysterious force at work within sunlight which caused chemical change. He had his suspicions as to the nature of the force, but could not come out with any theory which he could actually prove. He could show that the force could be provided by an electric battery, a heat source or a light source (the force of light observably 'decreasing as we go down the spectrum') and he knew from experiments by Melloni that the more intense the source of energy, the higher or lower the position of light or heat rays in the spectrum, and the greater or less the chemical change they effected. Nevil also noted that heat rays effected more change the nearer they approached the red end of the spectrum, while light rays had their strongest effect towards the violet end of the spectrum – 'the one principle increases inversely as the other does', the maximum effects of either being beyond the ends of the visible spectrum.

Thinking about photography, Nevil had already surmised that the effect of sunlight in the breakdown of chemicals was 'a force very analogous in many

Nevil Story Maskelyne with his hand on a camera (photographer not known)

of its effects, indeed so similar as to be almost identical with, electronic action.' Electrolysis, the splitting of molecules by electric current, had been in use for nearly 40 years, so Nevil was familiar with a number of the chemical effects of electricity and, since he believed that the atoms which compose each molecule were held together by 'the synthetical force of chemical electric affinity', he believed that they must be parted by electricity too. The idea that the atoms which compose each molecule were held together by electric force had been put forward a good decade earlier but had been discarded by most English scientists in the 1840s, largely because it could not be proved. Nevil thought that the energy content of light acted as a catalyst in effecting chemical change, since it was too weak to cause the change on its own. The word catalyst had come into chemical terminology ten years before, to describe small amounts of chemical which lessened the forces binding atoms together, to the point where they were ready to part. Nevil noticed so many exact parallels between the action of electric current and the action of light, that he was seriously wondering if the effects of light were not actually electric, or at least whether the forces of heat, light and electricity would not prove to be three forces 'produced and brought into play' by the one solar beam. There were so many analogies which he saw in his experiments. In the galvanic battery, for example, electricity produced 'secondary decompositions' which exactly resembled similar tendencies in certain chemicals, when exposed to the sun, to decompose and then re-form as new compounds. Another parallel lay in the readiness of particular salts to decompose under either electrolysis or light. This tendency, he noticed, corresponded with the position of each salt in what was known as the ascending salt radicle series, and from this he concluded that the force in light had exactly the same effect as a 'current of Galvanism of very feeble intensity and of small quantity'. Nevil saw a similar set of parallels between the effects of heat and electricity, 'that what we call caloric effects in fact are actinic, shall we say electric, effects'. He was of course putting forward an idea which he could not prove, so he crossed out most of his more interesting and audacious thoughts, which were to be left out of the subsequent abbreviated printed version of the paper altogether, and remain only in the manuscript. 1847 was not the moment for a young student to put forward a theory which contradicted the current scientific climate, especially when he had no proof.

By no means every scientist at that time had been convinced, like Nevil, by the theory of light waves, or the 'undulatory theory', as it was called then. The light wave theory assumed that each different colour in the solar spectrum of light is travelling in vibrations of different wavelengths and frequencies. Nevil considered that the visible red rays were long waves of high frequency – 'longer than ·000167 of an inch' and vibrating about once in every 458 billionths of a second. The visible violet rays he understood to be short waves – 'less than ·000026 of an inch long' and vibrating at a lower frequency of about one wave every 727 billionths of a second. His calculations were based on approximations arrived at some twenty years earlier by the scientist Fraunhofer, who had invented an ingenious method of examining the light rays of the spectrum, using a prism, a special grating of lines, and what he described as a telescope. Nevil tried this too, and he observed the famous pattern of spectral lines discovered by Fraunhofer, which corresponded exactly with the rainbow colours in their correct order. Nevil recorded this pattern of lines on photographic paper, but when he tried recording them through light passed through vapours of iodine or bromine he saw that they appeared in inverse order – the lines at the violet end of the spectrum now appeared last, if at all, when they would, without the vapour, have appeared first and strongest – and the thicker the vapour the more pronounced the reversal, so he suggested in his paper that it might be due to the vapour absorbing particular wavelengths of light (rather than transmitting them), and he added, 'I allude to this, as any suggestion that may throw a light on these mysterious bands has its value.' He had noticed an effect – that certain vapours absorb light – even though he could not explain its cause. It was not until two years later, in 1849, that the scientist Jean Bernard Foucault was to show one of the spectral lines (the D line) to be due to absorption.

Nevil mentioned in his paper that the energy content of a heat wave depended on the heat source, and that the higher the intensity of the heat source, the higher the frequency of the heat wave, and he added that 'here, as in electric phenomena, quantity is the measure of the number of rays, while intensity is the measure of the Quality of the rays.' He was very interested in the observation made by the scientist Edmond Becquerel, that a furnace could heat a substance like metal to a point where it emitted light as well as heat; that the heat had to exceed 1075 degrees fahrenheit before light became visible, and that the wavelength of the visible light shortened in ratio as the heat increased. Nevil wrote that the power of a spectral ray to effect change increased in ratio to heat and also, inversely, to light. He believed that infrared rays with the power to effect chemical change 'emanate from all the bodies in Nature, under ordinary circumstances, since all such bodies are capable of emitting heat'. He had also been led to the idea that substances are able to 'absorb light, more properly actinism, and to radiate it to one another in the dark'. Nevil was letting his pen go here, and thinking as he wrote, for he was describing light and actinism (the power to effect chemical change) as one and the same thing.

Sir John Herschel had put forward the theory in 1840 that sunlight is composed of three separate kinds of rays – heat rays, light rays and rays capable of effecting chemical change. Nevil preferred to see these rays of Herschel's as principles of the 'one solar beam', rather than as separate rays. He wrote that while he had great respect for Herschel, he thought the theory insufficient to account for the varied effects which energy of different wavelengths could have on different substances. The undulatory, or wavelength, theory gave him the idea that there might be 'two classes of undulations' – 'caloric' and 'actinic'. In unison, he thought, these two classes of undulations – or waves – could produce the power to effect chemical change, and in unison they could also produce light, but the light was stronger 'where the principles are equal, and weakest where either is in excessive or deficient proportions'. He had even come round, by the end of writing his paper, to the idea that light and 'actinic force' – the power to effect chemical change – were one and the same thing, but just perceived as two different effects 'caused by the same force, and even I may say by the same undulation'. His thinking had by now reached out as far as it reasonably could without stumbling on an electromagnetic theory of light. His perceptive imagination had taken him to the frontier of current knowledge and a little beyond. Fifteen years later, and armed with some knowledge of the forces at work inside the molecule, James Clark Maxwell was to apply mathematics where Maskelyne had applied imagination, and was to prove the relationships between electricity, light and magnetism.

That spring, the pressures were being steadily maintained on Nevil by Anthony Story Maskelyne, whose ambitions for his son had by no means diminished. He was, after all, investing money in Nevil's legal training, whether Nevil liked it or not, and he was determined to see a handsome reward in terms of filial success. Nevil was avowedly poring over points of law in his chambers, Anthony having instructed him to 'give up the scientific part of the pursuit', but there was no doubt that it was still science which held his creative thoughts and attention.

The Mirage

Who else should Nevil meet in London that March of 1847 but Fox Talbot himself. 'Yesterday in the street', wrote Nevil to his father, 'I met Mr Fox Talbot. At first we were polite and distant. I told him of my improvement in the process, and also of a little notion of mine of using a green liquid medium in the camera to prevent the solarization of bright objects. This tickled his fancy, and he shook hands with me, saying "I congratulate you upon that thought, it is one of the most ingenious ideas I ever heard of. Work it out, it is well worth it." . . . He was pleased so much at my idea that he has ever since been most kind to me. Murray, Faraday's assistant, said he never saw him treat anyone so before.'

Henry Fox Talbot was so taken by Nevil's creative approach to photographic science that he took his arm and led him off to visit Sir David Brewster, who was staying in London for a few days. Henry Fox Talbot was a good friend of Sir David's, and they kept up constant correspondence about photography, so much so that Sir David described St Andrew's, the Scottish university where he was principal, as the headquarters of photography, second only to Lacock Abbey itself. St Andrew's University, which had been built up largely by Sir David's own enthusiasm, was one of the more progressive academic centres in Britain at that time. Sir David was a kindly person who had been the first scientist to isolate red, yellow and blue as the three primary colours, which he had done by using Fraunhofer's method to analyse white light superimposed on light polarized through a sheet of mica. Sir David remembered the kindness with which he had himself been entertained by Nevil's grandfather the Astronomer Royal, to whom he had had a letter of introduction when he had first come south to London as a young man.

Sir David Brewster

The Roman Wal

Sir David Brewster and Nevil Story Maskelyne had two or three hours of conversation on scientific subjects, and the older man must have been deeply impressed. Nevil wrote to his father to tell him of this interview, but he was careful to open in a casual tone upon a subject which he knew could infuriate his father – 'which I mention to you more for your pleasure than thinking you will view it seriously. Sir David begged me to call upon him this morning with my pictures. I have done so, and since showed them to Fox Talbot. They both say they never saw such photographs in their lives. Sir David Brewster was charmed with them. Talbot's favourite was the little view of the Roman Walk. He says it is a Gainsborough in beauty so I gave it to him. I shall send him the negative tomorrow, with my compliments.' Nevil was thoroughly heartened by Sir David's approval and interest, and began to think he could succeed at science, but even he was astonished at the professor's next suggestion. 'He told me that the Chair of Natural Philosophy at St Andrew's, the college he has lately raised so much, is vacant', and Nevil went on to explain to his father that Sir David had actually suggested that he should apply for the post. The new Professor of Natural Philosophy was due to be elected by the eight existing professors, and Sir David, as president, had an extra casting vote. Sir David Brewster firmly promised Nevil his own two votes and had already secured him the promised vote of another of the professors, who happened to be in London. Nevil only had to persuade two more professors to vote for him and he would be elected. He had already been invited to go up and inspect the university, meet the professors and, if he liked the post, advance his cause by canvassing for their votes. The only serious opponent for the chair was John Couch Adams who had recently discovered the planet Neptune, but he did not have Sir David's support, and was in any case believed to be angling for a post at Cambridge. Nevil, beside himself with excitement, wrote in almost desperate vein, trying to convince his father of the attractions of the job. 'The salary is £350 at the lowest, to increase as my time at the college increases. 6 months in the year I am at liberty, from April 27 to Nov 4, . . . I am to give 2 hours a day in lectures, Saturday and Sunday quite to myself – apparatus found me – 10 days vacation at Christmas . . . the library is a fine one, and Government give £680 annually to its improvement. In fact Government have been rebuilding the whole thing and Sir David takes it up and is its principal. Such is his offer.' Nevil was writing as if he already had the post – for he knew it was the sort of job he could really throw himself into, in the much more liberal academic atmosphere of Scotland at that period. He couldn't believe his luck at having such an offer, together with the promise of powerful backing for election to the post. What was more, it would give him unlimited access to scientific equipment, with which he could set about trying to prove some of his more advanced theories on light and energy. He explained to his father that he would be expected to give courses of lectures in 'Mechanics, including Statics and Dynamics, together with their subdivisions, Hydro-statics and Hydrodynamics; Optics, which is my strongest point, whether practical (including Photography and Polarization) or theoretical; Pneumatics and Acoustics (which are my weakest point); Electricity and Galvanism, and not least Astronomy.' He had to teach all these subjects as applied science, rather as Robert Walker taught science at Oxford, but with a better salary, and with far more time for his own scientific and experimental work. He felt justifiably confident that he had done enough groundwork in most of the subjects and would enjoy working up the areas where he was weaker.

There was just one major stumbling block still to be negotiated – the attitude of Anthony Story Maskelyne. Nevil already foresaw the reaction at home. 'You and mother may burst out laughing if you like', he wrote bitterly, and he knew that what his father feared most of all was loss of social standing and respectability. 'I expressed a hesitation on the grounds of my friends, and the people who respected my family, not liking my sinking into the grade of a professor', explained Nevil tactfully, but he tried to improve the social appeal of the post, by pointing out to Anthony that in liberal Scotland professors were not relegated to the 'middle classes of gentility', but received into society 'with marked distinction and respect'. Nevil assured his father that the present professors, including Sir David Brewster himself, were very anxious to improve the tone of their several chairs. They wish to have *gentlemen*, even who have seen some society and of general information, filling them, and the liberal salaries, coupled with the cheapness of living at St Andrew's (with all its wild and beautiful sea scenery), enable them to do this. The neighbourhood is the best in Scotland.' In a last desperate bid to show Anthony the social acceptability of the place, Nevil added that 500 gentlemen had their names down as members of the St Andrew's hockey club. What more could his father want?

Nevil had, however, judged the situation only too accurately, and Anthony Story Maskelyne was not impressed. He wrote back, telling Nevil that he was not to contemplate such a post – the indignity to the family would be unthinkable – and he set out instead the attractions of a steady and well-paid legal career, leading to the life of a gentleman worthy of inheriting the Basset Down estate. Anthony was the head of the family and, like the father of any early Victorian family, he expected an attitude of deference from his son and heir. Nevil had told his parents that he would abide by their decision on his future career.

On 20 March 1847, he wrote back a dutiful letter, in which his anger and frustration were thinly veiled. 'You have and mother has, expressed each your opinion. The die is cast, the pretty little mirage is vanished'. Nevil, torn between filial respect and the bitterness of total frustration and despair, wrote 'You, from greater age can see further into the future than I can, and therefore, of course, draw better conclusions as to the far future. Your last resource, however, of an expatriated judge, is not a very entrancing one'. He saw that he would have to give up science and experiments, and devote 'years of unwearying heartbreaking labour' to the pursuit of the law. 'I shall sell everything in my laboratory for which I can get money, so that temptation shall be taken away, and the little rough room in which I have spent so many and successful hours shall be dismantled . . . My camera shall be my sole scientific companion, yet not a scientific one, I shall only make it an artistic one.' He added that he would probably be in Wiltshire on or before Good Friday, and would be spending a day or two on some experiments for his

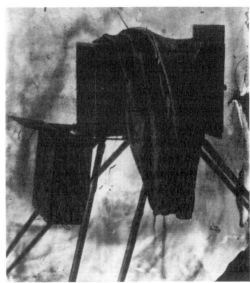

The large camera, fitted with its box

scientific paper, since he had already been asked to read it to the Ashmolean Society in May. He said that the paper was to be his swan song in the scientific world, and would foreshadow future developments in physics and chemistry.

After that he would have to face up to the years of legal studies and turn his back on his scientific interests – for the sake of the family name and fortunes. Naturally, he had been so involved in scientific circles up till now that there would be temptations – in fact his thoughts were already being distracted away from his law books by anticipation of a major scientific event, the summer meetings of the British Association for the Advancement of Science. Not only was this the big event of the year for British scientists, where they could spend several days hearing and sharing each other's most exciting research finds, but the 1847 meetings were to take place in Oxford itself. All Nevil's friends and heroes would be there and it was obviously already an event of enormous importance and emotional involvement to him, but he realized that his father would prefer him not to get mixed up with the scientific fraternity again. Out of a sense of duty, he resolved at first to try and stay away from the meetings.

The final temptation came when he was actually invited to present some of the ideas from his paper 'on the bearings of photography on chemical philosophy' to an afternoon meeting of the British Association, and a strong factor behind his decision to accept this invitation was the support he received from his mother. As the daughter of the late Astronomer Royal, who had spent all the earlier part of his life devoted to science and mathematics but very short of money, Margaret Story Maskelyne was in a position to understand the frustrations of her scientifically-minded eldest son. She could even act as something of a buffer beween Nevil and his father. As so often happened when he was under stress, the letter Nevil wrote home from Wadham College in June was to Margaret alone. 'My dearest Mother. The first day of the meeting is over and it is twelve o'clock at night on the floor of my bedroom here that I am writing this to you – to thank you for making me come, in spite of my own intentions.' He lived in Wadham College during the two weeks of the British Association meetings, and he told his mother that he had already spent part of the first day taking active part in a scientific debate involving photography. He had taken up the argument on behalf of Professor William Grove, a scientist who had been obliged to leave the debate in mid-stream, for an appointment. Nevil found himself floundering a bit to start with, trying to argue with Robert Hunt, author of the main photographic text-book of the day. However Nevil gained confidence as he went along, and was able to finish by proving the point which Professor Grove had tried to make – for which he received applause and some admiration. Robert Hunt came up to Nevil after the debate, saying that he had not realized the grasp he had of the chemical theory behind the use of silver bromide, which had been under discussion; so Nevil showed him the tree pictures he had taken at Basset Down, which Hunt 'at once declared to be better than any he had done or seen, although he had experimented with the same substances'.

Professor William Grove, who had abandoned the debate to Nevil, was himself a photographic enthusiast and a very capable scientist, and had earned the unstinted admiration of Faraday for inventing a battery (a nitric acid voltaic cell) which could produce from within its single cubic foot of apparatus a current of electricity as strong as that previously produced by a whole roomful of equipment at the Royal Institution. More recently he had invented a gas fuel cell battery, producing electricity straight from pairs of gases whose atoms, when constricted under certain chemical conditions, would burn and produce heat. William Grove had also become known for his recent work on the idea of one kind of physical force being convertible into another, and he would have loved to have continued working as a scientist – in his post as Professor of Experimental Philosophy at London University – but the pay of a professor was not nearly enough to support his wife and growing family. He had originally trained as a barrister, and this summer he reluctantly returned to the law, specializing mainly in patent cases, which often proved awkward because he kept noticing ways in which the patented invention could be radically improved, rather than concentrating on fighting infringements of its patent rights. Grove was a shrewd but rather introspective inventor, and his friends considered that he was a better scientist than barrister.

During the meetings, wrote A.H.Miers later, Faraday stayed at Wadham College with Nevil, who 'shewed Faraday what he had never seen before, the development of a photograph taken of the college from my window, a development from the absolutely white paper into a sharp and brilliant little negative.' The photograph was of the college quad, and Nevil reported that Michael Faraday's 'joy was that of a boy', on seeing it developed. 'He was my guest in the college at the time and next day he said he would return the compliment by shewing me two diamonds . . . which had been burst into cauliflower-like coke by forcing an electric current through them.' Faraday had been delighted to receive this package of carbon, brought by hand from the great French chemist Jean-Baptiste Dumas in Paris. Faraday rather hoped that it might some day prove possible to convert this coke-like carbon back into diamond again, but he realized that the experiment already represented an important discovery for science. He demonstrated the carbon to a British Association gathering on the Saturday at the end of the first week, but the following Wednesday he returned to London and was seized by faintness and confusion in the head, which forced him to put aside his researches and retire from society for yet another spell. Nevil presented his own paper 'on the bearings of photography on chemical philosophy' on the Monday of the second week and it was apparently well received.

A number of Nevil's former lecturers were at the meetings – Buckland, Daubeny and Walker, as well as Professor David Baden Powell, who used to give him lectures in mathematics. Baden Powell, now an elderly man, had been one of the best mathematicians and optics experts of his day, with particular interest in the undulatory theory and the dispersion of light. His students saw him as a lecturer with a total lack of physical energy, vitality or even ability to move a muscle, but on occasion he had proved alarmingly adept at outwitting even the brightest and most hardworking of his pupils, and he used to toss off highly successful sketches in a deadpan manner. At the British Association meetings, Professor Baden Powell had chosen to speak about shooting stars.

As well as being an academic high point of the scientific year, the meetings were a great social gathering. Prince Albert dropped in himself for a time, and the Prince of Canino – Lucien Bonaparte – came as a philosopher, and named a new species of bat. Baron Bunsen, Prussian envoy to London, had come to Oxford to read a paper on languages, and while he was there he held daily breakfast, lunch and evening parties, at which dukes, bishops and professors

Professor David
Baden Powell

mingled freely with the poorer students. This liberal style of continental entertainment was not familiar to class-conscious Britain, but it was very popular with the scientific fraternity. Baron Bunsen had brought with him a clever free-thinking young German called Max Müller (whose first name was Friedrich, but who was always familiarly known as Max - part of his surname). Nevil was almost exactly Max Müller's age, and they were to find that they were living close to one another in London. Max Müller had found rooms in Lincoln's Inn Fields when he arrived in London, and was studying ancient Sanskrit manuscripts belonging to the East India Company. Nevil was very sympathetic to continental ideas and lines of research, after the influence of Richard Congreve, his Wadham tutor, but theirs was still a contrary attitude to the one taken by most English academics just then. Nevil was to grow very interested in Max Müller's liberal views and the novelty of his largely uncharted research field – covering the developing relationships between the languages and legends of different cultures, and how one language grew out of another.

It was during the British Association meetings too that Nevil got to know Benjamin Brodie, already an accomplished chemist, and the son of an eminent surgeon of the same name – Sir Benjamin Brodie. Young Brodie, six years older than Nevil, was a man of presence and class, heir to a knighthood and used to having his way. He had gone to Lincoln's Inn after graduating, but had given up the law after a year or two in favour of science, which had interested him more. Nevil had heard him read a paper to the Ashmolean Society in 1843, but the following year Brodie had gone off to Germany to study in the laboratories of the already famous Justus von Liebig (whose name lives on in Liebig condensers), a charming and aristocratic scientist and a good friend of Ben Brodie's father– which had no doubt furthered the study visit. Liebig had long been a friend of Dr Daubeny's too, for they had both been made professors of similar subjects in the 1830s and their interest in the agricultural sciences had grown together. In 1839, just before Nevil had come to Oxford, a new faculty had been opened for Liebig at Giessen, a town to the north of Frankfurt. Young science-struck Britons flocked out, if they could afford it, to join the many German students studying under Liebig, whose methods and apparatus were achieving rapid progress in the field of organic chemistry. The 'Chemical Halls' at Giessen were hives of activity from morning till night – filled with future professors and with young industrialists eager to apply Liebig's methods to manufacture. Students came from every part of Germany, but one hall was almost entirely given over to British students, despite Liebig's fondness for remarking that Britain was not the land of science. Liebig's personal charisma inspired his students to throw themselves into energetic experimental research, and Nevil would have been in his element at Giessen, but it is unlikely that Anthony Story Maskelyne would have contemplated releasing family funds to send his son and heir to Germany, to rub shoulders with the sons of factory owners.

At Giessen, Liebig had directed Brodie to analyse the waxes produced by bees fed on different sugars, from which he had proved the existence of solid alcohols that could be shown to fit into chemical series with certain already known alcohols. This research backed up a recent (1843) observation by the French scientist Dumas, developed into a theory by Charles Gerhardt – himself a former Liebig pupil – that many organic compounds fell into 'homologous series', or families of like molecules, the compounds in each series reacting in similar ways but with varying intensities. It had been a useful breakthrough in the study of metabolism, for which Benjamin Brodie was soon to be rewarded with Fellowship of the Royal Society. Justus von Liebig was coming over to Oxford in person during the summer as the guest of Ben Brodie, who invited Nevil to help him entertain the great chemist. They were stimulating weeks, and it was not until after Liebig had finally left for Germany that Nevil was suddenly faced with the miserable reality of his situation. He had been moving among the top scientists of his day, accepted as one of them despite his youth, but he was actually only a poor and decidedly unenthusiastic law student.

Benjamin Brodie had been deeply disturbed when he had heard Nevil's story of frustrated ambition, and the two men became close friends. He shared some of his own frustrations with Nevil, for he too had suffered setbacks. Some years earlier, when he had wanted to continue his scientific career at Oxford, Ben Brodie had been thwarted by the compulsory rule of subscribing to the Thirty-Nine Articles of Faith. He had refused to subscribe, which had meant he could not become a college Fellow, nor a Master of Arts. Brodie was also annoyed by the rule that a college Fellow could not marry, for he confided to Nevil that he intended marrying in two years time. Oxford professors on the other hand, could marry, so Benjamin Brodie was just waiting until an Oxford professorship should come up, so that he could enjoy a scientific career at Oxford, together with a wife. Ben Brodie expected life to come his way, so he had taken a private laboratory in Regent's Park, London, until his coveted Oxford scientific chair fell vacant. Nevil would have liked to see Ben Brodie's ambitions fulfilled, but he knew that the chances of a professorship coming up for him in the next two years were rather remote, because neither Buckland nor Daubeny would be very likely to relinquish their posts before they died, and they were both robust enough to last some time.

The professorial posts were ill paid, but this was of no great consequence to Ben Brodie with his private means. He, meanwhile, could see a way of helping Nevil Maskelyne out of his predicament, and he devoted a great deal of energy to discussing the possibilities open to him. Ben Brodie's idea was to

Benjamin Brodie

invite Nevil to come and work in his own laboratory in London for as long as he liked, to concentrate partly on Ben Brodie's research and partly on his own. He set about persuading Nevil that this would be the best solution, though it would mean throwing in his legal studies, and Nevil found the offer very tempting indeed. It would mean working in Ben Brodie's pocket, which might be limiting, but he had been such a caring friend to Nevil and had taken so much interest in his future, that Nevil was finally only too glad to work with Brodie, and so escape from law to science.

The next step was to tackle Anthony Story Maskelyne, who believed Nevil to be on the road to the Bar at last. At the end of August, when Ben Brodie had convinced Nevil that his plan could work, Anthony Story was down on his Welsh property at Glanwysk, near the Brecon Beacons. Brodie sugested that they should go down and tackle him together, so they set off by train in the direction of the Welsh hills. Brodie's excellent social standing, confidence and commanding manner won the day with Anthony Story Maskelyne, and he had soon fixed up for Nevil to be released from his legal studies and supplied with a servant and an allowance even if a meagre one. Anthony even expressed pleasure at the future being offered to his son by this well-born friend of his. The embarrassment which could have arisen from Anthony's only offering a small financial alowance, was hastily overcome by Ben Brodie, who wrote straight away from Glanwysk to his friend Henry Halford Vaughan, with whom he shared his house in Regent's Park. He asked if Vaughan would mind Maskelyne moving in with them, and said he would give up his own bedroom to Nevil as a drawing room, and would use their present main drawing-room as his own bedroom. Ben Brodie told Henry Halford Vaughan that he realized he was taking a certain responsibility on himself when he offered Maskelyne this opportunity to work in his laboratory, but that he was truly anxious to do all he could for Nevil 'that his plans in life may succeed'. Vaughan raised no objections for he was an Oxford graduate and knew Nevil already, so Nevil moved to 13 Albert Road soon afterwards. Ben Brodie's support and help were deeply appreciated by Nevil in his hour of need, but of course the advantage was not entirely one-sided, for

Brodie had found himself not only a lively and loyal friend, but also about the most able and enthusiastic research assistant currently available. The friendship between Maskelyne and Brodie was of the typically intense kind enjoyed by Victorian men at that time. 'We went on arm in arm for a few years – when I honoured your heart far more than your intellect, and you found in me sufficient of both to make me your companion', wrote Nevil to Ben some time later, 'you helped more than anything else for those years of my life to gladden me when otherwise I should have been most unhappy.' Nevil mentioned the 'difficulties, pecuniary and otherwise' which he had suffered in the years he was befriended by Ben Brodie, and he felt enormous gratitude to him.

The one snag to the arrangement was that in accepting so generous an offer, and letting Ben Brodie negotiate with his father to release him from his legal studies, Nevil had unwittingly placed himself in deep moral debt. If Ben Brodie called out for help one day, Nevil might find himself faced with a true dilemma.

A Fermentation of Mind

The winter of 1847-8 was a very cold one indeed, and it was particularly grim for the thousands of people who were unemployed in the towns and cities of Britain. Despite the fact that the Corn Laws had at last been repealed, crop failure that summer had led to higher winter bread prices, causing hunger and discontent among the out-of-work urban industrial workers who could only get relief by becoming inmates of the parish workhouse, where the sexes were segregated and conditions were made deliberately unpleasant, to try and induce them to accept any job, however lowly, in preference to the work-house fate. This employment situation was exploited by many employers, who expected their workers to perform unreasonable tasks under rotten conditions, without giving them a fair wage for doing so. The frustration and destitute situation of so many workers led them into more militant and active support of Chartism and the rights of working people.

In the meantime, the potato famine had been dragging Ireland to her knees and reports had been coming back that one third of the Irish population had already died of starvation or fever, and that carts went about regularly collecting up the corpses of the stricken, whilst the public works employees themselves could hardly stand up to carry out this gruesome work, for weakness and malnutrition. Anthony Story Maskelyne donated £5 towards the Irish fund, and made several subsequent payments towards this form of relief, but Jowett mentioned in a letter to Brodie that Lord Lansdowne, a leading British politician, told his private secretary, Matthew Arnold, that he expected a million people to have died before the famine was over. Matthew Arnold, who had recently landed himself this particularly interesting job as secretary to Lord Lansdowne, was living, like Nevil, in London. Matthew Arnold had just seen his younger brother William off to India. Willy Arnold was an ardent and headstrong young man with a shock of dark curly hair like his father, Dr Thomas Arnold. He had given up Oxford after a few months of university life, getting into some minor trouble on the way, and had decided to find action and adventure overseas. He and Nevil may or may not have met, but they were to have grandchildren in common one day.

As the spring of 1848 advanced, so the conditions of working people worsened and the popularity of Chartism grew. Trouble was stirring on the continent too, where workers were starting to organize themselves. A young Anglo-Indian lawyer named John Ludlow had been in the fermenting city of Paris (where he had spent his own childhood), finding out how French workers formed themselves into associations to fight for better conditions. John Ludlow had always been a sensitive and socially conscious person, and he returned to England more than ever determined to help working people out of the hopeless situation they had got into. He said that he could see plenty of philanthropists going to the aid of people in their misery, but he saw nobody trying to help them *out* of their misery, for even the most concerned well-wishers were not thinking in terms of changing the basic structure of society in such a way as to release one class from dependence on the other.

Ludlow felt that social expectations themselves had to change, and he had already approached the chaplain of Lincoln's Inn, the Reverend Frederick Denison Maurice, who was known to be concerned about the plight of London's poor, and had asked him if he could see any way of helping the vast urban masses of people who were Chartists but not Christians. From this, a movement was to grow, and Nevil Story Maskelyne, already something of a radical from his Wadham days, was about to become involved in Ludlow's early attempts to help socially deprived people improve their own lot.

Angry movements on the continent, coupled with the troubles and tragedies of Ireland, spurred more people to attend Chartist meetings in England, and to join the organization. In February, a three-day workers' revolution suddenly broke out in Paris, just at the moment when Max Müller, the young German student of ancient languages, happened to be out there working on manuscripts in the Biliothèque Royale. Nobody's life was safe, Max later reported, for once the workers had gained control there was no government, no police and no soldiers, and he said he couldn't sleep at night for the sound of fighting, burning houses and cannon-roar. The municipal guards, he said, were hacked to pieces by the mob, bullets whistled past on all sides and blood ran in the streets. Barricades were built up from omnibuses, tables and pianos, only to be stormed, seized and then rebuilt, by the tough young soldiers of the working people, who wore ragged blouses and called themselves the Garde Mobile. Once they started winning, the Tricolore flag was raised above the Tuileries and the Marseillaise was sung on all sides, but – as always happened in Victorian times – people were curious to see the gruesome side of the event for themselves. Max Müller noticed ladies sallying forth in the thick of the fighting, just so as not to miss the spectacle, so he did the same, and Robert Mansfield came over to Paris for a week, to impress himself with the sight of the dead lying in dozens and the pavements slippery with blood. Max Müller fled the country with the manuscripts he had been studying, as soon as it was safe to escape after the revolution.

A street barricade during the Paris revolution

Back in Britain, the effect of all this violence and bloodshed was an increase in support for the Chartists, for the Paris workers had won for themselves, in three days, the sort of recognition which the Chartists had been seeking for years. It had been an impressive coup. Chartist demonstrations were staged in all the big towns in England that March, and the landowning classes began to show signs of panic, because it certainly looked as if a British revolution could be on the way. Given a stronger leadership, the Chartist movement could have escalated even more than it did, but Feargus O'Connor seems to have overestimated his own ability to rally support for the final crucial demonstration.

The plan was for a huge gathering of workers to meet in London on 10 April, to present a five-million-signature national petition for a People's Charter at the Houses of Parliament. The Establishment were thoroughly alarmed at the prospect, for the Paris revolution was still very fresh in their minds, so they set about a full-scale counter-offensive to keep the invading hordes from sacking the capital city. The working people were due to assemble on Kennington Common, south of the Thames, and march from there to present the petition at Westminster. In the end the number of supporters who rallied to Kennington Common on 10 April was far less than expected (whether you believed the figures given by the Prime Minister *or* those given by Feargus O'Connor). Strategically, too, they were ill-placed, because they had to cross the Thames by bridge to reach Westminster, and a bridge is easily blocked. The Duke of Wellington, who was now 80, took the military defences in hand, deploying his troops in convenient hiding places like the houses and gardens of Bridge Street and Parliament Street, ready to charge out and hold the Thames bridges against the Chartists if any trouble broke out. The British Museum took the threat so seriously that 250 museum staff were issued with cutlasses, 50 muskets and ammunition and a pike each – and they stockpiled stones on the roof, just in case it came to hurling them on any insurgents below. Thus armed, the museum staff, supported by two regular army officers, 57 other ranks and 20 Chelsea Pensioners, set about the defence of the museum against all comers.

John Ludlow was in two minds over whether to enrol as one of the 50,000 or more special constables created for the day to keep order, but he decided not to. Most of Nevil's set, however, jumped at the opportunity of seeing some action. Even Thomas Hughes joined up, after some initial doubts, but on the day he went and threw himself into a typical rugby-type scuffle in Trafalgar Square, and had to be rescued by police. Another of Nevil's friends, Charles Pearson, a King's College student and disciple of the Reverend F.D.Maurice, caught a chill whilst on truncheon duty and became so ill that he never fully recovered from the after-effects of the day. Robert Mansfield found himself guarding the site of what is now the Royal Academy, in company with the future Emperor Louis Napoleon. After spending dreary hours waiting, this little group went out on a night street patrol, during which one of them was picked up by the regular police for being drunk and disorderly.

The Reverend F.D.Maurice himself stayed in with a cold, but the writer Charles Kingsley came up to town from Eversley, the small Hampshire village where he was rector, to stay with his friend, Charles Mansfield, with the express idea of going and reasoning with Feargus O'Connor and his men on Kennington Common. Charles Kingsley hoped to persuade the Chartists not to do anything which might lead to confrontation with the police, for, he said,

Part of the
Chartist
procession

the poor fellows meant well, however misguided – and he would hate to see bloodshed. He went and looked out Ludlow, to ask if he would accompany him to Kennington Common to plead with O'Connor – a useless idea, to Ludlow's mind, but he agreed to go nevertheless. In the event, they were prevented from crossing Waterloo Bridge by the Chartist crowds surging back after being sent home by their leaders, so the tall young clergyman with the angular features and gentle stutter was reprieved from confrontation with the aggressive red-headed O'Connor. All in all, the day was rather a sad non-event, though many Londoners may have preferred it that way. One cab was spotted by the Buckland children, carrying a petition of barely two million signatures – and some of those forged – to Westminster through the later evening drizzle, but the only onlooker to remain totally unmoved by the day's upheavals was Frank Buckland's eagle, let loose from Westmister Abbey roof.

After the demonstrations, Charles Kingsley and John Ludlow walked to the house of the Reverend F.D.Maurice, in Queen Square, Bloomsbury, to plot immediate action. Within 48 hours the impulsive Charles Kingsley had placards pasted up all over London, addressed to 'the Workmen of England', and signed 'a Working Parson', in which he warned the workers against Chartism, and reassured them that the clergy understood the misery of their condition, and that a nobler life was round the corner. Ludlow, a more reflective thinker, discussed with Maurice the idea of forming a brotherhood of 'tried moral men' who would meet with Chartists and start to talk through the problem. Ludlow met Charles Mansfield staying with Kingsley at Eversley Rectory soon afterwards, and roped him into the group; and Charles in turn contacted his own friends, including Nevil Maskelyne. Thomas Hughes, who had been an ardent follower of Maurice's sermons for two years, also joined the band together with several other young barristers, and they all attended Maurice's sermons together for inspiration. Tom Hughes was a very honest, open and practical young man, who brought a down-to-earth atmosphere of sanity to this otherwise rather idealistic bunch of would-be reformers, who were all full of enthusiasm and hope, zealous propagandists and keen to bring in all the recruits they could. By 1873, looking back on those days, Thomas Hughes was to write, 'I cannot even now think of my own state of mind without wonder and amazement'. Ludlow was the one among them who had some idea of where the band of brothers should apply their energies in order to raise the workers both socially and spiritually. He saw himself and his friends as founders of a Christian socialist movement, and it was he who led the group to search for a suitable area in which to work.

While the Christian Socialists were looking around for the best way of tackling their appointed task, Nevil was also getting himself used to working in Ben Brodie's laboratory, analysing what would later be known as the fatty acids obtainable from different kinds of wax, ready for Ben Brodie to publish a paper on the subject in the spring. Nevil also worked on the use of phosphates in farming, and read a paper on this research to the Ashmolean Society the following year. Liebig had already made the study of artificial fertilizers very popular in Britain, by going round the country talking to landowners about his own discoveries in this field. In the evening, Nevil would sometimes go and look out his friend Charles Mansfield who was busy on his own laboratory work at the Royal College of Chemistry. 'Late into the night, for hours after other lights were extinguished at the College of Chemistry, the lamps under his retorts were burning', Nevil was to write later, in a preface to Mansfield's *Theory of Salts*, 'and he would be sitting there, marking in his notebook the temperatures told by his thermometers, and labelling the products he distilled'. For about ten months Charles Mansfield watched his retorts of boiling coal tar, and by March 1849 he complained that his wits were in a constant state of anaesthesia from inhaling benzole. He was noting down the succession of hydrocarbons which separated themselves from the coal tar, and had discovered that one of these products was benzole. In order to make it possible to extract benzene in commercial quantities, he eventually invented a method of extracting it by fractional distillation, followed by freezing and pressing. He also prepared nitro-benzene, by subjecting the benzene to the action of nitric acid, and his work from this time was to have extremely far-reaching consequences in the fields of fuels, dying, detergents, dry-cleaning and perfumes. Nevil Story Maskelyne, John Ludlow and other friends who came to see how he was getting on in his laboratory used to have lively conversations based on the ideas which passed through Mansfield's fertile

Charles Mansfield

The new façade
at the Royal
Institution

mind while he watched over his retorts. Through Charles Mansfield, Nevil became increasingly interested in the Christian Socialists and began to support some of their activities.

In April 1849, Charles Mansfield gave two lectures, one of which, 'On the Uses of Benzene', took place at the Royal Institution, and his friends turned out to hear him. Ludlow described Charles Mansfield lecturing – 'He stood there with a wonderful gracefulness of manner, in spite of his nervousness, never awkward for an instant, and looking so young too, among all the grave ugly scientists; and what was beautiful, as beautiful almost as Mansfield's own self-suppression, was Faraday's intense anxiety about him.' Charles Mansfield's other lecture, given at the Institute of Civil Engineering, was on his 'Patent Gas or Air-Light Apparatus', in which he had applied his benzene discovery in an ingenious way, to produce inflammable gas mixtures for lighting purposes, and he even went so far as to visualize the apparatus modified to fuel a 'combustion engine' sparked by electricity.

Nevil Maskelyne went to other lectures besides Charles Mansfield's at the Royal Institution, in fact he was in a good position to know what lectures would be given, because since the autumn of 1847 he had been a member of the Committee of Visitors for the Royal Institution, no doubt at the suggestion of Faraday. This body, which existed largely to audit the accounts and to keep a check on the running and repairs of the building, had lately been involved in alterations to the street frontage, which was receiving a fine colonnaded façade. On the committees at the Royal Institution, Nevil had found himself in the company of Ben Brodie, Henry Fox Talbot, Sir Charles Wheatstone of the electric telegraph, and William Grove, amongst others.

Nevil had been following Michael Faraday's 1848 lectures based on his most recent researches into light and magnetism, and he also followed current research trends in photography. By June 1848 a new process had been published, in which the negative consisted of a coating of albumen (egg-white) on glass. The albumen carried the photographic chemicals, and the idea was thought up by a Frenchman named Abel Niepce de Saint Victor, who had been striving to produce a more transparent and detailed negative. Nevil tried out the albumen process, but it depended on whole clutches of fresh eggs being available, which made it easier to experiment at Basset Down farmhouse than in London, where chickens were less evident. In August 1848, an article in the *Pharmaceutical Journal* mentioned that the substance called gun-cotton, (later to be known as cellulose) if dissolved in sulphuric ether produced a waterproof transparent membrane which adhered to a smooth surface. It would have served Nevil better than egg-whites for holding his chemicals to the glass, but neither he nor anyone else seems to have spotted its potential application to photography at this stage.

Back at Basset Down, beautiful Mervinia, Nevil's second sister, had, like him, gone against her father's will. Anthony had always been heartily against marriage for his daughters, but there it was - on 25 April 1848, Mervinia married and flew the nest with a young clergyman named Thomas Masterman. Ben Brodie too, after telling Nevil that he would be marrying in two years time, found himself unable to last out that long, and married Miss Thompson in the summer. Nevil was therefore obliged to move out of Brodie's house, so he took rooms at 11 Stanhope Street, near Regent's Park, which put him within easy walking distance of the Reverend F.D.Maurice in Queen Square and the Mansfields in Regent Street. Charles Mansfield (who had studied medicine for a time in his student years at Cambridge) was particularly interested in unorthodox forms of medical treatment, including hypnotism. He accompanied Charles Kingsley to Bournemouth for a month that autumn, to try and 'magnetize' him out of a violent attack of nervous depression. Whether by magnetism or by the friendly attention he gave Kingsley, he managed to pull him round by the end of the month, losing a good deal of chemical research time in the process, but he had to repeat the treatment at Ilfracombe during the winter, while Charles Kingsley completed a novel!

Both Charles and Robert Mansfield had become fascinated by hypnotism, and they were not the only ones – for in London it was the latest craze. Robert attended a lecture on this new art, known as 'Electro-biology' and decided that it was just one big confidence trick, but in the end he couldn't resist

Jenny Lind

having a go at learning to hypnotize people himself. After sending a young lady into a trance from which she could not be withdrawn until the following morning, Robert Mansfield decided to give up the practice. That winter he went to just about every performance staged at the old Opera House in the Haymarket, from which vast crowds were turned away every night, because it was the year that Jenny Lind, the 'Swedish Nightingale', hit the town. She drew the audiences wherever she went – and the smart London set were falling over themselves for Haymarket tickets. Another of Robert Mansfield's favourite haunts was the popular Cider Cellars in Maiden Lane. These supper rooms staged nightly performances of the gruesome song 'Sam Hall', in which the singer took the part of a man condemned to be hanged, acting out his last moments in the best traditions of Victorian melodrama.

Nevil Story Maskelyne's own social round included going to the Bucklands' parties, where one of the girls, Mit Buckland, used to wind snakes round her wrists – which not everyone found amusing. In the summer of 1848, Dr Buckland and his two daughters caught typhoid, after an ancient brick drain had accidentally been opened in Westminster. London only had very old brick sewers and cesspools at that stage so, once he had recovered, Dr Buckland set about getting pipe sewers put in for the 15 local houses, after which he embarked on a campaign for pure water and sanitation for London as a whole.

Conditions were bad for the underprivileged, and the Christian Socialists were opening night schools in areas where they were able to make satisfactory contact with working people. Nevil Maskelyne was asked if he would be prepared to give classes in photography, so he at once agreed to share anything he knew about it with the night school pupils. Like the rest of the 'band of brothers' and their friends, Nevil had never before been required to meet working people socially, because Victorian social codes forbade it. He and the other young scientists, barristers and clergy found themselves in a new and uneasy situation which they never entirely sorted out, but the more important result of their activities was that they were starting off a movement which would lead to significant social change in the future.

Charles Mansfield worked mainly at the night-school which had been opened up in Little Ormond Yard near the home of the Reverend F.D.Maurice but Robert Mansfield taught at one which had been set up soon afterwards in an alley to the river side of the Strand, near Charing Cross, and Nevil Maskelyne probably demonstrated photography in both. The problem with evening classes, as Charles Dickens had recently pointed out in connection with Mechanics' Institutes, was that they all too easily suffered from 'over gentility', by attracting clerks and shopkeepers instead of the craftsmen and labourers for whom they were intended (see P.Collins). The Christian Social-ists seem to have avoided this problem at first, by basing their work on small local communities, and they used to meet up with leading working men at night, in the Cranbourne Coffee Tavern, to plan the next moves. These meetings led on, guided by Ludlow, to the forming of a proper working men's association. The 'band of brothers' themselves used to meet at six in the morning, for purposes of policy making and general fellowship. They were a close-knit group, and his son wrote that when F.D.Maurice remarried in the summer of 1849 (his first wife having died some time before), 17 'true kind friends' from the Christian Socialist group – Nevil Maskelyne among them – gave him a collective present of books.

Punch cartoon
view of the
plight of the
working tailors

During the summer, *The Morning Chronicle*, a liberal voice among the daily papers, ran a series of powerful articles on poverty by Henry Mayhew, which confronted the middle and upper classes with some highly unpalatable facts which had been ignored until then. Amongst the outrages which the paper exposed was the so-called 'slop system' - a sweated-labour arrangement for tailors, shirtmakers and seamstresses (also described by Charles Kingsley in his book *Alton Lock*). To avoid paying decent wages to workshop staff in factories, the manufacturers of clothing put out work through their agents, to get the lowest tender possible from home-based clothing workers. The agents, or 'sweaters', took most of the money and the tailors lived in debt for their materials, half starved and in rags, while many of the thousands of women on slop work turned to prostitution for a living.

During the summer, the Christian Socialists, being young professionals, were on vacation, so it did not occur to them to do anything further before the autumn, when Ludlow would be back from investigating working men's associations in Paris, and talks with London's working men could be resumed. In September however, Charles Mansfield wrote eagerly to Ludlow telling him that 'Maskelyne is keen on Christian Socialist work', and should be involved in meetings to set up a Working Tailors' Association. Ludlow thought that the best plan would be for Christian Socialists to give money to set up workrooms and shops for the tailors, and to guarantee to order their clothes from these tailors. This gave rise to an interesting new style of dress among the avant-garde set, and liberal Oxford men could be spotted wearing 'strange-patterned and ill-fitting trousers from the C.S. tailor'. London Christian Socialists even went to the extent of wearing beards and wide-awake hats, which was considered a real piece of social effrontery. These eccentric and gifted people, like many another band of idealists, would probably have attracted a much greater following for their cause, had they not been such a bohemian set. The Mansfields and others of the inner circle affected fads such as vegetarianism or a yearning for phonetic spelling, both very practical ideas in themselves, but collectively they added to the impression that Christian Socialists were not like other people, and cared little for what people thought of them. Their less fanatical friends, who would have liked to help, were put off by the weird image of the enterprise.

Nevil Maskelyne was fully in sympathy with the Christian Socialist cause and wrote a note to Ludlow in the spring of 1849 to say he had left 'a hat, coat and trousers and certain boots' in his rooms for the neediest of the men attending Little Ormond Yard night-school, and that he was just off for the vacation to help his father cut peat in Wales. He added that he noticed the landlords around Basset Down 'croaking very loudly' against the effects of the Corn Laws, repealed only two years earlier. 'But what I fear will prove an evil is that they talk seriously of lowering wages next winter to five shillings a week. What our already nearly starved labour population will do I know not.' Nevil was often out of London by the spring of 1849 because Dr Buckland no longer always felt up to delivering his Oxford mineralogy lectures, and would ask Nevil Maskelyne to stand in for him as 'praelector' or lecturer, on an occasional basis.

While he was in Oxford, Nevil could catch up with the latest news on Oxford reform, for reform was certainly in the air at last, and a certain light trend towards liberality could be sensed. Arthur Stanley, one of Dr Arnold's greatest supporters and an ex-Rugby master, was now a tutor at Balliol college and had been preaching a series of sermons to the university, in which he had supported the views of Arnold, the principle of free enquiry and even the thinking of the German theologians – who were considered most dangerously radical by almost every contemporary critic who had heard of their existence. Benjamin Jowett, another of the forward-thinking Balliol set, and a close friend of both Arthur Stanley and Ben Brodie, had travelled abroad with Stanley and become a supporter of the German philosophers Hegel and Bauer, whose ideas included the concept of God being part of a universal system, rationally laid out – which rather did away with any 'naïve' view of an Almighty Ruler on high, acting by divine will as He alone saw fit; and Jowett also liked the German theologians' explanation of the New Testament in terms of history, as opposed to myth and miracle. It was all very strong meat for an Oxford don at the time, and looked perilously close to atheism – though Jowett was himself criticizing Brodie for unbelief. Benjamin Jowett wanted to liberalize education too and to throw out the prevailing teaching philosophy – that students should take only one given, classic, authoritative view of any given subject – in favour of students being allowed to compare and contrast one opinion with another. Jowett was following the mood of the German professors, who were currently taking a leading rôle in revolutionary up-heavals against the German established order. Another of the Oxford dons who had just returned from the continent even more liberal than before was the Wadham tutor Richard Congreve. He had come back from Paris converted to 'Positivism'. Positivists were followers of Auguste Comte, who viewed the whole of human kind as part of a system within which humanity itself was the supreme being, and in which science and technology contributed to the progress of social order (which would be harder to envisage today). The philosophy was a kind of humanism, and would have been an unacceptable intrusion on the Oxford scene only five years earlier. Positivism had much that was attractive to Nevil Maskelyne, with his admiration for Greek human-ist culture and his passion for science. The young free-thinking German scholar, Max Müller, had just arrived in Oxford to live, so as to be on hand for proof-correcting while the Oxford University Press proofed his book on Sans-krit texts, and he added to the more liberal atmosphere. By the end of 1848, Stanley, Jowett and Congreve were all agitators for Oxford reform, and a

Max Müller

Cambridge group worked simultaneously to get syllabuses introduced there in Moral Sciences and Natural Sciences.

All through the 1840s, ordinary undergraduates had received no word about any of the great discoveries of the past 50 years in scientific fields like physiology and chemistry. Unless they specifically asked to join a particular course of lectures given by a professor, all scientific news, or even any mention of science, had been blocked from them by the power of the theologians. The Tractarian era had kept an effective muffler over Oxford student ears for a good decade. Now, however, Dr Daubeny, Dr Walker and Dr Henry Acland who lectured in medicine, had started writing pamphlets suggesting that science should be included in the general syllabus for all undergraduates at Oxford. Two years before, Ben Brodie had written to his friend Henry Halford Vaughan, prophesying that the public would sooner or later demand real knowledge for its students and if the existing Oxford system could be shaken at all it would be shaken to its very foundations. Ben Brodie, writing to Jowett, had visualized a 'fermentation of mind' ahead at Oxford, an introduction of new books and new ideas.

Now, the science professors were beginning to bring Brodie's vision to life, for Daubeny and Walker were asking for undergraduates to be able to choose to read for a 'school', or degree, in natural sciences or in mathematics with physics, at the same time as preparing their classics school. They wanted to see professors given more lecturing power, and college tutors pulling back all that teaching they had lost to private tutors. There were rumours of new legislation afoot, to undermine the entrenched ways of Oxford, and by early 1849 there were proper plans being made to change the examination system. The university authorities were making an effort to promote a few changes themselves before anyone else could step in and do it for them, so they quickly voted in a Natural Science school, as one of three alternative schools (degree subjects) to be read up at the same time as the original classics school. The other two alternatives were to be mathematics and modern history, but Henry Halford Vaughan – Ben Brodie's friend with whom he used to share the London house – who had just been made Regius Professor of Modern History at Oxford, had had to fight to get his subject accepted at all, let alone the kind of wide-ranging and critical syllabus he wanted.

Nevil Maskelyne spent the summer term of 1849 back in Oxford, completing the residence requirement which would qualify him for the degree of Master of Arts. That June Dr Buckland, in a letter to the Duke of Wellington's secretary, recommended Maskelyne for the Radcliffe Travelling Fellowship, for which the duke had a vote. 'He is passionately addicted to Chemistry, Physiology and High Branches of Mathematics', wrote Dr Buckland, 'and his original researches in Natural Sciences give assurance that he should be appointed to the vacant Fellowship and thereby get the means of continuing his studies in the schools of Germany and France. He will do more to carry out the designs of Dr Radcliffe than has been done by all his Fellows of the last 40 years.' Needless to say, in the science-shy climate of the day, the Fellowship did not come Nevil Maskelyne's way, so he threw himself instead into yet another Oxford reform project – the fight for a university museum for the natural sciences. It was an idea thought up by Dr Henry Acland who, besides being a lecturer, worked as a general medical practitioner from his centrally placed house in Broad Street. Dr Acland's university post was the 'Lee's Readership in Anatomy', which meant that he taught in the very Anatomical Theatre at Christ Church College which Dr Carus had so roundly condemned for being centuries out of date. The progressive Dr Acland, who had taken Dr Carus' remarks to heart, had tried to modernize the place by, amongst other things, introducing microscopes into his lectures, sending them round on a little table railway. Using the microscope – a new and unfamiliar toy in Oxford – he could demonstrate the construction of body tissues; but, according to H.M. Vernon, the aged Regius Professor of Medicine Dr John Kidd stared through the microscope in amazement, saying that in the first place he did not believe in what he saw, and that – even if it were true – he did not think that God intended us to know it. Dr Acland was made to stop the microscope demonstrations, on the grounds that he was being paid to lecture, and that this was not lecturing.

Dr Acland therefore turned his energies to updating and adding to the Anatomical Theatre's comparative zoology collections, which included the bones and pickled organs of a wide range of creatures. Dr Pusey, the veteran of the Tractarian movement, had stables close to the Anatomical Theatre, which he helpfully lent to Dr Acland for preserving his giraffe and other specimens, though the stench was terrible. Dr Pusey, reported Vernon, could not resist informing Dr Acland that he had noticed that the pursuit of Natural Science 'led to a temper of irreverence and often of arrogance, inconsistent with a truly Christian character', and that he himself discouraged its study.

The more grandiose university museum which Dr Acland envisaged for Oxford was to be a centre for research, lectures, demonstrations, displays and libraries, all devoted to natural science – a place where the great scientific finds and ideas of the day could be brought to the notice of the ordinary student. Dr Acland's museum plans were given a send-off by a small meeting held at New College in May 1849, and Nevil Maskelyne was appointed secretary to the 20-strong action committee, which had swelled to 60 members by the end of the month. He seems to have carried out most of the early spade-work for the museum campaign single-handed. He found out all he could about lighting and use of space in existing museums and about how to arrange exhibits to the best advantage, and he visited various London museums to research their lighting and display tactics, in order to write out a detailed report on the subject. He also had to interview each one of the existing professors of science subjects in Oxford, to sound out their estimated needs for rooms and equipment in the proposed museum, so that he could write a pamphlet about it for the rest of the committee. He found a surprisingly varied response to his questions. Professor Walker was bold enough to ask for a lecture hall to seat 250 people, and a large room where he could display his splendid collection of working models and apparatus. Professor Daubeny's first requirement was a laboratory for himself, with another one where he could demonstrate to 20 students. Dr Acland was the only professor who thought in terms of students doing research of their own, and modest William Fishburn Donkin, the Professor of Astronomy, assured Nevil he would be perfectly happy with a wooden hut in the grounds.

The museum idea was bitterly opposed in many quarters, and no funds were to be had from the university authorities, least of all when they were to hear of the architect's estimate of £30,000 for building it. Undaunted, the museum's action committee called a large public meeting for 19 July in the Sheldonian Theatre, to beat up support for the idea of a museum for the natural sciences as a public university institution, to be paid for and supported from university funds. Crowds of people came to the meeting but nothing further happened because, yet again, there was not enough money – the promised donations being pretty small.

In September 1849, Dr Acland secured the help of a young 'conservator', Viktor Carus, to help him with the collecting, identifying and preserving of specimens for the Anatomical Theatre. Young Viktor Carus was a recently qualified doctor, and was very interested in comparative zoology and anatomy, but he was also pleased to come to Oxford because his close friend Max Müller was already there. Viktor Carus, a gentle musical youth, had spent all his teenage years in the company of Max Müller, who had come to live in the Carus household at Leipzig after his own father had died. That first winter in Oxford, the two friends saw less of one another than expected, because Viktor Carus was sent to the Scilly Isles for many months, to collect

Viktor Carus

and classify marine specimens, and Max Muller returned to Germany for a holiday with his elderly mother from October till March.

It was in any case a bad time to be in urban England, because cholera broke out in London at the end of the summer. The Christian Socialists determined to set about relief work, inspired by reading the articles written by Henry Mayhew in the *Morning Chronicle*, which described the open sewers of the Jacob's Island district of Bermondsey in London's East End. 'In the bright light', wrote Mayhew, the sewer 'appeared the colour of a strong green tea, and positively looked as solid as black marble in the shadow – indeed it was more like watery mud than muddy water; and yet we were assured that this was the only water that the wretched inhabitants had to drink. As we gazed in horror at it, we saw drains and sewers emptying their filthy contents into it; we saw a whole tier of doorless privies in the open road, common to men and women, built over it; we heard bucket after bucket of filth splash into it, and the limbs of the vagrant boys bathing in it seemed, by pure force of contrast, white as Parian marble. And yet, as we stood doubting the fearful statement, we saw a little child, from one of the galleries opposite, lower a tin can with a rope to fill a large bucket that stood beside her. In each of the balconies that hung over the stream the self same tub was to be seen in which the inhabitants put the mucky liquid to stand, so that they may, after it has rested a day or two, skim the liquid from the solid particles of filth, pollution and disease. As the little thing dangled her tin cup as gently as possible in the stream, a bucket of night soil was poured down from the next gallery.' The Christian Socialists went down to Jacob's Island to work out the most practical way of organising relief work among the victims of cholera. Charles Mansfield enlisted the help of a medical friend, Dr Walsh, to try to provide medical treatment and advice, and Mansfield also arranged for a supply of butts of fresh water to the area, but John Ludlow later wrote that the people of Bermondsey were such a down and out lot that they stole the brass taps from the water butts and sold them, so that the water just ran out onto the ground. Still, they used the money to buy gin, which, as the philosophical Dr Walsh remarked, probably preserved them from cholera better than the water could. Dr Walsh lost several wealthy

Punch cartoon depicting conditions ripe for cholera in London

patients from his smart West End practice when it became known that he was also working in Bermondsey doing such staunch work on sanitation, treatment and health education during the cholera outbreak, but the poor Jacob's Islanders themselves never did fathom out why those young gentlemen should have wanted to come and help them.

By early November the cholera epidemic was over in London, but at about that time Dr Buckland, at the Deanery in Westminster, began to succumb to a malady of a different kind, from which he was never going to pull himself round. He began to sink into a state of apathy and depression. Poor Dr Buckland had slowly been losing his enthusiasm for life over the last two years for, as he bitterly remarked when he first arrived in London, he had spent 44 years trying to encourage a love of science at Oxford, and had failed. However much his friends might try to point out that this was not entirely true, Dr Buckland could not rally himself round. This hitherto confident, ebullient and humorous figure had to leave Westminster for a country rectory at Islip, near Oxford, where he gradually withdrew to the point where he could rarely be induced to look at anything more than the Bible and the 'Leisure Hour'. Nevil was particularly hurt at Dr Buckland's tragic decline, because the cheerful support and enthusiasm of his old Professor of Mineralogy and Geology had meant a great deal to him since his own teenage years. By the middle of the summer of 1850, Nevil Story Maskelyne had been offered the post of Deputy Professor of Mineralogy at Oxford – for Dr Buckland, however ill, continued to hold the position of professor.

Nevil was surprised and not a little embarrassed at the offer, wrote A.H.Miers later, because he saw that this was just the opportunity which could help Ben Brodie into Oxford professorial circles, so he suggested that Brodie was better qualified for the post and should have been invited first. Ben Brodie, however, knew how to play his cards and he turned the offer down. So Nevil went and talked the matter over with his friend Michael Faraday. A.H.Miers quotes Nevil's words to Faraday, 'I told him that I had collected minerals at one time and had only superficially studied them, but had no fear as regards the subject of mineralogy alone'. Nevil told Faraday he was more worried about crystallography, the study of the chemistry and structure of crystals, since he had not worked this up more than any ordinary chemist would. His work in Brodie's laboratory these days left him with no time to do his own research there, but Faraday's answer was, 'Accept the offer, and, as you have several months before you, come here [to the Royal Institution] on such evenings as you may have. You shall have a room and light, and I will get from the library any books you may need.' Nevil, of course, accepted the generous offer, knowing that with Faraday's help he would soon be able to work up his knowledge of crystallography.

He agreed to take up the post of Deputy Professor of Mineralogy that autumn, on the proviso that he should have a laboratory for teaching the chemical analysis of minerals, but laboratory space was rare in Oxford, and Nevil soon found that he and the redoubtable Dr Baden Powell were both after Dr Daubeny's old lecture theatre and laboratory under the Old Ashmolean Museum in Broad Street. Dr Daubeny had left it now, in favour of a grand new neo-classical laboratory and lecture hall which he had built himself at his own expense, beside the main gateway to the Botanic Garden, on ground belonging to his own college, Magdalen. He was delighted with his move to this new setting amongst the flowers and elm trees, not least because

The Oxford
Botanical Gardens

he no longer had to shuttle back and forth between the Botanic Garden and his Broad Street lecture theatre. He had grown heartily sick of lecturing in the Old Ashmolean basement anyway, saying in an 1853 address that it was 'thoroughly unworthy of a great university, being dark, inconvenient and confined'. For years he had fought for better facilities, because he had always thought it wrong that chemistry should be 'relegated like a sort of occult science or Black Art, to underground rooms'.

In the end Nevil won the toss for Dr Daubeny's basement against the claims of Dr Baden Powell, and was only too grateful for his underground prize, even though Dr Daubeny had taken all the chemical apparatus with him to the Botanical Gardens. Nevil was told that the university authorities would convert part of the basement into a laboratory suitable to his needs, and that they would do up the old quarters of the Museum Keeper for him to live in. It may have been a dreary place to Dr Daubeny but it was quite a palace to Nevil Maskelyne, who would now at last have both a laboratory and a home to himself. Placed between the Sheldonian Theatre and Exeter College, he would be right at the centre of all that was happening in Oxford. He was only 26, and he was used to a fairly meagre allowance, so the low pay of £100 a year would be no great hardship if it was going to be his lifeline towards independence from his father and from his benefactor Ben Brodie, for whom Nevil had done three years of energetic work.

Signs of Change

Installed beneath the renaissance building of the Old Ashmolean Museum in Broad Street, Nevil found himself in the grand possession of six living rooms, 'offices', a small lecture theatre and a laboratory, which the university had converted for his chemical analysis classes from one of Dr Daubeny's living rooms. During his time at the Old Ashmolean Museum, Dr Daubeny had busily added four rooms, two of them entrance lobbies in the area below street level, between the front of the building and Broad Street. After Nevil arrived, a pair of curved flights of steps was added to the front façade, sweeping up and out from the Broad Street entrance, to meet at a landing before the main door of the museum, which gave more light to Nevil's basement door below. The last recorded use of the basement for an experimental laboratory had been in the seventeenth century, when it took up the whole great vaulted front chamber, with two 'faire rooms' adjoining, for a chemical store and library. Nevil was delighted to be returning it to some of its former scientific uses, even if he still had to fight for one more asset which the professor had had in those much earlier days – a chemical assistant.

He wrote to ask his father for any furniture he could spare, but Anthony suggested saving carriage charges by buying it locally in Oxford. Though no significant player himself, one of the items Nevil acquired was a piano, because a number of his scientific friends were exceptionally gifted musicians. He learned to appreciate the music of his fellow-guests when he was round at the house of the Professor of Astronomy, Dr William Fishburn Donkin, who despite a rather quiet, retiring disposition was a very able mathematician, astronomer and musician. The Donkin family made Nevil very welcome at

The Old Ashmolean Museum, from an 1834 engraving

Professor William
Donkin

their house because he was, like his host, a lively-minded scientist with liberal views, and there he met many others of the radical set.

Dr Donkin, who was a Northumbrian, played the organ, piano and violin, besides composing music, and he had once written a setting to William Wordsworth's poem 'She dwelt among the untrodden ways', which Wordsworth had come to listen to when he was visiting Oxford. With a Double First in classics and mathematics, William Donkin had become an expert on Greek music from classical times. Max Müller, who was a close friend of Donkin's too, said that the delicate Professor of Astronomy was dying all the years he knew him, and was fully aware of it. It was Donkin's semi-invalid state which somehow made it perfectly acceptable for him to give musical performances at evening parties. This was not normally considered a suitable activity in the academic man's world, although Max Müller also got away with it by being a foreigner.

Max must have been the most musically gifted person in Oxford at that time. Weber the composer, an old friend of Max's parents, had been his godfather, and the Mendelssohns had been family friends too. By the age of six this lively child had started learning the easier Beethoven sonatas and Felix Mendelssohn, on a visit to Max's home town of Dessau, had sat the child on his knee at the organ, working the pedals himself, while Max played the keys. As a boy, Max had often been invited to musical evenings, and remembered tiptoeing in and catching the sound of the beautiful music as he reached the staircase. Max's father had died when the child was young, and his mother had found it an increasing struggle to feed and clothe him. Viktor Carus' father was a physician and surgeon and comfortably off so the Carus family had invited Max to come and live with them as the friend of their only son Viktor. The two boys already got on well, so Max left the deprivations of his own home for the comparative prosperity of the physician's household. Max and Viktor used to go to school together, and they played a good deal of music together too. Max used to sing in a choir under Mendelssohn while he was with the Carus family, and he learned the cello and piano. Viktor was a fine violinist, and when the two boys were about 15 they gave Dr Carus a birthday surprise by playing him the whole Kreutzer sonata by heart.

Now, reunited in Oxford, Viktor Carus and Max Müller would join Nevil Maskelyne for walking, on the afternoons when they were all free, discussing all kinds of things on the way. Nevil later realized how many of the interests he developed during his life had been inspired by those conversations, ranging over religion, fossils, molecules, mythology and every kind of far-reaching topic. The three of them would sometimes spend an evening in what Nevil called his 'queer little rooms' underneath the Old Ashmolean Museum, with Max playing the piano and Viktor the violin. That winter, Max Müller was, like Nevil, made deputy to a professor whose health had broken down – the Professor of Modern Languages. He started his lectures after Christmas in the newly-built Taylor building, speaking about a mediaeval German folk saga – the Niebelungenlied – comparing it with other myths and legends of neighbouring Norse and Icelandic cultures. G.Muller later wrote that Nevil heard these lectures and told her that he noticed that 'through the whole ran the sad refrain, so often recurring in the sad music of the poem' and he enormously admired his friend's lucid explanation and his deep feeling for his subject. Nevil could see that Max was breathing new life into Oxford lecturing, and he used to sit, fascinated, at the back of the lecture room, where he was supposed to listen out for errors of accent and syntax for Max, who wanted to correct himself where he could. However Nevil usually became too engrossed in the lectures to notice many mistakes. Max had so much experience of life already, and had known both poverty and tragedy as a young child, as well as receiving the warmth and encouragement of the Carus family when he came home from school every day in his adolescent years. Nevil had known none of these and, although they were exactly the same age, he couldn't help viewing Max as though he were someone older by several years.

Nevil Maskelyne's own course of mineralogy lectures had been taking place on Monday afternoons in the Clarendon Building, and Mark Pattison, a

The Clarendon
Building

young don who came to the first of the series, said it was masterly in outline and showed great grasp of the subject. Nevil had been working up the study of crystallography, and had started teaching chemical analysis to a few students in his basement laboratory. His first pupil was Leslie Thomson, whose real name was William, but who seems to have been known to all his Oxford friends as Leslie. He was a tutor at Queen's College and a specialist in logic, which meant that he didn't take things for granted. E.M.Thomson later wrote that when, for example, he noticed certain similarities between the rising sap of plants, the spread of moisture through soil and the diffusion of vapour in the air, Leslie Thomson would jot down the query 'do chemists fully understand the laws of capillarity?' This first student of Nevil's set his enquiring mind to the problems of chemical analysis, so becoming the earliest of a whole string of young and later distinguished men to try out supervised laboratory experiments for themselves. These cellar classes were the first of their kind to be held in nineteenth century Oxford – and they caused quite a stir among university members, curious to know what on earth analytical chemistry might be.

Nevil gained some useful teaching material in February 1851, when the university allowed him £140 to buy a good collection of minerals which happened to be on offer. The name of the eager young science professor began to get about, in fact science as a whole was beginning to be accepted by a few more people now in Oxford. The Tractarian movement was becoming less vociferous, mainly because most of its members had been 'perverted' – to use the jargon of the day – meaning that no less than 85 Oxford clergy and laiety had transferred their support to the Church of Rome (and so had 49 from Cambridge) and a mildly anti-Tractarian reaction was setting in.

The stagnant state of studies at Oxford and Cambridge universities had caused the government to order a Royal Commission of Enquiry into the problem and, just before Nevil came back to Oxford, men had been appointed to the tricky task of being commissioners. They had to tackle the ramifications of statutes laid down in Elizabethan days, as well as the independent traditions of each individual college – for each one was used to running itself as a society, and wanted to stay that way. The university governing body was made up of college heads who were a closed community of elderly men, content with the present system, decidedly against change and nearly all of them clergy. College tutors were often capable men but teaching at a very basic level, and they had very little inducement to stay on, since they had to leave if they married, so it paid them to look for a parish as soon as possible. Money payments, in the form of fellowships and scholarships, were nearly all available to clergy only, and many were limited to men from a particular county or school, or to 'founder's kin', so the colleges easily filled with privileged but lazy and uninterested members who contributed very little to the advance of knowledge. Oxford, of course, still only accepted members of the Church of England as students.

The two most active members of the Commission of Enquiry into the state of the university were Arthur Stanley of Balliol College, its secretary, and Francis Jeune, the Jersey-born Master of Pembroke College, who was married to a niece of Ben Symons, the entrenched Warden of Wadham – who had shown rather less hospitality towards the Jeunes since they had become embroiled in the Commission, being himself very suspicious of reform. In fact the poor Jeunes found themselves cut on every side but, as Mrs Jeune observed, it was a healthier way of life, because they scarcely received a single invitation out to the lengthy and substantial dinner parties enjoyed by more popular members of society. As soon as Francis Jeune had taken up the cause of reform he was off to London very frequently, and he and Arthur Stanley missed only one of the Commission's 88 meetings each.

There were some signs that the university authorities were bending slightly to the spirit of reform, and one person who benefited from this was Dr Daubeny, who, early in 1851, was promised £400 for building two hothouses so that he could grow orchids and other tropical and heat-loving aquatic plants like the massive Victoria water-lily. Nevil took photographs of Dr Daubeny's lush botanic garden, using the calotype method, but by early 1851 he was also using the new collodion photographic technique.

Collodion was described by Maskelyne at the time as being a fluid like sherry, produced by dissolving 15 grains of guncotton in 9 fluid ounces of sulphuric ether to one ounce of 60% proof alcohol. To this collodion you then added 5 grains of potassium iodide dissolved in a little alcohol, and about 3 ounces of sulphuric ether to make it run freely over the glass of your negative. The glass had to be scrupulously cleaned and then held flat by a corner while the pool of collodion was poured into the centre, tilted to run the liquid to one corner, then circulated to the other corners, the excess liquid being poured back into a jar from the last corner. Once the collodion had hardened, through the evaporation of the ether, the glass plate could be sensitized with the photographer's favourite chemicals, which meant immersing the plate for some minutes in dishes of solution, then washing off excess ether before placing the glass plate wet in the camera. If the light was good, the picture could be made at once, without a long exposure, which made collodion handier than the calotype process for everyday portraiture. The development of the plate usually involved pyrogallic acid, rather than the gallic acid used for calotypes – a solution of crystals from either of these acids would combine readily with oxygen and deposit a brown powder when exposed to light.

The collodion process had been envisaged by a M.le Grey in Paris the previous year, and Frederick Scott Archer, a London photographer, had worked out the method in practice by the autumn of 1850, publishing it in March 1851. Nevil Maskelyne had certainly been practising collodion photography before 19 April 1851, because he took a successful collodion portrait of Viktor Carus outside the Old Ashmolean Museum before Viktor Carus left the country for good before Easter 1851, in time to start lecturing in comparative anatomy at Leipzig University in the summer term. Nevil's negative of Viktor Carus was made on mica rather than on glass, and he used thin sheets of this highly stable base material for a number of his negatives as well as for making collodion direct positives – achieved by adding a little nitric acid to the pyrogallic acid at the developing stage. These positives showed the picture the right way round, as far as light and dark areas were concerned, and could be painted on the back with black varnish, to darken the shadows – an effect called ambrotype. Nevil sandwiched together mica ambrotypes he had made of the front and back of a medal, to make a complete photographic facsimile of it. Mica was widely used by scientists for polarizing experiments, but Nevil Maskelyne seems to have been the only photographer regularly using it as a base for photographic negatives and positives at this date, and it would have been an excellent transparent lightweight material for the purpose had it not been so brittle.

Photographs of the front and back of a medal, from which an ambrotype was made

Nevil can have had little time to spare for photographic experiment towards the end of March 1851 because, in addition to his Oxford teaching, he gave a Friday evening lecture on 28 March at the Royal Institution in London – the second of the 1851 series – on 'The connexion of chemical forces with the polarization of light'. Charles Mansfield took John Ludlow and his mother along to listen, and they heard Nevil try to explain how certain crystals, which had identical atoms in identical proportions, could still be different in their molecular structure. One way of demonstrating such a crystal difference was by seeing which way a crystal would rotate polarized light – to the right or to the left. Certain crystals, he pointed out, built themselves up in such a way as to be exact mirror images of similar crystals with identical atoms. Depending on whether one of these crystals had built itself up to a left-handedly or a right-handely asymmetric pattern, it rotated polarized light to the right or else to the left.

These mirror-image crystals which showed the effect so clearly had recently been named hemihedric crystals by a French scientist, Delafosse, who had also thought up the profound concept that molecules might be loosely linked in space within a crystal. Louis Pasteur, too, had just been experimenting with pairs of hemihedric crystals which he had obtained from two acids with the same chemical content and reactions; the salt crystals of one acid rotated polarized light to the right and the others to the left, and when he mixed solutions of the two together, they ceased to cause rotation at all. This revealed to Pasteur, as Nevil pointed out, that the molecular structure of two otherwise identical substances could be different. Nevil had long been interested in seeing a proof that this was possible, and he had been hankering after it in his 1847 paper. Louis Pasteur had generously forwarded his own finest crystal specimens from Paris, to illustrate Nevil's talk but, as luck would have it, the specimens did not arrive in time, so Nevil, who had arranged for them to be displayed at the Royal Institution, urged his audience to look at them as soon as they turned up. He explained that the specimens were exremely rare because half of them were products of racemic acid which had only been found once, and then by accident, in the cream of tartar from a particular vintage of wine from the Vosges.

The Royal Institution lecture was just before Easter, and the summer term started later in April, a few weeks after Viktor Carus had left. Now that his friend had returned to Germany, Max Müller's musical circle was sadly reduced, so he was pleased to note the arrival in Oxford that May of 'two little singing birds from London'. These upright young ladies were the daughters of Dr R.W.Jelf, Principal of King's College, London, who was also a canon of Oxford's Christ Church Cathedral and consequently had a house in Oxford too, where Mrs Jelf spent a good deal of time with her daughters, who enjoyed singing Mendelssohn's songs, which naturally made them very popular with Max Müller.

Nevil's summer course of lectures was given in the Clarendon Building, next door to his basement home, on 'the minerals which constitute volcanic and plutonic rock', and the lectures, which took place three times a week for four weeks in May, were no doubt well illustrated with his new range of rock specimens. May was a wet, cold month that year, and magic lantern shows were a popular indoor amusement at Oxford parties – particularly magic lantern slides showing foreign lands, because interest in overseas activities was increasing daily with the approach of opening day at the Great Exhibition in London. The Great Western Railway had decided to run an excursion train from Oxford to give university members and their families a view of the exhibits before general opening time. Several of the science professors decided to give public lectures in preparation for the trip, and to give the proceeds to a fund for sending Oxford mechanics to see the Great Exhibition. Nevil gave the first of these public lectures one Thursday evening in his basement lecture theatre – on the ores of the various precious metals, and how they were extracted and used in different countries of the world.

Nevil himself was deeply interested in the technology on view at the Great Exhibition, and impressed at the huge scale of the display and the way it could take in several Hyde Park trees of forest proportions, and he bought himself

The Great
Exhibition

some of Delamotte's professional photographs of the 'Tropical Transept', the 'Great Aspidistra' and the 'Aboosimbel Figures'. He also noted the great wealth of colour in the halls, in the exquisite fabrics coming off the Indian looms, the decorative ceramics from Tunisia and on the girders and columns of the Crystal Palace itself, where colour had been used to accentuate form, to emphasize the lightness and space of the whole structure. The Great Exhibition was expected to herald a great era of peace and prosperity in the world, and it made the insular British more aware of people living and working overseas, for even the radical Nevil Maskelyne had clearly assumed that all foreigners beyond the Mediterranean were at best semi-barbaric, and he was consequently surprised at the excellence of their craftsmanship. Later in May, the Great Western Railway laid on another excursion, this time to mark the opening of a new railway connecting Oxford with Buckinghamshire, and Nevil was invited to share in a banquet to celebrate the event. Starting with turtle soup, followed by fish, and lubricated with moselle wines, claret and champagne, it must have been a cheering occasion for the low-paid young professor.

The status and pay of professors was strongly under discussion by this time, because the Royal Commission had called for evidence on the subject. Evidence had already been returned by a large number of college heads and professors, including Nevil Maskelyne, who, together with Henry Halford Vaughan, Professor of Modern History, asked that professors should be paid enough to enable them to marry on their academic salaries. These two likeable and lively young men had no significant worldly goods to share, and this certainly put them at a disadvantage in the marriage stakes, but their radical activities and the righteous tone they brought to their campaigning irritated those in authority, and Mark Pattison, a mutual friend, wrote to his wife that Francis Jeune, Master of Pembroke, was heard sarcastically asking why Maskelyne was the most unpopular man in Oxford. 'Is it', he wondered, 'because he gets with Vaughan and thus comes away saying "How we apples swim"?' Few Victorian papas would contemplate relegating their daughters to a life spent in the basement below Broad Street, on a salary of £100 a year, and it would of course be unthinkable for Nevil to marry below his station, so he was caught either way. Whilst on the subject of pay, Nevil took the opportunity of urging pensions so that professors could eventually retire, for, as he pointed out, not all science professors could keep up with the most recent scientific and technological developments to the moment of their death and, in any case, retirement could be something pleasant to look forward to in later years. It was this lack of pension which caused Dr Buckland to cling to his two professorships, even though all his work was being done by deputies. Counter-evidence was of course put forward by the anti-professor lobby, who said that since most professors were college Fellows, and therefore clergy, they could retire to college church livings, where they would need no pension.

Several academics urged a general pay increase for professors, so that the services of eminent men could be bought for Oxford. As it was, they said, few undergraduates ever saw a professor at all, and those who did were often more attracted by the general showmanship of the lecturer than by the

Broad Street
from the
Old Ashmolean
Museum

content of his courses. This was probably true – because professors had to work ten times harder to attract audiences than the tutors did (tutors' lectures being compulsory), but it could be argued that a little showmanship never came amiss in serious lecturing anyway. Benjamin Jowett was sure that professors should not be forced to submit to religious tests, which excluded non-Anglicans like Liebig or Faraday. In any case, he didn't think that scientific men felt any particular *hostility* towards the churches.

Nevil felt concerned about support for scientific research, and he wanted to see scholarships available so that his own students, for example, could have funds available for equipment and materials for chemical research. Like several of his colleagues, Nevil thought that there should be more science professors, to cover the subjects already taught but in more depth, for he considered that Dr Walker's physical science lectures alone should be made the work of three professors.

Nevil's own salary was put on trial in June 1851, when the university reviewed the salaries of certain public lecturers and professors, and decided in principle that the pay of these men should go up. However, when it came to the vote, only one professor, Dr Walker, got his rise. When it was proposed that Nevil Story Maskelyne, Deputy Professor in Mineralogy, should receive a salary rise from £100 to £250 a year, the votes broke even, 57 for and 57 against, so he didn't get it.

One voice which came out surprisingly firmly in the cause of the new studies at Oxford was that of the aged and infirm Duke of Wellington, who, following correspondence with the Prime Minister, Lord John Russell, decided he could still perform a few useful services as Chancellor of Oxford University, by speaking in the right quarters in favour of scientific subjects like physics and chemistry. The duke was canny enough to realize that the Anglican body in the university might not yet be ready for the imminent spread of scientific learning, but he set to work nevertheless, to soften up those government members who might cause trouble by baulking educational reform. The duke also tackled his own deputy at Oxford, the Vice-Chancellor, Dr Plumptre, who was one of those who thought the university should aim at

Probably the
Duke of Wellington

higher things than mere education. Nevil Maskelyne seems to have taken a somewhat faint photographic portrait of the Duke of Wellington in his 'robe and collegiate cap' (which had been borrowed by Prince Albert in 1847 for the British Association meetings), and the star of the Order of the Bath – a decoration the duke had received in 1815.

A job came up in Oxford that July, which Nevil would have found a very useful additional post to his professorship, but he was only one of four people who applied for it – the job of Radcliffe Librarian in charge of the beautiful circular renaissance building at the heart of the university. Dr Acland got it, despite having a thriving medical practice and a professorship himself, or perhaps because of these prior advantages. Dr Acland was not the only professor to combine his academic teaching with a busy medical practice, and Dr Daubeny struck out at this habit in his evidence to the Royal Commission, saying that he believed professors should be paid enough to render such additional employments unnecessary. Success, however, breeds success, and Dr Acland cheerfully took on the Radcliffe Librarianship plus everything else. He was a very active man, full of good will – described by Goldwin Smith as 'always kind and apt to be gushing' – but although he usually coped well with a heavy work load, he was sometimes driven to bouts of temperament if he didn't get his way. Viktor Carus, who had lived with the Aclands for the later part of his time in Oxford, had found he had had to provide a good deal of sympathy and support for the household, with its constant stream of patients waiting in the hall.

Dr Acland had been tantalized to hear it revealed at a committee meeting that June, that the university authorities had £60,000 tucked away – the accumulated profits of the Oxford University Press, left behind when the press had left the Clarendon Building for new premises. Dr Acland set his sights on that money, but was refused at first because of the doubtful morals of using the proceeds of Bible and prayer-book sales for anything so secular as the promotion of interest in science.

It was religious issues, not scientific ones, which still held most people's attention, so everyone noticed in September that the Reverend F.D.Maurice was being confronted over his religious beliefs, and that his suitability as Professor of Divinity at King's College, London, was being challenged. He was openly questioned by the Reverend R.W.Jelf – father of the two little singing-birds, and brother of the unpopular Oxford proctor, W.E.Jelf. An article in the *Quarterly Review* followed the matter up by accusing Maurice's Christian Socialist friends of putting out propaganda in favour of Chartism, Red Republicanism and Communism which could well lead to anarchy, infidelity and, indeed, immorality. To the Christian Socialists, the attacks on Maurice seemed unfair, because their revered Bible-study leader had recently been hanging back and protesting at the more organizational and socialist aspects of their work, and had even tried to stop John Ludlow from publishing his paper, *The Christian Socialist*, partly because he had feared it might encourage the setting up of some breakaway sect. Maurice's name was nevertheless associated with socialism and with dangerously angled theology and, although he did not actually lose his Chair of Divinity at this stage, his position was precarious.

John Ludlow, meanwhile, had become involved in setting up consumers' and producers' cooperatives, and Ludlow did not always see eye to eye with them. He was particularly anxious to uphold the cause of the downtrodden craftsmen, by keeping the producers' cooperatives stronger than those for consumers (the shopkeeping side). Ideally he would have liked to see the one depending on the other but if, as he feared, the consumers' side should grow too powerful and lose sight of the original aim of helping the producer, he considered that the Working Men's Association should part from the consumers' cooperatives altogether.

Events began to overtake John Ludlow's idealism early in 1852, when the powerful new trade union, the Amalgamated Society of Engineers, asked the Christian Socialists for practical advice on setting up a Working Men's Association workshop to absorb surplus engineering labour while they campaigned to keep down overtime. By the autumn, some of the newly joined Christian Socialists had set up contracts between trades unionists and the managers of Working Men's Associations and consumers' cooperatives. Ludlow suddenly realized his ideals were being undermined, for not only was the Christian side of the work being swept aside, but he suspected that the craftsmen's profit-sharing agreements were no longer being honoured, so on 30 October he called a meeting at which he protested strongly, and called for the resignation of the newcomer Christian Socialist organizers. However, since only the loyal Charles Mansfield would support him, John Ludlow gave in his own resignation a few days later, and it was accepted on 13 November.

Charles Mansfield was able to share all this Christian Socialist trouble with Nevil Maskelyne when he came to stay with him in December. Maskelyne was unable to leave Oxford, since he was lecturing there regularly that winter but from Oxford Charles Mansfield wrote to John Ludlow to tell him that Maskelyne offered him a bed at the Old Ashmolean Museum if he wanted to come and stay. By this time, not only had Ludlow fallen out with the Christian Socialist movement, his life's work, but the Reverend F.D.Maurice, after cross-questioning by a committee of clerics, had finally been found unsuitable as divinity professor at King's College, London.

Charles Mansfield was still full of inventive ideas, and had been writing up a concept he had for propelling an aircraft by means of a steam engine heated by pumping benzene through a specially designed carburettor. By this year, 1852, his restless, fertile mind was already envisaging smokeless coal, domestic central heating, harnessed tidal power, purified water supplies, pollution-free rivers, fertilizer made from treated sewage, and vehicles which no longer relied on animals or steam. Charles Mansfield gave 25 lectures at the Royal Institution that winter, on his 'Theory of Salts' – a highly complex and philosophical system of ideas which attempted to explain the chemistry of these crystals. At the end of the series he introduced his mother to Michael Faraday, who confided to Mrs Mansfield that Charles 'puzzled him sometimes dreadfully'.

Charles Mansfield had become involved in plans to build a hall for the Working Men's Associations, to provide them with a central meeting place. An extension was to be built for it, on top of the building at 34 Castle Street which was already the home of the Working Tailors' Association that Nevil Maskelyne had helped to initiate. The architect for the extension was Francis Penrose, a cousin of the Arnolds and a close friend of Charles Mansfield since their student days at Cambridge. Francis Penrose had spent most of the five years since he had left university in travelling the continent, staying for months in each city, so as to learn all he possibly could about European architecture. Latterly, he had concentrated his efforts on measuring up the

Charles Penrose

classic Greek buildings of Athens, and had enlisted the help of the crew of H.M.S. Amazon to hoist scaffolding around the Parthenon, so that he could lower plumb-lines and so make accurate measurements. From them he was able to work out the mathematics behind the hyperbolic curves of the Parthenon columns – presumably a useful collection of information for anyone wishing to embark on a full-scale Doric temple and determined to get it right.

Francis Penrose wrote out volumes of notes, so that his eventual book, *The Principles of Athenian Architecture*, was to remain a standard work for about a hundred years. Now, in 1852, he had just been appointed Surveyor to the Fabric at St Paul's Cathedral in London, which Sir Christopher Wren had never quite completed. Francis Penrose's brief was to complete the interior of St Paul's as Wren himself would have done it – a challenge he took up eagerly – but funds were not made available to carry out the designs and, when money was at last found, someone else's designs were used instead. It was to be a bitter blow for this highly sensitive architect, who had always been shy in company and very easily hurt. Francis Penrose came to visit Nevil Maskelyne at the Old Ashmolean Museum, whose classic façade no doubt made him feel at home.

In December 1852, Nevil's pay rise was at last voted in, and he suddenly found himself earning £250 a year instead of £100 so that, even if he was still rather low in the marriage stakes, he had at last gained real independence. That same winter saw an advance for Max Müller, for he was awarded an honorary M.A. degree and membership of Christ Church College – a real honour at the time for a non-Anglican foreigner. George Butler – Nevil's friend who used to enjoy steeplechasing in their student days – was back in Oxford that winter too. He had returned as a Fellow of Exeter College, right next door to the Old Ashmolean Museum, but in December he decided to marry, which meant that he had to give up his college Fellowship and could no longer live at the college. He had not taken Holy Orders, so he could not be vicar of a college living either, so he and his bride, Josephine, had to take rented accommodation in Oxford and live off George's private tutoring. Josephine was a girl of exceptional personality, depth of character and intelligence, who was to have no difficulty in adapting to tenant life for the next five years. George Butler still enjoyed riding, and he and Josephine would set off on horseback together for hours at a time, enjoying the summer evenings in the woodlands around Oxford.

George and Nevil were fellow-members of the Ashmolean Society, and the Butlers' little house was to become a haven for the young professors. Nevil would go round there with Max Müller and William Donkin, who both played music with Josephine – herself a very good pianist. When Arthur Stanley was in the house, they avoided playing because they knew he hated music, but Josephine made sure there were extra buttered tea-cakes when he came, because he loved those. Nevil was getting less time for socializing now though, because he was lecturing three afternoons a week that spring (on the chemical analysis of minerals and soils) and his laboratory was being increasingly used for public analysis work. In the interests of agricultural research, Nevil was currently analysing some samples of mineral phosphates of lime from the United States for Dr Daubeny.

In March 1852, Nevil Maskelyne gave a paper to the Ashmolean Society, in which he showed that he was well up in his thinking on atoms and molecules. He said he believed a chemical molecule to be 'a group of the ultimate chemical units of the element, whether these be atoms or not'. The early nineteenth century chemist, Dalton, had imagined atoms to be actual ultimate physical particles of matter, but most scientists since then had (unfortunately for progress) been rather afraid of Dalton's physical atom theory, and preferred to think of atoms as little chemical concepts, possibly even forming continuous undivided matter. Nevil had long been torn between the two standpoints, and to some extent he still was. However he was aware of the importance of space and volume in relation to atoms and molecules, and he was particularly interested in the fact that certain compounds could, without altering their chemical content, change into a form 'in which the same amount of matter occupies a higher volume'. The 'cauliflower-like coke' which Faraday had exhibited at Oxford had been a good example of this, because after being converted – by heat – from diamond, it took up much more space.

At this stage – March 1852 – Nevil Maskelyne believed that the correct formula for water was H_2O, although this formula had been abandoned for decades by most scientists, in favour of HO. The confusion had first arisen from one false assumption made by Dalton himself earlier that century – that a molecule was formed only when a single atom of one element was paired with a single atom of another element, *except* where two or more combinations of the same elements were known (even though it had been queried at the time, in 1815, by the English scientist William Prout). It was this arbitrary rule which had led Dalton to express water with one H and one O, even though he had himself managed to separate the elements of water and had observed that they produced two volumes of hydrogen to every one of oxygen. If Dalton had only met the Italian chemist Avogadro in 1811, he would have heard of Avogadro's hypothesis that one volume of a gas (such as hydrogen) contains the same number of particles as the same volume of another gas (such as oxygen) – but not enough people seem to have met Avogadro, working away modestly beyond the Alps, so his accurate discovery went unnoticed for years, and Dalton went on thinking that water was HO.

When working out the weights of different types of atom relative to one another, Dalton balanced his two volumes of hydrogen against a single volume of oxygen (following his own HO formula) and found the oxygen eight times heavier. Dalton's measurement was pretty accurate but, being based on the wrong combining number of atoms, it caused great confusion among the retorts for years, and gave chemists, including Nevil Maskelyne, a lot of unnecessary thinking on the way.

Dalton, however, had not been the only one studying the water molecule, for back in 1808 a French chemist called Gay-Lussac had been working simultaneously, but from the other direction. Instead of separating out hydrogen and oxygen from water, Gay-Lussac had formed water by combining two volumes of hydrogen with one volume of oxygen – and he had assumed from this that the formula for water was H_2O. At the time however, Dalton, being a man of strong personality, had won the argument in major scientific circles, and HO had stuck.

ontemporary
chemical
workbench

Nevil Story Maskelyne had by now come round to the view that Gay-Lussac must have been right all the time, and that the formula for water was indeed H_2O. Nevil stated that he thought the combining molecule of hydrogen consisted of two 'atoms', and he also thought that, after separation from water, the volume of a single hydrogen atom equalled the volume of a single oxygen atom. Nevil had been attracted to the H_2O view by various recent observations made by himself and others, especially in the study of ethers and alcohols, where it was known that certain groups of two or more atoms would stick together, while moving from one molecule to another. Such groups were called 'radicles', and it had been found that in certain cases one radicle could be substituted for one atom of a molecule. Influenced by a French scientist named Laurent, Nevil Maskelyne regarded oxygen as the central atom of any molecule of the 'water type', and he believed that hydrogen atoms or radicles grouped themselves around this central oxygen atom. It had been found that any two of a particular series of radicles could be substituted for the two hydrogen atoms of H_2O, to form alcohols. This, as Nevil pointed out, would be physically impossible if Dalton's single hydrogen equivalent was also Dalton's ultimate and indivisible atom – because it would have to be split in half.

Nevil Maskelyne's belief in the H_2O formula was further strengthened by the fact that a number of acids, previously supposed to have one atom combining with a salt-radicle, had now been found to have two. Working with minerals – inorganic compounds – which have a relatively simple chemical make-up, Nevil was in a good position to try out his theories. Now that he had accepted the H_2O formula, he was beginning to hit on the idea that atoms of one particular kind of element might be combining in certain different set ratios with the atoms of each other kind of element, and he backed this up by mentioning seven recently discovered combining powers for the element manganese. Nevil confirmed his ratio idea by writing out the formula for salts of iron, using fractions to express some of the combining ratios – which was the best way he could think up for doing it at the time, with no proper atomic weights to refer to. His formulae agreed in essence with the formulae used today, though they look rather curious the way he put them onto paper. It is interesting that one year later, in 1853, Benjamin Brodie was still thinking in terms of hydrogen as a 'double atom'; that he was still wondering if such a thing as a single hydrogen atom could be said to exist, and was referring to 'the compound molecule of hydrogen H H' and to 'hydrogen gas H H'.

It was an exciting time for chemistry because several scientists were beginning to stumble upon the theory of valency – the concept that an atom of one element will only combine with a fixed number of atoms of another element. We know now, for example, that oxygen only combines with two hydrogen atoms, whereas nitrogen only combines with three hydrogen atoms. If only they could have been sure of that in the mid nineteenth century, they would have been on much firmer ground. Nevil Maskelyne was up there with the front runners, and they were all closing in on the threshold of modern chemistry, but the door was still closed.

Oxford opens out

By May 1852, Charles Mansfield had been driven into what he described in a letter to his sister Anna as a 'changeable state' and Nevil Maskelyne, who was now giving three mineral analysis lectures a week in his basement laboratory, had little time to help his friend. One of the things which had upset Mansfield was Charles Kingsley's insistence that he should give up his mistress, to whom Kingsley objected firstly on the snob grounds that she was too common, and secondly because running a mistress was immoral anyway, Charles Mansfield, writes E.R.Ward, had always been helpless before the charms of women, and had even left a wife tossing about on the choppy seas of his past – something of a scandal in those days. It was while he was so upset at the loss of his mistress that he resolved to fulfil a longstanding ambition and visit a country he thought of as Arcadia itself – the far-distant South American state of Paraguay. It was a particularly exciting moment to choose to make the voyage, because the country, after being closed to outsiders for many years due to political instability, had just been opened up, following the overthrow of its dictator Rosas. So on 10 May Charles Mansfield set sail from Southampton for the exotic shores of Paraguay, Brazil and the River Plate.

Although Charles Mansfield was a close friend of Maskelyne's at this stage, there was no question of Maskelyne getting away with him to the southern hemisphere, for he was daily being drawn closer into the university reform struggle. The Royal Commission's report on university reform was made public that summer, and in it Arthur Stanley set out the proposals his committee had arrived at. The report, generally known simply as 'the Blue Book', was sent off for the perusal of Queen Victoria and her ministers, but it was July before the Chancellor of Oxford University himself – the Duke of Wellington – received a copy. After examining it for a week, the duke advised the dyed-in-the-wool university authorities to go ahead and accept certain of the Royal Commission's reform ideas, but the authorities stiffly replied that they were unable to think about his letter until after the long vacation. This turned out to be a bit late for further action by the duke, for he had died before the vacation was out, and his voice would no longer be heard upholding the cause of science behind the parliamentary scenes. Now that the Royal Commission report was written, Arthur Stanley was underemployed, so he was offered the post of canon at Canterbury Cathedral, where he was to work up a great enthusiasm for the history of the place. Nevil Maskelyne was among Arthur Stanley's many Oxford friends who came down to stay with him at Canterbury, to chat over reform tactics in these congenial cloistered surroundings.

In the same July that Arthur Stanley left Oxford, Dr Acland enlisted the help of Maskelyne and one or two other fellow-scientists in preparing for a one-day conference he was organizing for medical men – the Provincial and Surgical Association – in Oxford. For their evening's entertainment he planned a soirée in the Radcliffe Camera, which was to be adorned in grandiose style, with the object of impressing his visitors with Oxford's achievements in the natural sciences. At the foot of the grand staircase he placed a vast blossom of

Cloisters at
Canterbury

Dr Daubeny's Victoria water-lily from his new botanical garden hothouse, accompanied by two of its huge round leaves. In the magnificent circular library of the Radcliffe Camera, Acland hung a central chandelier, supported by light from numerous assorted lamps, to show up the fine portraits of Oxford scientists, lent by colleges. Dr Walker staged a demonstration of Foucault's pendulum experiment and an exhibition of his own collected instruments; Acland displayed choice specimens from his 1,000-strong Christ Church anatomy collection and Nevil Maskelyne contributed what *Jackson's Oxford Journal* described as a 'splendid collection of daguerreotypes'. The visiting doctors were, we hope, impressed. Dr Acland had reason to be pleased with himself that year, because he had at last persuaded the university authorities to promise the £60,000 windfall from the Oxford University Press for the building of his new University Museum for the Natural Sciences.

While Dr Acland was adding success to success, Henry Fox Talbot took an unfortunate step. That summer Fox Talbot had reached the conclusion that the new collodion photographic process – which was gaining popularity daily – was covered by his own photographic patent and that commercial photographers who used collodion without his leave were flouting the patent by not paying him dues. Fox Talbot had already had to waive his calotype patent for amateur photographers because they were not observing the patent anyway; but he was openly indignant about professional photographers who used the collodion method in their studios without paying patent dues, in fact he forbade them to do so, and some obeyed his wishes. Many however refused, on the grounds that a patent on the calotype method of photography did not cover collodion as well.

Nevil Maskelyne though was sorry for Fox Talbot, and believed he really was being done down over his patent dues, for had not Fox Talbot, after all, been the genuine inventor of the photographic negative from which many positive prints could be made? Maskelyne felt that the mere matter of the choice of chemicals or of the base material on which they were spread, was quite secondary to the invention of the negative-positive process itself. The commercial photographers, naturally enough, took an opposite view, and the whole conflict was to come to a head a year or two later. In the meantime Nevil Maskelyne's thoughts returned to his friend Charles Mansfield, from whom he had started receiving letters telling of the strange things he was finding on his voyage, including the oranges of Pernambuco, which contained a second smaller orange. By August, Charles Mansfield had reached Buenos Aires and wrote back asking Nevil Maskelyne to send out a camera so that he could record some of the astonishing things that he was seeing. The letter did not, of course, reach Nevil for another three months, by which time Charles Mansfield had arrived in Asuncion, Paraguay, after travelling 700 miles by boat up the river Parana, to the interior of the continent. He stayed in Paraguay for two and a half months, fascinated by the latin women as much as by the flora and fauna, and it is doubtful whether he ever met up with the box containing a camera which Nevil Maskelyne despatched to Charles' first port of call, Pernambuco, half a continent away.

Chacra, near Asuncion, Paraguay (from Charles Mansfield's book)

John Ludlow was receiving letters from Charles Mansfield too, and wrote back with the latest Christian Socialist news, for Ludlow had not lost interest in the movement when he had resigned the previous year. Since Mansfield had left the country, the Christian Socialists had become involved with a new Cooperative Society formed to invest workers' savings, and Ludlow had worked hard behind the scenes to smooth the path of a government bill designed to legalize Industrial and Provident societies. In a November letter to Charles Mansfield, Ludlow told him that he had been asked to come back and work with the Working Men's Association and the Cooperative Societies again, and had decided to do so. The top floor lecture area for the Working Men's Association in Castle Street had now been successfully built to the designs of Francis Penrose, the St Paul's Cathedral expert; and one of John Ludlow's first moves, on returning to the Association, had been to secure the services of Nevil Maskelyne for a lecture in photography at the new hall that December. The lecture was to be one of a series, starting at eight in the evening and costing 2d an attendance (6d with reserved seat). Ludlow told Charles Mansfield that Maskelyne's lecture, to his mind, was quite the best of the series, both clear and interesting, and that he had an audience of 50, 'very attentive indeed but without a swell among them'. Ludlow added that he was glad to see that Lord Goderich's talk on insects had not been as successful as Maskelyne's on photography, 'because it shows after all, the working men not to be such todies [sic] as we had expected'. With the amount of lecturing he now did at Oxford, Nevil Maskelyne had clearly learned how to get through to his audience, but young Lord Goderich from Oriel College was no mean speaker either, and would one day be Viceroy of India, and, on the way, one of the negotiators of the Treaty of Washington which, in 1871, was to lead to the Alabama settlements – huge sums of gold paid to the supposedly neutral British, in restitution for having fitted out the warship Alabama for the American Civil War.

Back in Oxford later in the same December, 1852, Maskelyne's earliest chemical analysis pupil, Leslie Thomson, was to perform the annual ritual of singing the boar's head carol at Queen's College. This was a Christmas Day performance which had gained a quite astonishing popularity, attracting an audience of no less than 600 people, who watched the steaming, rosemary-bedecked boar's head carried into the college hall to Leslie Thomson's baritone chant, backed by Magdalen College choristers. Leslie Thomson, tall, dignified and substantially built, had a strong deep voice and a real feeling for music, as well as wide cultural interests – small wonder that he was destined for an archbishopric later on.

During that winter two other brilliant students joined the flow of those learning chemical analysis with Nevil Maskelyne – Charles Pearson and Henry Smith, who were both friends of his already. Charles Pearson had studied at King's College in London, and was a disciple of the Reverend F.D.Maurice. He had had to abandon his King's College studies though, after being so ill from catching a chill during special constable duties at the Chartist demonstrations of April 1848. Now, after a fresh start, Pearson had emerged from Exeter College, Oxford, with a first class degree in classics, and had his eye on studying medicine, learning some anatomy, physiology and analytical chemistry on the way. He was joined in the basement laboratory by Henry Smith, who had enrolled for the classes because his college, Balliol, wanted him to teach some chemistry there the following year. As a child, Irish-born Henry Smith had been something of a scholarly prodigy, educated by his mother and then by very good tutors, but he had been a delicate boy, and had spent only the final years of his schooling at Rugby, under Dr Arnold. After taking a Double First at Balliol College, Henry Smith had had to decide whether to plump for further studies in mathematics or in classics, but his eyesight was poor for prolonged classical reading, and the college offered him a maths lecturing job, so maths it was.

Henry Smith was to become Nevil Maskelyne's lifelong friend, and the two complemented each other for humour and vitality. Nevil could be quick-tempered and impulsive, and he readily turned to sarcasm, a habit learned early in life when trying to counter his father's aggressive moves, but under-

Henry Smith

neath Nevil's brusque manner there was a modest and humorous personality, well able to laugh at himself and at life in general. Henry Smith was full of Irish wit, plays on words and a readiness to appreciate the humour in any situation, but Benjamin Jowett was later to note (in the preface to Smith's *Collected Mathematical Papers*) that a slight irony was always playing around in Smith's mind too.

Maskelyne and Smith would spend hours together in conversation and repartee, for theirs was a compatible humour. During their sojourns in the laboratory Henry Smith would discuss his idea that atomic weights and the properties of elements must have a mathematical relationship to one another which could be worked out in theory, anticipating the results of experiments. 'His conviction that such a numerical and mathematical basis underlay the phenomena of chemistry was even stronger in the case of crystals', Maskelyne was to recall. 'At my suggestion he undertook the discussion of the principles involved in the parallelism of zone-axes and face-normals in a crystal system with rational indices.' Like many another genius, Henry Smith did most of his advanced work early in life and would soon be working on his theory of numbers and theory of elliptic functions, together with certain new processes in geometry.

He and Nevil Maskelyne would sit up studying together at night, drinking more and more tea as they worked, and filling up the teapot with hot water until no tea was left in it. In the laboratory, Nevil Maskelyne trained Henry Smith to approach mineral analysis in a reasoned and meticulous way, but they would break off for long and interesting talks over the bench, for Henry with his Irish blood loved nothing better than a good chat taken through to its conclusion, and would never stop a conversation for a clock. He had no problem in setting others at their ease, and would often break into fits of laughter as he talked, so the Old Ashmolean Museum cellar saw some lively fun as well as earnest discussion in those years. Balliol College were building a chemistry laboratory underneath their new Salvin Building, where Henry Smith would teach his students, and his lectures were soon to become well known for the amusing manner in which he gave them – one demonstration for example finished with the words 'It is the peculiar beauty of this method, gentlemen, and one which endears it to the scientific mind, that under no circumstances can it be of the smallest utility.'

Both Henry Smith and Charles Pearson were enthusiastic supporters of Nevil Maskelyne's views on university reform and became interested, too, in his work for the Working Men's Association in London. Both of them joined him that spring of 1853, by lecturing at the Hall in Castle Street. Charles Kingsley was teaching there now too, and so was another of Nevil Maskelyne's friends, Mountstuart Grant Duff. Maskelyne was still in sporadic touch with Matthew Arnold, and had bought volumes of some of his recently written poems, including 'Sohrab and Rustum' which he particularly liked. Matthew Arnold was now married and living in London, but travelling about a good deal as an inspector of schools. He still appeared in Oxford from time to time and Max Müller described him as being a man full of dreams and schemes, whose 'Olympian manners began even at Oxford, there was no harm in them, they were natural, not put on'. Early in 1853, Matthew Arnold had seen his ardent younger brother, William, return from India on long-term sick-leave with his wife Fanny, already pregnant with her second child. William Arnold had become disillusioned by the corruption he found in India and by the added vices he saw being brought in by Europeans, but he was determined to go back and do what he could to help the Indians to help themselves through education – an ideal in the Arnold tradition and somewhat after the Christian Socialist's way of thinking too, but by no means the normal way of thinking for an empire educational administrator. William even went so far as favouring teaching in the vernacular, and teaching local religions rather than introducing Christian missionaries. Perhaps the fact that he had kicked free of the Oxford traces after only a term of college life had left him with a more open mind.

The struggle for science at Oxford still went on, and by the beginning of that year, 1853, the University Museum project had been properly launched with the appointment of a delegacy to work out the precise buildings and rooms required. As secretary to this first delegacy, Nevil Story Maskelyne had to find out the kind of museum display areas, lecture rooms and equipment considered necessary by the people who would use them. He didn't have to look far to question the natural science professors on their needs because Acland, Daubeny and Donkin all sat with him on the same delegation committee, and so did Richard Greswell, who had secured major bequests of money and a vast insect and butterfly collection for the new museum. Mr Strickland, Buckland's deputy in geology, was a member of the delegacy too.

Nevil Maskelyne wrote out a report stating that the purpose of the museum would be to provide for 'teaching and studying the Natural History of the Earth and its inhabitants', for which it would need public exhibition rooms, lecture rooms, studies for the professors, work rooms for students, somewhere for the curator to live and a common library for all departments. For his own Department of Mineralogy, Maskelyne suggested a lecture room to seat 100, to be shared with the Department of Geology; two museums, one for rocks and one for minerals; a 20 foot by 20 foot laboratory, a store room and a sitting room for himself, to face south so that he could use his goniometer in sunlight, for measuring the angles of crystals.

It was firmly written into the report that every part of the building should be provided with gas supplies, water, heating, ventilation and fireproofing, with mains fire hydrants and drainage. It was a practical and carefully researched report which Maskelyne put together, and no doubt deserved the acceptance it received. However, this time the architect estimated that the museum and accessories would cost about £48,000 – or £57,000 with galleries, fittings and furnishings. Since all this was within the budget, and left some money for buying land on which to build, the delegates looked round for an empty plot. There was land available opposite the Clarendon Building in Broad Street, but it would have cost £30,000 to acquire this prime city-centre site, so the delegates looked at Merton College's offer of two fenced fields in the University Parks – four acres in all. An outcry was raised at the proposal to develop these fields because, although they were under the plough at the time, university walking enthusiasts claimed that it would mean snatching away yet another attractive and healthy country area suitable for afternoon walks.

The enclosure of open grazing country, in favour of cultivation, had rapidly been narrowing the choice of Oxford walks over the past two years. The 'Cowley Enclosure' had cut off most of the extensive Cowley Marshes; Bullingdon Common had gone, and Port Meadow was about to be put under cultivation too. Even Bagley Wood, with the old Gobble Oak at its heart, was no longer available to the botanists and poachers who used to roam about beneath the mysterious shade of the old trees – so it is hardly surprising that there was an organized protest against building on the University Parks. In fact a further objection was raised, that the site was too far out of Oxford, remote from the colleges and therefore inaccessible to professors and students. However, the Royal Commission had recommended the science museum idea in principle, so the museum delegacy won the day and bought the site.

By the time the Parks site was purchased (December 1853), a third delegacy was directing operations, with George Butler as its secretary. During the past year, George Butler had been working closely with his friend Nevil Maskelyne and the other museum planners, and Josephine Butler as usual found herself

Probably Josephine
Butler

entertaining numbers of scientific men in their little house. Josephine was a brilliant young woman with perceptive views on social justice and the rights of women, views which had partly been sparked off by witnessing a man beating his wife. This incident had led her to think deeply on the position of women in the society of her day, and later to embark on an energetic life devoted to winning equal educational and financial rights for women and to establishing homes for prostitutes. Josephine was to initiate a Europe-wide movement against licensed brothels – as being a form of slave trade for which children were even sometimes expressly reared – and she was to have laws passed in Britain to take away the right of the police to arrest women on the street on suspicion of their having venereal disease.

Josephine saw Oxford University as a society of celibates living behind college walls and failing to communicate with those outside, and she thought the judgements of university men were made with masculine prejudice. 'There were original thinkers', wrote Josephine years later, 'but afraid to go outside the celibate mass opinion', and she regretted the absence of normal home life in university circles. One family whom Josephine did know, however, were the Skenes, who brought to Oxford not only normal home life, but three capable and attractive girls. This remarkable family had arrived in Oxford shortly before Nevil Maskelyne had come to live at the Old Ashmolean Museum. They had been brought to the city by old grandfather Skene, who had been a great friend of Sir Walter Scott in his younger days. Grandfather Skene had once lived at Rubislaw in Scotland, and Scott had written 250 lines of poetry in memory of their comradeship and their walks over the border country together (the introduction to the fourth canto of *Marmion*). Sir Walter Scott described the Skene family as being full of old-fashioned kindness and good humour, and old James Skene had been no mean scholar in his time, for he spoke fluent French, German and Italian, had written books and was a Fellow of the Scottish Royal Society. Although the Skenes originally hailed from Scotland, grandfather Skene had taken his wife and his one remaining unmarried daughter, Felicia, out to live in Greece for six years – partly for Mrs Skene's health and partly to be near their married son and his young family. This son, Felicia's brother, had married a Greek beauty of ancient princely family, when both of them were young – his bride had been only 16 at the time – so their daughters were not so very much younger than their aunt Felicia.

In Greece, Felicia had enjoyed a highly adventurous time, riding out into the Greek hills with her father, writing poems and travel books, and receiving singing lessons from the maestro of the Athens opera, who trained her up to sing like a prima donna – a powerful addition to domestic musical evenings around the candlelit piano. When old James Skene 'the white-haired laird' had returned to Britain with his wife and 33-year-old daughter Felicia, he had also brought along with him his half-Greek grandchildren, to finish their education – so now the two beautiful young Skene granddaughters were taking Oxford by storm. Felicia, though a robust young woman of immense character and accomplishments, had no looks to compare with theirs. She became a personal friend of Dr Pusey, took on the job of parish worker at St Thomas the Martyr church in Oxford, near the Skenes' Beaumont Street home, and made a name for herself locally for her fine sung renderings of the works of Handel.

The two younger Skene girls, Zoë and Janie, known respectively as the

pretty one and the clever one, were much in demand for evening parties,
picnics and university dinners, and the young professors and dons would try
to position themselves in such a way that they contrived to take the clever
Janie down to dinner, but sit opposite the pretty Zoë. They would even hang
round the door of any shop she might enter, to catch a glimpse of her as she
came out. Zoë, who became known as the 'Greek slave' for her Levantine
beauty, attended Nevil Maskelyne's lectures in mineralogy, which must have
increased their popularity, and he took a number of photographs of the Skene
girls, but it was Leslie Thomson, Nevil's first chemical analysis pupil, who
managed to steal the heart of the beautiful Zoë. In 1852 they had become
unofficially engaged, but this coup of Leslie's was vehemently opposed by
Zoë's Greek mother and her aristocratic Athenian family. Not only had they
no faith in the young clergyman's suitability, but they received a visit from a
young English peer, to whom they showed a photograph of Zoë, and who as a
result asked for her hand in marriage. In accordance with local custom, a
marriage was arranged without Zoë's consent or knowledge. Some of the
sorrow which lay behind Zoë during the three years of her forbidden engagement to Leslie Thomson shows through in photographs taken of her by Nevil
Maskelyne.

Through his continuing interest in photography, Maskelyne was on the
committee of the Photographic Society which had been started up in London
that January. On 21 April 1853, he gave a lecture to his fellow-members, on the
subject of his calotype camera, which he had adapted for handling large
numbers of sheets of paper. Each sheet of paper could be exposed in turn by
sliding it behind a board secured by a button. A focusing glass was placed next
to the glass screen holding the paper, to get the image in focus, and the rest of
the operation was rather like a conjuring trick, with the photographer's hands
disappearing into a black cloth to remove an 'excited paper' from a large box
which hung behind the camera, place it in the camera and replace an exposed
sheet into a compartment of the hanging box. There were other minor pro-
cedures, like the removal of the focusing glass before exposure, and the last-

minute positioning of the paper. It sounds like a complicated routine by today's standards, and even Nevil Maskelyne's fellow-members of the Photographic Society voiced misgivings over whether his 'very ingenious construction' might not be a bit of a handful to use.

Charles Mansfield burst back into the scene that spring, returned at last from South America. Remembering Nevil's fondness for animals, Charles had arranged for an ocelot to be shipped to him from Buenos Aires, and Nevil kept it for several years before it turned savage. Now that he was back, Charles Mansfield saw a good deal of Nevil, and returned to chemical research, working partly with Professor Hofmann at the Royal College of Chemistry and partly in a small private laboratory he had set up for himself beside the Regent's Canal in London. Both Nevil Maskelyne and Thomas Hughes were down in Weybridge staying with the Mansfields that summer, and in October Charles Mansfield was back again staying at the Old Ashmolean Museum, but he was suffering from a temperamental bout which, combined with a sudden urge to devote himself to good works for others, rather than to chemistry, set him so much on edge that he fell out with Maskelyne for the time being and wrote to tell John Ludlow that 'all sympathy between Maskelyne and myself has vanished, he is as affectionate as ever, but we live in two different worlds'. Later that autumn though, Mansfield and Maskelyne seem to have been on friendly terms as usual.

Early that autumn of 1853, Nevil Maskelyne suddenly heard of the death of his opposite number, Hugh Strickland, Dr Buckland's deputy in geology. He had been returning from the British Association meetings at York and had broken his journey to examine the geological strata in a cutting beside a railway tunnel when he stepped back out of the way of one oncoming train, right into the path of another coming the other way. It was sad news for Oxford because Mr Strickland, although some years older than Nevil, was a comparatively young academic and an inspired geologist and zoologist.

Oxford was opening out a little now, due to better communications by rail, and was even relaxing very slightly in favour of music and the fine arts. John Ruskin had been writing books which were causing people to appreciate the

A collector of
engravings

100

works of Turner, and he was just turning his attention to the pre-Raphaelites, Millais and Holman Hunt. Mr Combe, director of the Clarendon Press, and a local pre-Raphaelite enthusiast and collector, had Holman Hunt working away at his painting 'the Light of the World' in his Oxford house. Nevil Maskelyne possessed a number of Ruskin's meticulously illustrated volumes on architecture, but he never got caught up in the Victorian passion for the gothic style himself. Another practising artist about Oxford in those days was John Pollen of Merton College, who used to leave little drawings on college staircase walls, to indicate that he had called on someone in their rooms, but had found nobody there. John Pollen used to give numerous lectures to local societies, on art and architecture, particularly on the use of colour in buildings – ranging from colour in mediaeval churches to colour in the great mosques of the Middle East, which he had noticed during his far-flung travels. At an evening party, John Pollen had once egged on the redoubtable Felicia Skene into singing Handel's 'Waft her angels', promising to follow it himself with a rendering of the muezzin's call to prayer, which he carried out cross-legged on the floor, rocking back and forth as he gave out the long wailing call. John Pollen's most admired work was probably his painting carried out on the Merton College chapel ceiling, which included cherubs based on the Magdalen college choristers.

Collecting works of art was becoming popular enough in Oxford to support a picture dealer, James Wyatt, in the High Street, who attracted the custom of connoisseurs like the Radcliffe Observer, Manuel Johnson, a keen private collector of Italian engravings and Dutch etchings – which Max Müller and Nevil Maskelyne used to enjoy – and Mr Griffiths, the Sub-Warden of Wadham College, who had endless portfolios of collected drawings which he loved to show to friends, 'a taste a little irksome and boring', remarked Mrs Jeune in her diary, after being subjected to a whole evening of the gentlemen examining Griffiths' portfolios.

Nevil Maskelyne followed up the art craze by giving his autumn mineralogy lectures on the ores and minerals used in the arts, demonstrating the states in which such minerals can normally be found. Lectures on religious topics were, however, still the controversial crowd-pullers, and Leslie Thomson gave a very popular series of lectures that term, on the Atonement. Frederick Denison Maurice had been in the national public eye again too, over some theological essays which he had just published. They had not been at all well received by the Anglican authorities and in November 1853 Maurice was at last thrown out from his post as Professor of Theology at King's College, London. In some distress, he turned to his friends in the Christian Socialist movement and the Working Men's Associations, who rallied round so loyally that 967 workers presented him with an address in their Hall of Association that December, in token of their sympathy and support.

As before, it had fallen to the lot of the Reverend R.W.Jelf to judge Maurice's theology. Jelf was a remarkable man, highly respected on all sides for his integrity and impartiality, in fact he had been the one person to whom both Pusey and Newman had written for advice on points of doctrine during the Tractarian troubles. Dr Jelf had been involved in judging Pusey's condemned sermon too, but he had always avoided being theologically overthrown himself. A diplomatic and courteous man, Dr Jelf held the post of Principal of King's College, London, for 24 years and was a Canon of Christ Church, Oxford, for most of his working life as well. He was now 55, but as a younger man he had spent nine years in Germany, tutoring the son of the blind King of Hanover.

Viktor Carus, who had now been back at work in Germany for two years, had just finished a meaty book about the work he had been doing on comparative anatomy whilst in Oxford and the Scilly Isles. Dr Jelf might not have approved, for in his book Viktor Carus managed to anticipate some of the arguments which were to lead Charles Darwin to write his *Origin of Species*, by pointing out relationships between existing creatures and fossil forms. Darwin was in fact to write to Viktor Carus a decade later, after seeing his book, to tell him that he only wished he had known of this work at the time when he had been researching his Theory of Evolution. Oxford was by no means ready for Darwin yet, in fact the reformers still had a great deal of work to do to gain recognition for scientific innovations of any kind, let alone really controversial ones.

Into the Fight

At the close of 1852 everyone had become worked up about university reform in Oxford after hearing about the Queen's Speech in the House of Commons, which set out the main areas of reform that the government wanted to see debated. These included alterations to the university's decision-making machinery, the number and financial state of students, and the use of college funds for university purposes. Copies of the Royal Commission report were to be circulated at Oxford and Cambridge, for examination by all interested parties.

The university decision-makers themselves – mainly college heads – naturally appointed a committee to look into the report, so the numerous band of working college tutors revived a Tutors' Association to look after *their* interests. Francis Jeune, a college head interested in reform, gathered up a separate group consisting of middle-of-the-road reformers, while the extreme radicals formed a tight group to work out their own more drastic policies and course of action. The formation of these four diverging groups gave promise of many months of exciting reform battles at Oxford

The names of the principal members of the radical group were Chretien, Congreve, Donkin, Jowett, Maskelyne, Pattison, Goldwin Smith and Wilson, and they met together on a regular basis with the aim of reviving the professoriate and of reducing the influence of the clergy in the university. Nevil Maskelyne's basement rooms saw a good deal of the radical set – his friend Mountstuart Grant Duff was dining there with him in February 1853, to meet up with Richard Congreve and Max Müller (who was supportive, though careful to keep out of the political limelight). Soon after joining the radical group of reformers, Mark Pattison dined beneath the Old Ashmolean Museum in the company of Nevil Maskelyne, John Conington, Henry Smith, Richard Congreve and Mountstuart Grant Duff, and described the atmosphere as one of 'cosy abandon, not unpleasant but that I am not quite as home with them yet'. One of this group, John Conington, was known to be Oxford's 'foremost wearer' of clothes made by the Christian Socialist tailors.

Five radical university members were known to be in favour of immediate expansion of the university to take more students, whether attached to a college or not. The five were Henry Halford Vaughan, Richard Congreve, Mark Pattison, Nevil Maskelyne and John Conington; in fact Maskelyne was now playing an active and central rôle in university reform, and his signature was inevitably among those on a document received by the university authorities that spring, supporting the Royal Commission's report as far as it went, but urging yet more power for the university (and therefore for the professors).

In April 1853 the Royal Commission's report on university reform was praised in a parliamentary speech, for its proposals to alter the university decision-making machinery, the rules for Fellows and the regulations for the intake of students. These points were all strongly supported by Dr Jeune's party and by the radicals, but the Tutors' Association deplored them with equal vigour. By the end of 1853, the university authorities excited a fresh burst of interest in the status of professors at Oxford, by issuing a report recommending a few more science professors, with better salaries, and they also recommended that the teaching of mathematics should be shared between professors and tutors. The tutors' side had anticipated this sort of offensive, and had prepared a report of their own, in which they stated that the rôle of professors was to point the minds of undergraduates to higher things – as an antidote to the commercial spirit of the times. Professors should be there 'making the University a centre and source of unproductive thinking, a means of reform to society in general'. Thinking about the matter further, the tutors said that they would like to see rules drawn up, obliging professors to write 72 lectures a year, in six volumes, and to be sure to keep their teaching subordinate to that of tutors, But the tutors showed a surprising generosity when it came to salaries (which, after all, would not have to come from college funds) and recommended that professors should be paid £500 a year.

Dr Pusey, who had strong views of his own on the matter, considered that the professors of chemistry, geology, mineralogy, anatomy, physiology and botany were communicating knowledge efficiently enough through their lectures and should continue to do so, but that all other subjects should be learned from books rather than from professors' lectures – which would leave professors free to keep on studying and studying until they became a great living body of learning. Dr Pusey refused to believe that, by lecturing, a professor could stimulate great minds, produce minds capable of advancing knowledge, or even make anyone able to write better books. In Pusey's view, the purpose of lectures was limited to imparting knowledge, which was all that science students needed anyway. Henry Halford Vaughan, the Professor of Modern History, disagreed with Pusey, pointing out that science involved understanding and memorizing, and being able to compare, deduce and make leaps of the imagination – not just absorbing facts. Henry Halford Vaughan was a popular and successful lecturer, who actually claimed an attendance of 500 at his last course of lectures, though a number of these had been observed to be women, and therefore not undergraduates. The Principal of St Mary Hall was sure that if professors became the main lecturers it would cause 'injury to all sound learning' and encourage 'superficial and unprofitable teaching'. This particular college head, Dr P.Bliss, was supposed to have published the university's new science degree syllabus, but he had sat on it for so long that Nevil Maskelyne had had to write and ginger him into getting it printed, so that students of that school could have some idea of what to study for their exams.

University reform, though, was not the sole problem facing Oxford in January 1854, for not only had the new year come in with some of the coldest recorded days that century, but a terrible cloud of gloom hung over the whole country, due to the likelihood of war starting up in the Crimea at any moment. Russia now seemed like a fearsome great bogey, threatening the freedom of Europe, and British people were full of righteous indignation against Tsar Nicholas I for holding most of his nation in serfdom and for having taken away the liberty of the Poles and suppressed the Hungarians.

Tension had been building up around Turkey for many years, and Britain had some grounds for fearing too strong a territorial hold in the Middle and Near East, which seemed uncomfortably close to India. Late in 1853, a minor squabble between the Russians and the Turks had set light to the whole long-smouldering Near-Eastern situation. The Turks attacked the angry Russians in Moldavia (near the present-day Russian-Rumanian border) and in November 1853 the Russians countered by destroying the Turkish fleet, near Sinope in the Black Sea. British public feeling waxed indignant against Russia and, despite divided opinion in the British cabinet, Britain and France each sent off fleets for the Black Sea at once, and told the Russians to withdraw from Moldavia, expecting that they would.

Max Müller wrote to Baron Bunsen that he thought the Russians would give way if they could find a way of doing so without loss of face but, looking around him at Oxford, he noticed that British patience was growing short, 'and once they begin war here, diplomacy can do nothing; for it is the people that make war here, not the sovereigns and ministers'. Max had judged the situation shrewdly enough, for the Russians, under pressure from Austria, had quietly pulled out of Moldavia. By that time, however, the British and French were in no mood to be stopped, and the Crimean War was set to begin.

Back in Oxford during that extremely cold winter, Max Müller was keeping

Skating on the Thames (at Richmond) during the winter of 1853-4

warm by skating, walking and playing racquets – 'which makes one perspire even more than camomile tea' – but many of the poor and elderly stayed in bed much of the day and night, to stave off the freezing cold. Food, clothes and coal were very expensive and snow lay deep on the ground, but the extreme conditions did not deter the Oxford reform committees from meeting. While the old guard of the college heads argued in favour of celibacy for Fellows, power for the clergy and strict college discipline for students, the 'chief talent and young blood' of the university organized itself to push through radical reform.

Nevil Story Maskelyne, as one of the latter group, wrote to Lord Palmerston in February to explain to him the position of science professors at the time, and to point out that, although an examination syllabus for natural sciences had recently been introduced, students had made little success of science studies so far because not only were there not enough science professors, but the college tutors actively discouraged students from thinking of taking up any but the traditional courses. Nevil Maskelyne gave the Prime Minister, Lord Palmerston, a list of five new professorships which he considered should be created – medicine and pathology, zoology, practical chemistry, mechanical sciences and mathematics. He also recommended that the university should have special powers to create 'extraordinary' chairs if it seemed important to secure the services of a specialist in some branch of study not already represented.

Nevil Maskelyne held out strongly to Palmerston against one man being allowed to hold two or more professorships at the same time. As soon as the professors could be better paid, he said, they should be restricted to one job each, and he explained how Dr Daubeny currently held the three professorships of chemistry, rural economy and botany, while the Regius Professor of Medicine, Dr Ogle, held four other paid professorships – one each in medicine and clinical medicine and two in anatomy. Even comatose Dr Buckland still held the chairs of both mineralogy and geology, and Nevil himself, as he pointed out, had just been allotted £100 a year for four years to superintend the study of chemical analysis in the public laboratory (his cellar). This post, Nevil suggested, should ideally form the work of a newly-created Professor of Practical Chemistry – a job he would dearly have liked for himself.

He set out his proposals in the form of a neat table which cannot have failed to put its message over to Lord Palmerston. The Prime Minister's thoughts, however, were by now largely centred on the impending Crimean War, and it was Gladstone, current M.P. for Oxford University, who took up the fight for the proposed reforms, in preparation for a bill on the subject to be introduced in Parliament in March.

The tutors were now fighting to make sure that only they and the college heads could possibly be in the majority on the elected governing body of the university. They had opposition though, for on 15 February, 41 liberals, including Nevil Maskelyne, signed a petition in favour of an alternative constitution which would give professors more chance of being elected. The radicals certainly hoped that Gladstone would still be enough of a liberal to ignore the tutors' protests and push the Royal Commission's proposals through wholesale, but he did not.

The University Reform Bill's first reading in Parliament showed that Gladstone was trying to please all sides by compromising, but in fact he pleased none. As it stood, the bill allowed more professors onto the governing body, but only a quarter of all college Fellowships were to become 'open' to all comers, and then only on a short-term basis and at the college's discretion. All Fellows had to be celibate anyway, and at least three-quarters of them still had to be ordained members of the Anglican clergy. It was stipulated though, that Fellows must now be either tutors, disciplinarians (like proctors) or on the staff of Oxford churches – as opposed to being undergraduates or layabouts, as had sometimes been the case up till now. Half the Fellows still had to come from particular traditional counties or schools, which meant that the restriction no longer applied to the other half – and this did free a few places, though it still gave clear preference to those from certain privileged schools. The existing élitist character of the old universities had been upheld, so a counter-petition was drawn up at once, signed by Henry Halford Vaughan,

Dr Daubeny, Richard Congreve, Nevil Maskelyne, Arthur Stanley and Professors Walker and Baden Powell – Oxford radicals to a man. Mr Gladstone was irritated, accusing them of being dreamers who should not expect the English legal system to force their 'spick and span' professoriate upon Oxford.

Lord Derby, the Duke of Wellington's successor as Chancellor of Oxford University, was himself a prominent politician and was beginning to wonder where he should stand in the controversy, so he consulted a legal friend, the Earl of Devon. The earl wrote back that he personally considered that professors were a useful accessory to university education, whom he would like to see have more influence and more chance to work efficiently, but in his opinion it would be politically risky for Lord Derby to go along with them too far, as this might widen the rift between the professors and the university authorities – and Lord Derby needed to keep in with *them*. The earl also confessed to feeling 'some jealousy' at the idea of opening up college Fellowships to all and sundry.

Professor Edward Hawkins, who had been Provost of Oriel College for over 25 years, threw in a firm request of his own at this stage, telling Mr Gladstone that every tutor and college head should be bound by the Thirty-Nine Articles – which would guarantee orthodox Anglican teaching for every undergraduate. At the same time though, he wanted to see abolition of religious tests for undergraduates, whom he regarded as too immature, in many cases, to be sure of what they were subscribing to, especially when they first arrived at university. Edward Hawkins was a well-known Oxford character of forthright views, who had not been afraid to offer severe criticism to Newman over erroneous theological points in his early sermons – so teaching him to weigh his words and stick to the point. In fact, wrote Canon Tuckwell, all Hawkins' students were encouraged to discuss clearly and only to make statements which were worth making. He was known to be very fierce about smoking too, and he disapproved of the liberal-thinking Benjamin Jowett, so much so that the story went round that Edward Hawkins had tenderly cared for a dog which had bitten Jowett. Strangely enough, though, it was Edward Hawkins

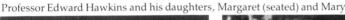

Professor Edward Hawkins and his daughters, Margaret (seated) and Mary

who was to put in a plea for the admission to Oxford University of 'Dissenters' from non-Anglican faiths, saying that if he were a village schoolmaster he would not throw them out, and would even excuse them from learning the creed. Now that he was growing older, crabby Edward Hawkins tended to become more and more scrupulous, always obsessed with details, but he, his Somerset-born wife and two daughters had been very kind and welcoming to Max Müller and Nevil Maskelyne over the years.

In March, several professors met together to see what could be done to strengthen their electoral power, for time was running out. Daubeny, Donkin and Maskelyne were there, among others, and four of the older men present were chosen to meet the politicians Lord John Russell and Mr Gladstone on 1 April, to put their case. By then, however, the University Reform Bill had already passed its second reading in the Commons, so Maskelyne and the radical set felt that the remaining aim for the professors, for the time being, should be to fight to seize education out of the hands of the clergy and into their own.

It was a bad moment for trying to attract the attention of politicians to such local causes, for on 8 April the Oxford town clerk stood on Carfax in the city centre, to proclaim that Britain was at war with Russia. It was a long-awaited announcement, for Britain's younger generation had been on the lookout for a good aggressive scrap for the past 40 years. On 26 April there was a national day of fasting and humiliation for the Crimean War, and then the fight was on. Oxford student numbers began to drop away, as young men chose the army rather than college life, and many current undergraduates left for the battlefield too, many of them never to return. It was a natural call to the young, healthy and adventurous, and they responded cheerfully, eager to throw themselves into the jingoistic fray. Janie Skene was out visiting her father and her Greek mother in Constantinople when the war broke out. Constantinople was important as a naval base, and Janie's father was with the

Embarking for the Crimean War

British diplomatic service there, so he became very involved in the war and was injured in the process.

Back in Britain, the Christian Socialists had been engaged in a less newsworthy, but perhaps more constructive fight, to start up a Working Men's College in London. This had long been an ideal of Charles Mansfield's, and the Reverend F.D.Maurice, deprived of his professorship at King's College, had decided to devote his energies to getting a Working Men's College started. Attracted by the challenge of the project, Charles Mansfield announced to Ludlow that he would give up chemistry altogether, in favour of 'a more humane profession'. In fact he didn't completely give up chemistry, but he certainly threw himself into the campaign to gather funds, pupils and teachers for Maurice's new college. Premises were found for it in Red Lion Square, in a house recently abandoned by the failed North London Needlewomen's Association. Maurice was anxious not to mix up the name of Christian Socialism with that of the Working Men's College, because he kept fearing that Christian Socialism might turn into a breakaway religious sect.

John Ludlow had long been puzzled by the attitude Maurice took towards his Christian Socialist ideals, but Maurice's thinking had foxed other people too. Listening to a Maurice sermon was said to have been like eating pea soup with a fork, and Benjamin Jowett, when asked to comment on one of Maurice's sermons, had said, 'Well! all that I could work out was that today was yesterday and this world the same as the next.' Many an intelligent man had listened to Maurice's sermons without understanding a word of what he was talking about, but his fervour and his passionate nature more than made up for his 'hopelessly confused reasoning', and he was remarkable for having inspired such a following for so long. It says something for Maurice's compelling leadership that in July 1854 he managed to attract a meeting of about 1,500 trades union members to hear his plans for the Working Men's College.

The college actually began taking students that autumn, and Charles Mansfield taught there, along with Mountstuart Grant Duff, Dr Walsh of the East End cholera campaign, John Ludlow, Charles Pearson, Francis Penrose the architect, Dante Gabriel Rosetti, John Ruskin and others. Charles

Charles Mansfield
about 1854

Mansfield protested vigorously at the inclusion of Ruskin, whom he considered a humbug, but Maurice and Ruskin had become friends, so Ruskin stayed. He took charge of the drawing classes and used to take parties of students out on walking excursions into the countryside towards the villages of Highgate, Hampstead, Harrow and Perivale, where they could breathe the fresh air and listen to the song of birds among the copses and meadows, with an occasional pause to jot down a quick impression of a cloud or a farm gate.

In the early days of the college, Nevil Maskelyne taught some science, but the subject never made much headway at the Working Men's College because of the amount of equipment it needed, and at that stage Nevil Maskelyne had little time to spare from Oxford. Thomas Huxley taught science there later for a while, and algebra was well taught from the start by Mr Litchfield, a friend of James Clark Maxwell, the mathematician. The Working Men's College students were 45% craftsmen, mostly Chartists, which was not a bad proportion at the time, but for Nevil Maskelyne and Charles Mansfield it was also a good social meeting place with their fellow-teachers.

Robert Mansfield was currently on the trail of action, in his usual dauntless way, and was frequenting the officers' mess of the 46th regiment, who were quartered at Windsor at the outbreak of the Crimean War. Robert, with his horsey conversation and racy jokes, was a popular honorary member of the officers' mess, and when the regiment set sail for Balaklava on 15 October 1854, he went down river with them in the steamer *Prince*, returning to London with the pilot. Robert Mansfield later heard back from his cousin, Colin Campbell, an engineer with the regiment, that the steamer had put the men off at Balaklava, but the port had been so overcrowded that the ss. *Prince* had had to lie offshore overnight. A fearful gale had blown up and the steamer had been dashed to pieces on the rocks, killing the crew and losing all the

A storm off
Balaklava Bay

regiment's equipment, so that the men had been left without winter clothing, tents or stores, in bitter wind and driving snow. Most of them, according to Robert Mansfield's cousin, had simply perished without a complaint.

Janie Skene travelled with her mother from her parents' home in Constantinople, to visit the wounded at Skutari, and she was so shocked at what she saw of inadequate relief that she wrote home about it to her grandfather James Skene, in Oxford, who had her letter published in *The Times* to stir up awareness of the problem. Florence Nightingale was out there campaigning to get positive political action to improve supplies and sanitation in the Crimea. One of the Skutari nurses wrote home to Oxford asking people to send out flannel and clothing for her patients. She reported that the hospitals had been awaiting a consignment of potatoes from France for months, but that the patients would be particularly grateful for chocolate, brandy and gelatine, while the nurses themselves would appreciate wine to fortify them before they went on the wards. Sebastopol, once described as 'that formidable fortress of the villainous Muscovite', was under siege by the late autumn of 1854, with the British army encamped on the bleak plain in front of it, and Russian forces holding firm within.

Felicia Skene, who was Florence Nightingale's nurse recruiting agent in Oxford, would dearly have liked to go out to the Crimea to nurse the wounded but, despite her 30-odd years, her parents would not hear of it. Felicia by this time had first-hand experience of serious nursing, because August 1854 had brought a raging cholera epidemic to Oxford. While Dr Acland spearheaded the offensive against the disease, Felicia Skene trained up nurses to work in his temporary hospital – three old cattle sheds in a field, one shed for cholera, one for smallpox (which was rife as well), and the third to give sleeping shelter to other members of afflicted families. Felicia Skene often tended cholera victims all night, alone in the house with them, and she described the stench as being enough to knock you down. She could scarcely bear to look at some of the smallpox patients, who were often so mutilated as to look more like logs than human beings, but even so, she would nurse them and would lay out the dead when necessary – even following them to the

Felicia Skene

grave if no relative was left. A policeman walked up and down outside her house at night, so that she could leave the door on the latch for people to call her quickly without waking the rest of the Skene household. Max Müller gave Dr Acland a hand to start with, but he soon caught cholera and had to turn patient for a while.

From the scientific point of view, the outbreak was carefully monitored. It was suspected that bad sanitation was in some way connected with the disease, but cholera was thought to be carried by the wind, so Manuel Johnson, the Radcliffe Observer, made daily records of wind measurements for Dr Acland at the Radcliffe Observatory in Oxford. The readings from each of his meteorological instruments were automatically recorded onto photographic paper, because the long strip of sensitized paper was slowly moved behind the instrument by clockwork, picking up a strip of light from a lamp. The thermometer, barometer and other instruments cast shadows, so Manuel Johnson could check and note down exactly how the wind force, temperature, humidity, wind direction or air pressure had been behaving – simply by developing his photographic papers. Dr Daubeny was working on the possible causes of cholera too, and came up with the likelihood that some minute living organism lay behind it – possibly a fungus – which was coming very near to the truth.

Because of the cholera epidemic, Oxford University started a week later than usual that autumn, but by mid-September the university authorities were already being instructed to put the proposals of the University Reform Bill into effect. The university decision-making body, known as Congregation, now had to be selected from a wider spectrum, to include the heads of colleges, Canons of Christ Church, the Radcliffe Librarian and Observer, the professors and museum-keepers and the public examiners. Nevil Story Maskelyne was among the ten Wadham men eligible for election to this newly-constituted body, which at last excluded from membership all those hordes of country clergymen who used to travel to Oxford to vote against anything which looked like disturbing the old order.

Things were moving in Oxford, and Dr Acland put on a public exhibition in the Radcliffe Camera in November, showing all the 32 designs which had been submitted for his new museum for the natural sciences. It was the heyday of the Victorian architectural revivals, and the choice was between the classic and the more popular gothic styles. In the end Dr Acland, George Butler and their fellow committee men chose a 'Rhenish Gothic' design which included a soaring glass roof, supported on slender cast-iron columns, with spandrels in decorative wrought-iron work. The final lofty expanse of space inside was to be reminiscent of something between a mediaeval cathedral and a London main-line railway station. One detail of the plan was to use samples of many different British rocks for the corbels, and to carve each one in the shape of a different plant – an idea which caused much innocent amusement among those of the Oxford community who wished to sponsor a carving of their favourite plant. John Ruskin joined Dr Acland in devoting endless energy to the museum project, to make sure that it became the perfect embodiment of the New Studies.

Dr Acland was at the same time becoming increasingly concerned at the plight of the sick and wounded in the Crimea and in December he put out an appeal to the undergraduates, asking for unwanted boating jackets, cricket and racquets trousers, shooting jackets, plaids, overcoats, dressing gowns,

Encamped
before
Sebastopol

jerseys and slippers. The winter seemed harder than ever, and the sufferings of the men encamped before Sebastopol must have been fearful. It was very practical of Dr Acland to think of collecting warm clothing, but if it ever arrived at all, it could not have reached the Crimea before the spring, and was certainly not in time to have saved the victims of the ss.*Prince* disaster. The Thames froze over and the frost lasted for weeks on end. Many Oxford families were plunged into sorrow and mourning as the lists of the Crimean dead came back, and the local churches were hung gloomily with black.

The winter brought influenza as well, and Nevil Maskelyne had a heavy attack of it, but it was a better winter for him in other ways, for he was made a Fellow of the Geological Society, and he also acquired a chemical assistant in the shape of a young foreign Doctor of Philosophy named Carl Ewald. This assistant was soon to find himself put to doing some unusual experiments, on behalf of Mr Fox Talbot's photographic patent. Henry Fox Talbot, who still maintained that the collodion process was covered by his patent, was growing more and more angry at the professional photographers who used the process without paying him patent dues. He had long decided that his position was strong enough to take one of these photographers to court over infringement of patent rights, and had written to Nevil Maskelyne late in the previous summer, to ask for his technical help in preparing evidence for a case against a Clerkenwell photographer who worked under the name of Laroche. Nevil Maskelyne was asked to try and prove that the collodion process was in essence the same as the process covered by the 1841 patent, so he and his assistant fell to and carried out exhaustive experiments into the precise nature of the chemicals involved.

One clause of Fox Talbot's patent had covered the making of 'visible images on paper' and the strengthening of these images 'by further liquids', which Fox Talbot claimed to his lawyer, J.H.Bolton, he had first achieved in 1833 by obtaining and fixing direct positive images. He sent Nevil Maskelyne one of these early direct positive prints on a slip of card, to show that he had succeeded in fixing it (it still exists, though only Talbot's word dates it). Another clause of the patent covered the use of potassium bromide as a fixer, but this was no longer relevant since most photographs were now fixed with 'hypo' (Sir John Herschel's discovery). The patent had also covered the 'obtaining of photographic portraits from the life, by photographic means, upon paper', but the clause which Nevil Maskelyne had been particularly asked to experiment on covered 'the employment of gallic acid, in conjunction with a solution of silver, to render paper which has received a previous solution more sensitive to light'. Fox Talbot wished to cover any technical loopholes because, while the use of gallic acid was involved in his patent, pyrogallic acid was not, and the collodion process mainly used the more sensitive pyrogallic acid, in conjunction with silver nitrate solution.

Back in 1847, Nevil Maskelyne had himself singled out gallic acid, in his paper on photography and chemistry, as being the most important single factor in calotype photography, so he now set out to examine its relations with pyrogallic acid, to see if he could demonstrate that the two were essentially the same. He already knew that they had common properties when exposed to light, for solutions of either acid would then absorb oxygen and deposit a brown powder. The light-sensitive properties of gallic acid had been known for centuries, for it acted like 'invisible ink' and had even formed the basic ingredient of the ink used for writing the Book of Kells in the Dark Ages.

In the 1850s, gallic acid was squeezed from boiled oak-apples – galls or growths which grew around the eggs of gall-wasps, for the larvae to eat. Liquid from the oak-apples was boiled up and then cooled to form silky strands of gallic acid. Pyrogallic acid was formed in those days by heating up either tannic acid or gallic acid in a retort, to distil it. Tannic acids and gallic acids were known to behave in a similar way, and Nevil Maskelyne believed that they had at least a radicle in common. During the actual court case, Fox Talbot's opponents argued that the gallic acid clause ought not to have been included in the original patent because the Reverend J.B.Reade, another photographic pioneer, had invented the gallic acid part of the process anyway, by both using it before Fox Talbot did and by mentioning its use in a lecture in April 1839 (though it is now understood that Sir John Herschel had been both using and mentioning gallic acid in the same context earlier still). Apart from Nevil Maskelyne, all the members of the Photographic Society sided with Laroche, the London studio photographer who was – according to how you cared to view the situation at the time – either pirating or simply practising collodion photography. William Grove, Queen's Counsel and inventor of the Grove battery, acted for Fox Talbot in the case, and Professor Hofmann of the Royal College of Chemistry, Claudet the photographer and William Miller, Professor of Chemistry at Cambridge University, all promised to give witness for him.

In the courtroom, the case became long and tedious and was scarcely comprehensible to the court dignitaries, since it involved so much new science and technology. When it came to summing up the evidence, the judge brushed aside the matter of similarities between gallic and pyrogallic acid as being unimportant, and stressed instead the point that gallo-nitrate of silver was used in Fox Talbot's calotypes, whereas pyrogallic acid was used in the collodion process. This was in fact a red herring because silver nitrate could be – and was – used in both processes, either combined with or separate from either acid. William Grove, who probably understood the case better than anyone, being lawyer, scientist and photographer, thought that the judge had gone astray here.

If the judge was mystified by the case, the jury was even more so, because the chemical side of photography might still be in the realms of alchemy as far as the man in the street was concerned. The trial itself had centred round the use of gallic and pyrogallic acids and the use of paper or glass as bases on which to spread chemicals. In the end, when they reached their verdict, the jury wanted Fox Talbot to be warmly reassured that he had truly invented the calotype process, but that they had nevertheless decided to return a verdict against him. Their opinion was that Laroche had not infringed Fox Talbot's patent by practising the collodion method of photography in his commercial studio.

It was a highly popular verdict in the working photographic world of the day but Henry Fox Talbot was both hurt and vexed by it, for he would now lose all the patent fees to which he had become accustomed and some of the acclaim for the invention of photography as well. Fox Talbot's invention had been the negative-positive process which, as he pointed out in a letter to his solicitor (quoted in chapter one), he had first carried out from fixed negatives in 1834 – but that had not been the point on which the trial had turned. Nevil Maskelyne wrote to Fox Talbot from Oxford, saying how much he regretted the way the trial had gone – 'Indeed I have not for long been annoyed by anything so much, but I feel that it might have been worse and that, besides taking away from you the naturally ripened fruit of your discovery, they might have taken, or rather stolen, away the honour of having planted and reared the seed and tender plant. I hope you will now let your mind grow quiet on the subject. I fear it must have cost you much, not in pocket only but in time, trouble, and not a little in that mistrust and bitterness against one's fellow-men, which these kind of annoying and really selfish assaults upon one are so apt to engender'. And he added, 'From the beginning – since I became a man – I have always looked on this photographic idea as one of the true poet-ideas of this marvellous age –and on you as its herald and enunciator. My sympathy is of little value to you – but you will always have it.' Maskelyne thought that it was unfair of the photographic fraternity to have turned against Fox Talbot when without him they might have had no photography at all, but he was also mature enough to see that patents are only as good as the jargon they are written in, and that Fox Talbot had lost his court case and should try to forget it. As he suspected though, the unfortunate inventor found the defeat constantly preying upon his thoughts, and was to remain preoccupied with it for months to come.

Nevil Maskelyne himself had plenty to occupy his mind at that time for he was working up a paper on the Koh-i-Noor diamond, said to have belonged to every mighty Indian ruler since the fabulous age of Krishna. In his paper, read to the Ashmolean Society on 12 February 1855, Nevil Maskelyne tried to re-establish the British claim that the diamond which had come to Britain on the fall of the Sikh empire was indeed the real Koh-i-Noor. This flawless diamond was currently set in the Indian Empire tiara in the jewel room at Windsor, but many Indians questioned its authenticity, for they still refused to believe that Queen Victoria possessed the true diamond of the Great Mogul. Sir David Brewster of St Andew's University had examined the stone at the British Museum in 1851 and had agreed with the Indians that this was not the Koh-i-Noor. M.M.Gordon wrote that he said he based his view on the traditional story that the Great Mogul's diamond had originally weighed 787½ carats and had subsequently been ruthlessly reduced to 280 carats by a seventeenth century Venetian diamond cutter. The diamond which Sir David Brewster had examined in 1851 had, reported Maskelyne, weighed only 186 carats, and had since been further reduced to a mere 103 carat brilliant, for use in the imperial tiara. In his paper, Nevil Story Maskelyne outlined his own re-searches into the historic background of the diamond, involving languages, weights and measures, prices, ownership and contemporary descriptions of the Koh-i-Noor through the ages, and he made out a convincing case for its authenticity. It was a research project of such historical depth that he could only have written it with the help of his friend Max Müller, with all his knowledge of the legends and languages of Indian history.

Chemistry and chemical analysis were still Nevil Maskelyne's foremost interests and took up most of his Oxford time, and his friend Charles Mansfield was now back at work in his own chemistry laboratory too, down by the Regent's Canal in north London. Charles Mansfield was preparing coal-tar hydrocarbons for the great Paris Universal Exhibition, to be held in the summer and he was using the apparatus he had invented and patented himself for distilling coal tar. All exhibits had to be in Paris by 15 March, so by mid-February Charles and his assistant were putting in many hours to get the work done on time. It was around one o'clock on the afternoon of 17 February that a sudden thundrous explosion was heard in the neighbourhood, fol-lowed by the collapse of the laboratory building. Charles Mansfield's young assistant had made an error with the apparatus, causing the naphtha to boil over and catch fire.

Charles had at once seized the still in his arms and made for the door, which was shut fast, so he tried hurling the heavy apparatus through the window, but it was too late. His hands were half burned away, and the still dropped. He and his assistant climbed out of the window and made towards the canal, and someone rushed up and rolled them in the snow to quench the flames. To the crowd who collected, reported the *Journal of Gas Lighting*, they looked so dreadfully burned as to appear more like shrivelled mummies than living humans. Charles Mansfield, after walking nearly a mile on a woman's arm to reach a cab, spent nine days in fearful pain in Middlesex Hospital. Nevil, his close friend for so long, was horrorstruck at the news of the accident, and came to Charles' bedside, as did a constant stream of his many Christian Socialist and scientific friends. When Dr Hofmann, his old chemistry profes-sor, visited the hospital, Charles managed to make a humorous situation out of the tragedy by getting out the remark, 'Here you see the ashes of Charles B.Mansfield.'

Charles died before the end of February, aged only 35, and the lad who had been with him died the same night. Nevil Maskelyne wrote to his older friend, Ben Brodie, to tell him how he had seen Charles in hospital – 'You know how dear a friend he was and if you have ever lost one whom you loved you will know how I feel, who never before did so. I suppose I shall presently feel less oppressed, but at present I may say that no event of my life has ever so deeply affected me . . . As I looked on his mangled face in which no one feature could I trace of those I used in course of their expression to love and in others to reverence; I could not but ask the often asked question – is the immortality of the soul a mere beautiful fiction of man to soften agony and give an artificial aim to life?'

Thereza

Death was hanging in the air; Nevil Maskelyne had been thrown into a state of acute depression following the loss of his friend Charles Mansfield, and news kept arriving in Oxford of yet more young men dying in the Crimean campaign. Further sad reports of the suffering before Sebastopol were brought back in April by William Flower, a surgeon acquaintance of Nevil Maskelyne's who returned wounded from the Crimea. However Oxford University life went on as usual, and a science professorship fell vacant that spring – a rare career opportunity provided by the resignation of Dr Daubeny. He had decided to give up his prestigious Chair of Chemistry and settle for being Professors of Botany and Rural Economy only. His decision would have been influenced partly by the growing feeling against plurality of professorial posts and partly by the fact that each professorship was to be rewarded with a minimum of £300 a year from now on.

Nevil Maskelyne's friends all urged him to stand for the vacant post, but there was another and far more powerful contender in the wings, in the shape of Benjamin Brodie, who had not only assumed Nevil Maskelyne's loyal support for his candidature, but expected him to organize all his election lobbying. Brodie had rather pushing ways, which meant that Nevil Maskelyne was more popular as a person among his contemporaries, so the radical Oxford set went on trying to press him to go forward as a candidate despite Brodie. Much as he would have valued and enjoyed being Professor of Chemistry at Oxford, lecturing in a subject which was his first love and major interest, Maskelyne decided to honour the great debt of obligation which he felt he owed to Brodie. His university friend Mark Pattison had Maskelyne to lunch and, while they walked together afterwards, he heard of his 'resolution to give up the Chemistry Proff., though his only chance of anything. Talks of New Zealand etc.' Maskelyne knew that his one real career opportunity was slipping through his fingers, but he equally knew he could not bring himself to stand in the way of Brodie, after all he had done for him in the past. Benjamin Brodie had in fact cooled noticeably towards Nevil Maskelyne in the last 18 months, probably because of his young friend's obvious academic success at Oxford, which threatened to thwart Brodie's own ambitions.

Nevil wrote in May to tell Ben Brodie how the lobbying for candidature was going, pointing out that his own supporters, who numbered 'many persons', had been trying to put his name forward, but that he had explained to them that he himself would resign at once if elected. He was meanwhile energetically whipping up support and votes for Ben Brodie, and had enlisted Henry Smith's help for the campaign.

Brodie was in many ways a stronger candidate than Maskelyne would have been – being older, more influential, a Fellow of the Royal Society and a former secretary to the Chemical Society, as well as having been taught by Liebig. However Maskelyne had to explain to Brodie in a letter that it was still as much as he could do to persuade enough men to vote for Brodie, and they could only be persuaded to vote at all because Maskelyne explained that by doing so they would be countering the 'theological vote'. This was because Brodie was an agnostic and the election campaign, watched by *Jackson's Oxford Journal* followed hot on an attempt (that March) to restore compulsory religious tests for professors. The theological side tried various cunning means to try and stop Brodie getting in as an agnostic, and it was the very fact that the election was something of a political hot potato which acted – paradoxically enough – in Brodie's favour, by ensuring a good turnout. Maskelyne's radical friends, who had not intended voting at all, wanted religious tests for professors less than they wanted Brodie, who would undoubtedly have lost, in the opinion of his friends, had it not been for Maskelyne's efforts on his behalf.

He had fought for Brodie, he told him afterwards, because the recent death of Charles Mansfield had made him see the importance of 'acting with singleness of purpose for the happiness of another'. Maskelyne went on to tell Brodie that in this knowledge 'You will know why I have given up to you what I might have had by holding up my finger any day in these last two years. You owe me nothing but what you long ago paid.' Nevil added that while he had been disappointed at how much Ben Brodie had cooled towards him over the past ten years, 'I look into the next ten with a cold shudder – with a feeling that I am now too old to form again such friendships as these – that require the enthusiasm of youth to kindle them . . . Hopeless and aimless, poor in my circumstances, and with health weaker every year, and being undermined by the long sleepless nights in which I think on these things' – Nevil Maskelyne was writing the letters of a thoroughly depressed person, whose physical health was probably no worse than anyone else's, but who was sick with misery in the aftermath of bereavement and the reality of frustrated ambition.

Nevil Maskelyne was worried when he realized that even his chemical laboratory could become redundant with Brodie's arrival in Oxford, and he wondered where to turn if this should happen. Ben Brodie offered a few suggestions, which included contacting Thomas Graham, a revered elderly chemist friend who had just been appointed Master of the Mint and might be able to use a chemist who could analyse minerals. Nevil replied, 'your suggestion of a berth at the Mint, cold and cheerless as it sounds – and such as are like it – are the only things that seem to meet my view. Your life is happy', he wrote to Brodie, 'Can you have another wish! I know not what it can be. Wealth, wife, Home, Family, Position in the world – reputation – helped on by all these – the ambition you revealed to me eight years ago ripened and accomplished! Good God, what else can you be wanting?' But Ben Brodie did still want several things, for he wrote and asked Nevil Maskelyne to look out for a house for him in Oxford, and to secure him a good laboratory. 'How coolly you write', Nevil replied, 'to ask if the requisite accommodation is to be found there!! Princelike man – I suppose all the world is to minister to you!' In the end Henry Smith, no doubt wishing to ensure that Nevil Maskelyne was not driven from his Old Ashmolean Museum basement laboratory, vacated his own laboratory at Balliol College so that Brodie could work there. The cellar laboratory at the foot of No. 16 stairs, underneath the new Salvin Building at Balliol, was perhaps not quite what Brodie had in mind, but a man with Brodie's style was unlikely to stand for this sort of treatment for long. Dr Daubeny hung on to the university chemical apparatus, rather than passing it on to his successor, but this was presumably unimportant to Brodie, who had all the equipment from his own London laboratory, without much space at Balliol for putting it all.

A view of Oxford showing Broad Street. Exeter College is in the left foreground, with the Old Ashmolean Museum to its far right. Across Broad Street, Dr Acland's house is just behind the large horse-drawn wagon. Wadham College is in the right middle distance, with the new University Museum beyond it.

Although it had been a bitter time for Nevil Maskelyne, his life was not all so disappointing, for he found himself giving Dr Buckland's geology lectures for a while, as well as those in mineralogy, and from 1855 he was appointed lecturer in physics and chemistry at Exeter College – a convenient arrangement because Exeter was right next door to the Old Ashmolean Museum. He also received recognition through being appointed a university Public Examiner, bringing his youth and reviving enthusiasm to the new Natural Science school, which was beginning to take its proper place as a recognized part of university academic life. Charles Mansfield had bequeathed Nevil all his chemicals and laboratory equipment, which Nevil was able to put to good use by completing a detailed long-term programme of research he had started in Brodie's well-equipped London laboratory two or three years earlier. He was examining the fatty acids obtainable from the alcohols derived from the waxy coating of the leaves of the Brazilian canaúba tree (Copernicia cerifera) and had already completed a study of cerotic acid obtained by oxidizing 'Chinese wax'. He pursued this examination of the 'solid fat acids' by doing detailed experiments into the vegetable tallow from the Chinese plant Stillingia sebifera, a source of palmitic acid, which he analysed very carefully. Organic chemistry was just around the corner at this date and, as so often happens, scientists were anticipating the next stage, by becoming interested in the perplexing percentages of carbon in their formulae.

Nevil Maskelyne was also interested in current studies on the silicates, whose chemical formulae had for some time been in question, and his Old Ashmolean Museum laboratory was still open daily from 10 till 5 for public analysis work, and on certain days a week for chemistry instruction. In the summer term Nevil Maskelyne gave an illustrated course of lectures on the paleozoic strata of the Malvern hills, the mezozoic strata of the Vale of Severn

Stillingia sebifera, the object of chemical experiment

and the Oxford area, and the eocene strata of the Isle of Wight. He also led excursion lectures, in the true Buckland tradition, to places like Shotover Hill and Culham, both near Oxford, with the added attraction of a weekend in the Malvern Hills in late May.

On 19 June, the irrepressible Dr Acland held yet another of his soirées in the Radcliffe Camera, to launch the actual building of his new museum. It was a hot and crowded affair at which the new Chancellor of Oxford University, Lord Derby, made a tedious speech (after protesting his unwillingness to make a speech at all). Mrs Jeune noted in her diary that as Lord Derby finished listing all the benefactors to the Oxford museum project, Mr Gladstone whispered to Dr Jeune, 'Now for the malefactors', for the museum had never been short of critics and opponents. The following day, the museum foundation stone was laid by a resplendent Lord Derby surrounded by choirs and crowds, who were obliged to listen to another of Lord Derby's orations, as well as having to kneel for a long prayer. However, by the end of this ceremony the new museum was well and truly launched and the workmen were able to move in with bricks and mortar, so George Butler thoughtfuly arranged for their comfort by fixing up a temporary kitchen and reading room on the site.

The other social event of the Oxford summer, though on a smaller scale, was the marriage of Leslie Thomson to the beautiful 'Greek slave', Zoë Skene, whose hand he had won at last. For three years Leslie and Zoë had remained engaged, with 'much sorrowing' at the Greek family's refusal to allow the marriage, but old Mrs Skene, Zoë's grandmother, had stood by her throughout, and by 1855 she had advised Zoë, 'if you had the courage, it would certainly be best to do as people here want Lord Raglan to do with Sebastopol, and try a *coup de main*, I do not think your mother would stand a storm of tears'. This sound counselling brought Zoë the reward she desired.

At about nine on the warm July evening before the Thomson's wedding day, Josephine Butler was wandering alone through the lush flower-filled gardens of St John's College where she had earlier been drawing Solomon's lilies for a design for the capital of a pillar for the new museum. As she admired the lilies gleaming white in the dusk, she heard the sound of voices and came upon Zoë and her bridesmaids relaxing in a little group in the cooler evening air, and Zoë lightheartedly invited Josephine to bring her little son as 'best man' to the wedding next day. Once they were married, the young couple moved to a smart parish in London, but by the autumn they were back in Oxford again, because Leslie had been appointed Provost of Queen's College. Leslie's sisters, Isabel and Annabel, used to turn up in Oxford, and were among the young ladies whom Nevil Maskelyne photographed, but his income was still too low to satisfy the parents of the kind of girl he might meet socially, and he still had no better home to share than the basement beneath the Old Ashmolean Museum. His father was in no position to help him financially either, having recently taken out heavy mortgages to buy Salthrop House and various farms near Basset Down which had belonged to the late Duke of Wellington.

During the summer, Nevil Maskelyne was invited to stay in South Wales, by John Dillwyn Llewelyn, a fellow-member of the Photographic Society, who had just won a prize for his photographs at the Paris Universal Exhibition. The Llewelyn family lived at Pellergaer near Swansea, and had grown rich on the discovery of coal seams under their land. They occupied an elegant regency country house, with beautiful gardens and landscaped grounds grouped around lakes in a wooded valley, with moorland sweeping up and away beyond to the Welsh hills. John Llewelyn could well afford to live the life of a gentleman these days, serving as a magistrate, training the local militia and taking an interest in the old Glamorgan county lunatic asylums. He had married Emma Talbot, first cousin of Henry Fox Talbot, and had been able to devote time and energy to photography from its earliest days, learning to modify and improve his calotypes by experiment.

Thereza, his eldest daughter, helped him with his experiments, and they were now inventing ways of carrying out the collodion process dry – rather than placing dripping wet plates in the camera just before exposing them to the image. Wetting the plates at the last moment meant that if you wanted to work outdoors you had to cart a dark-room tent and tankfuls of chemicals about the countryside, so John Llewelyn, who liked to record sea scenes, plants, cliffs and caves, was determined to find a foolproof way of using collodion plates dry in the camera. Like another of their mutual Photographic Society friends, Maxwell Lyte, John Llewelyn lived in good honey-bee country, close to miles of rolling heather, so honey was a plentiful ingredient and they both experimented with it. For the past 18 months, John Llewelyn had been trying out a substance which he called 'oxymel' – a mixture of honey with vinegar or acetic acid. The prepared collodion plate had a final immersion in this oxymel – diluted one to four with water – and could then be kept, ready for action, for over a week. The plates were placed in the camera just as they were, and were then developed, using pyrogallic acid. They reacted more slowly to light than wet collodion plates, but the pictures they produced were of excellent quality, so dry collodion plates treated with oxymel were well worth taking on field trips.

By 23 November 1855, Nevil Maskelyne had sent John Llewelyn a bottle of glycerine to try out as a substitute for honey, but John Llewelyn, who had never seen glycerine before, wrote back to say that while his fingers were burning to experiment with the stuff, he was not sure where to begin. He finally decided to try it out with acetic acid and alcohol, and obtained very good results to start with, which excited him. By 12 December, however, his results were less good, which, he suggested to Nevil Maskelyne, might have been due to decomposition or deterioration in the glycerine. Whatever the real trouble, the process kept leaving 'spots, stars and comets' on the prints and John Llewelyn concluded with perhaps a certain smug satisfaction that it was 'not indeed an easy matter to beat the honey'.

Later in the summer vacation of that year, when Nevil Maskelyne was on

Reading out the news of the fall of Sebastopol. Left to right standing: Anthony Story Maskelyne, Agnes, Peggy Tait; seated: Antonia, Margaret, Charlotte and Edmund Story Maskelyne

holiday with his family at Basset Down, a mighty headline hit the papers – 'Capture of Sebastopol'. Anthony Story Maskelyne read out the account from the *Times* newspaper to his assembled family. The months-long seige was over at last, leaving behind it a terrible toll of starvation, pain and death – for 20,000 men had died in this emotionally charged but ill-organized war. It had been a harrowing enough time in Britain, let alone out there on the Crimean battlefields, and the Story Maskelyne family shared the national feeling of relief that it was over.

Back in Oxford that autumn term, Nevil Maskelyne prepared to sit for the first time as one of three examiners for the final Honours School in Natural Sciences. That November they were able to award two Firsts and three Seconds, so the standard was starting to rise. Ben Brodie was still going through the official throes of securing his Chair of Chemistry. Although his candidature had long been approved, thanks to Maskelyne's efforts on his behalf, he still had to win through a subsequent election, this time against a St Mary Hall man who opposed him on behalf of those who favoured religion in their professors. Ben Brodie won again, and took over the Aldrichian Chair of Chemistry that winter, with an improved salary, and Nevil Maskelyne, who had by now pulled himself out of the bitter, depressed state he had plunged into after Charles Mansfield's death, stopped resenting Brodie's success and did some constructive writing for *Fraser's Magazine*. It published two of his articles that autumn, one on the science and theory of colour and one on the 'New Metals', which discussed the various grades of iron obtained from earths by means of heat or electricity – so releasing yet more metals. Nevil Maskelyne also mentioned the metal aluminium, lighter than either zinc, iron or silver, but still the price of gold, because it could be produced only a globule at a time, and was therefore by no means a household proposition yet. Maskelyne's interests had always ranged in this way into the field of industrial technology far beyond the tight academic circles of Oxford, involved though he was in university life and politics.

Oxford that winter was surrounded by flood water, and Christmas saw Mrs Jeune – wife of the Master of Pembroke – busy in the city centre parish of St Aldates as usual, giving out blankets and coal vouchers to the needy poor in their cold damp homes, whilst many of the more prosperous families of heads of colleges were enjoying Christmas trees, magic lantern shows and dancing. Music was a much more acceptable pastime in scholarly circles now, and even reactionary old Ben Symons and his wife followed up a dinner at Wadham by entertainment on the piano and harp. The Liddell family, who arrived at the deanery at Christ Church College that February 1856, managed to give two musical evenings in the very week of their arrival in Oxford, without even relating them to dinner-parties. Nevil, who knew the Liddells from Buckland parties at Westminster, was among those who were very pleased to see them replace old anti-reform Dean Gaisford at Christ Church. Dean Liddell had been headmaster of Westminster School in Dr Buckland's day, and had just completed nearly ten years there, but his younger daughter Alice – later to be the inspiration of *Alice in Wonderland* – was not yet born at this stage. Max Müller of course quickly involved himself in the Liddells' musical circle, and his mother, who was staying in Oxford during the summer of 1856, was taken to many of the Liddell's music parties, as well as joining the round of picnics, boat trips and other festivities enjoyed by the young professors and their social set.

The Oxford household who offered the most hospitality to Frau Müller was that of Manuel Johnson, the Radcliffe Observer, who had that year become both Fellow of the Royal Society and President of the Royal Astronomical Association. Manuel Johnson had fallen into astronomy by chance in the first place, as a result of being stationed on the island of St Helena in 1821 as a 16-year-old lieutenant. The bleak environment offered few other pastimes, so, encouraged by the governor of the island, he had thrown himself into the study of the stars until he had become skilled enough to be sent off on training trips to Capetown, and eventually an observatory had been built for him on St Helena itself. He had worked away at collecting data for a catalogue of the fixed stars of the southern hemisphere but, after 13 years on St Helena, his garrison had been disbanded and Manuel Johnson had been sent home to England on a pension. He had used the money to read for a degree at Magdalen College, Oxford, and had then fallen straight into the post of Radcliffe Observer, simply by being in the right place at the right time – for the previous astronomer had died shortly before Manuel Johnson graduated. He and his wife Caroline welcomed the young professors to their home, having no family of their own, and had been particularly generous to Max Müller, as a young foreigner. Max Müller had become curator of the Bodleian Library that year, and his friend Maskelyne came by a new title too, for as well as being Deputy Professor of Mineralogy he became Assistant Professor of Chemistry – presumably on the strength of teaching chemical analysis, whereas Brodie taught chemistry in general. Ben Brodie and his wife lived in an impressive residence called Cowley House and were fast finding their feet in the Oxford social round.

One old friend who turned up again in May 1856 was Robert Mansfield, who had been invited out to the Crimea the previous January by his army friends, and had set sail for the Mediterranean in the frigate *Leopard* (commanded by a relative of his). Although Sebastopol had capitulated by the time he reached the Crimea, the war was not yet officially over, so Robert was astonished, after docking at Balaklava, to find himself eating a splendid dinner of soup, turbot and a good joint of mutton, followed by apple tart and cream, all provided by his friends of the 46th regiment who had – of course – the only cow in the Crimea.

From Balaklava Robert Mansfield rode on to the front, where fighting had now ceased, in order to look out his cousin Colin Campbell. Although he found the camp swarming with rats, in these last weeks of the war he saw plenty of food among the British troops – including tongues, hams and other delicacies. Robert woke twice in the morning to find his beard and moustache frozen and his bed covered with fine snow which had drifted in through cracks in his hut. He was astonished at the quantity of 'shot, shell and grape' which lay strewn over the area between the British battlefront and the defences of Sebastopol, and reckoned that it was no exaggeration to say that he could have walked the whole way and trodden on one piece of ammunition at every step.

At last in early April, the news of peace had reached the camp, so Robert Mansfield had assembled a party who were to be the first to sally forth on an expedition towards the Crimean interior which had not been disturbed by strangers for three years. They had set off on 12 April and were soon encountering Cossacks, Tartars, deserted châteaux, fighting Turkish stallions and even the summer residence of the Tsar himself. Robert Mansfield, well satisfied with his visit, had left the Crimea on 1 May, and was back in England again before the summer vacation had started.

Peace had been proclaimed in Oxford on 30 April and had been celebrated with civic processions, bonfires and a certain amount of drunk and disorderly behaviour. The university Commemoration Week events in June included 'Illuminations for the Peace', along with the balls and breakfasts, theatres and parties and the Jenny Lind concert. Max Müller spotted Zoë Thomson entering a marquee in Worcester College gardens and exclaimed 'There is Mrs Thomson, the beautiful Zoë! – all Oxford has been in love with her'. Max Müller and Leslie Thomson gave a river boat party to Nuneham later that week for their many friends, and the revellers returned to Oxford around midnight.

The summer's festivities over, Nevil Maskelyne sorted out how to spend his vacation before the British Association meetings started in late July, and decided to visit his Photographic Society friend, John Llewelyn, in South Wales, with whom he had arranged to carry out some photographic experiments. Nevil's sister Charlotte had already intended visiting South Wales in mid July, to meet her old governess, Miss Deutschik, who was now tutoring the children of the Traherne family – cousins of the Llewelyns of Penllergaer – and had been governess to the Llewelyn children too. Nevil and Charlotte arrived together at Penllergaer on 21 July 1856, in time for Nevil to accompany Mrs Llewelyn and two of her six children, John and Emma, to the Swansea Regatta Ball. Thereza, the eldest daughter, who had never taken to dancing, stayed at home and noted with relief that the party, who didn't return from the ball until the small hours, seemed none the worse for it at breakfast time.

Nevil Maskelyne happened to have arrived at Penllergaer on the same day as Mr Bentham, the great nineteenth century botanist, who was a frequent guest at Penllergaer and used to give Thereza Llewelyn useful advice on her pressed flower collection. Thereza was a remarkable young woman, now aged 22 and already an expert botanist in the Victorian manner – word-perfect at the latin names of every plant she had ever found – and she had found more

Thereza Llewelyn.
(Photo.
J.D.Llewelyn)

The observatory and laboratory at Penllergaer. (Photo. J.D.Llewelyn)

plants than most of us identify in a lifetime. Botany was not Thereza's only interest either, for she was so enthusiastic about astronomy that her father, recognizing her real talent, had built her a large observatory in the grounds, equipping it at first with a telescope with a four-inch achromatic lens, and later with a more powerful one. By now she had become a highly experienced photographer too, preparing and processing her own sensitized papers and plates, and helping her father in his experiments with new chemicals. Thereza also made daily local recordings for the British Association for the Advancement of Science, filling in their printed tables with details of rainfall, atmospheric pressure, humidity, temperature and ozone levels.

When he left Penllergaer, Mr Bentham the botanist took with him Thereza's most recent set of record sheets, to be deposited with the correct scientist at the British Association meetings at Cheltenham. Nevil went on to Cheltenham on 29 July, to help Dr Daubeny with preparations but, the day after Nevil had left, Thereza was bitterly disappointed to learn that she was not, after all, to be allowed to accompany her Uncle Traherne to the British Association meetings as she had expected. 'I am sorry for it', she wrote in her diary, 'as I should have enjoyed the lectures etc, etc, very much, but I ought not to think about it, as I know every thing is always ordered for the best!' Even the eminent woman scientific writer, Mary Somerville, was careful to avoid appearing at such public scientific occasions because she feared her presence there might encourage other women to attend, and so lower the professional scientific tone of meetings. Such reasoning must have been hard for a science enthusiast like Thereza to accept.

Shortly after the British Association meetings had finished in mid August, the news reached Nevil Maskelyne that Dr Buckland had died at the age of 73, released at last from the atypical cabbage-like existence of his later years. As a result of Dr Buckland's death, Nevil Maskelyne became eligible for the permanent post of Professor of Mineralogy, to which he was in due course appointed. This meant that his position was at least secure, even though it was not a 'resident' professorship, which meant in effect that it was not well enough paid for the professor to be expected to live and work in Oxford all the time, nor depend solely on this salary for his income, nor indeed receive any of the pension rights for which Nevil Maskelyne and others had been fighting.

Well-paid or no, September saw Nevil travelling to the continent and writing letters home about his travels, which Charlotte Maskelyne read aloud to Thereza and Emma Llewelyn, whom she had staying with her at Basset Down at the time – their first visit. They were shown Nevil's laboratory in the thatched farmhouse, and his shaggy little dog Paws joined them for some of their walks round the farms, where they saw the latest cheese-making equipment in use and admired the prize cows – the kind of beasts which looked as though they were trying to bridge the gap between the eighteenth century breeders' ideal and the modern dairy shorthorn.

Rose Mary, a prize Basset Down cow

Soon after Thereza and Emma Llewelyns' visit to Basset Down, sad news came to the Maskelyne family that Tom Masterman, husband of Nevil's attractive sister Mervinia, had died, leaving a family of young children to bring up. The widowed Mervinia had to fall back on her father for support, and she brought her children to live on the attic floor at Basset Down, where her mother's friend, Peggy Tait, helped her to look after them. This was to fill the old grey house with a new lively atmosphere, as the young Masterman children threw themselves into discovering the ways of the badgers, squirrels, goldfinches and other wildlife of the surrounding Basset Down woods.

When he returned to Oxford that autumn, Nevil Maskelyne was pleased to learn that Arthur Stanley, after his several years at Canterbury, would soon be returning to Oxford as Professor of Ecclesiastical History and as a Canon of Christ Church. Arthur Stanley and Benjamin Jowett, who had for so long been viewed as suspect extremists of radical theology, were beginning to gain in academic respectability. Jowett was still a supporter of the progress of science, but he had begun to question whether scientists were not just as prejudiced as theologians, each in favour of their own cause. In fact, thought Jowett, scientists should feel grateful to the German philosopher Hegel for having chosen science as a basic ingredient for his scheme of the future progress of mankind. The current *avant-garde* philosophy in Oxford was English Positivism, as taught by Richard Congreve, Maskelyne's former Wadham tutor and longstanding friend, and by Congreve's younger disciple, Frederic Harrison. Jowett, who did not entirely approve of the Positivists, said that they were making use of science to prop up their beliefs – teaching that it was through science that mankind would determine its own ascent and positive progress. Although he had long known and admired Richard Congreve as a person, Jowett was growing uneasy that his Positivist teaching might lead his followers to atheism, and Congreve himself realized that his human-centred preaching was no longer entirely consistent with Anglican teaching.

Another of the unorthodox and original religious thinkers in Oxford at the time was Benjamin Brodie who had been a close friend of Jowett's all through the 1840s; but, from the time he had started working in Liebig's laboratory at Giessen, Brodie had started worrying Jowett by writing him letters in which he tried to explain some of his atheistic theories. Ben Brodie was also developing unconventional and highly complicated views on atomic theory, which he was trying to elaborate into a convincing system. He was now installed in his basement laboratory beneath Balliol College and was starting some sound research on graphite, but his chemistry lectures failed to attract many students. He gained some unpopularity among his colleagues too, for the rather high-handed way in which he demanded speedy completion of his new premises in the half-built University Museum, and kept asking for more and better facilities there. The museum delegacy in fact became thoroughly agitated by his requests, and declared that Brodie could not take priority over the other professors. As usual, however, Brodie got his way, and £600 was voted towards extra accommodation for him. His laboratory at the new museum was to be built after the design of the abbot's kitchen at Glastonbury Abbey, a rather fanciful idea which had no doubt been fostered by John Ruskin, who had become closely associated with Dr Acland over the design of the museum. By 1858 the museum delegacy had to inform the university authorities that not only had £1,650 been spent on chemical fittings for Brodie, but that he still wanted more. Nevil Maskelyne should perhaps have learned something from the success of these forceful tactics, but his modest personality was never going to make him that kind of exploiter of a situation for his own gain.

Leaving Oxford behind for a short time, Nevil Maskelyne took a train journey down to Nice after Christmas, by way of Dijon which was still under snow. He was not sure whether to believe a Greek travelling companion who told him to expect a dramatic temperature change before they reached Marseilles, but he soon found himself peeling off one coat after another in the unheated compartment, and finally even opening the window. He was amazed at the warmth of the south of France, and struck by the number of plants growing lush, green, sweet-scented foliage even in early January, but it was the unusual sight of the constellation Orion high overhead which really brought the southern latitude home to him.

He was not long in the warmer climate, for by 8 January he was back in

London exhibiting his camera to members of the Photographic Society and explaining to them about a new box attachment he had designed for it, to hold his dry collodion plates. This box had four fixed sides but a moveable top and base. A pile of sensitized plates was loaded into it and, each time the bottom plate was dropped into the camera slide, each plate in the pile would drop down one place, aided by a mechanism of little barrels and pegs, so that they were used consecutively. This saved lifting each glass into the camera separately under a black cloth. Nevil Maskelyne still believed glycerine could be made a viable alternative to John Llewelyn's oxymel process, for dry collodion plates, and he aired the subject in the May issue of the *Philosophical Magazine*.

John Llewelyn decided to visit Oxford in late March 1857, because he remembered it as the time of year when the delicate brownish purple fritilleries used to bloom on Christ Church Meadows in his own student days. His visit had two aims – to find out how his two sons were progressing with their studies and to visit Nevil Maskelyne's laboratory. He brought with him his two elder daughters, Thereza and Emma, together with the inevitable manservant and maid, and they all lodged at the Angel Hotel from 24 March. John Llewelyn and his boys dined with Nevil Maskelyne the first night, and the two photographic enthusiasts spent the next day out photographing Oxford views while the girls were taken on a sightseeing walk – particularly admiring the view of Magdalen Tower from the bridge. Nevil joined them all for a meal that evening and afterwards showed them what Thereza described as 'some very beautiful experiments with double refracting spar, and tourmaline, making polarized light; which I hope I shall remember'. The following morning Thereza and Emma were shown the buildings of Dr Acland's new museum rising rapidly from their site, and Thereza considered that the new museum would be very attractive when it was finished. They walked back past Wadham College, which the girls had not yet seen, before preparing to take a train for a visit to London. They extended a warm welcome to Nevil to come and stay with them at Penllergaer during his vacation, so he made plans to travel down to south Wales with his youngest sister Agnes just after Easter.

They joined the Penllergaer house-party on the evening of 16 April, spending a very merry evening playing at 'Proverbs', and Nevil had a long conversation with Thereza, persuading her that – according to a pet theory of Ben Brodie's – sleep is necessary for the *mind* rather than for the body, which only needs rest. The following day John Llewelyn had a severe headache, a malady which often laid him low and which was probably due to the noxious photographic chemicals he used; so the rest of the party amused themselves in drawing and music, interspersed with games of Blindman's Buff and Shuttlecock and Battledore. In the evening, Thereza showed the others her microscope, having spent the past few days cutting and preparing glass slides of specimens for it. Nevil was very impressed by the hot-houses at Penllergaer, which were heated by surplus steam piped across the fields from a farm steam-engine. There were orchid houses, a pineapple house and several other hot-houses for growing bananas, tea, coffee, cocoa, rice, guava, ginger, oranges, lemons, limes and festoons of scented vanilla pods.

Down through the wooded valley below the house, the Llewelyns had constructed two beautiful lakes, inspired by the Norwegian fiords which John Llewelyn had admired when working as a courier in Norway many years before. Nevil Maskelyne was taken to watch an otter fishing in the lower lake, arching its supple back when it dived, and Thereza showed him the owl's nest she had located a few days before, where the baby owls were just fledging. When they approached the Canada goose's nest of feathers and leaves on a grassy promontory, the goose made a dramatic stand, hissing and flapping its wings at them, and revealing four large white eggs. Late in the evening, Thereza headed a visit to her observatory to locate the double star *i cameri* which appeared yellow and blue.

On 20 April Nevil spent the whole day with Thereza, helping her with photography in the laboratory in the grounds near her observatory – her father having gone off to Quarter Sessions as a magistrate. Thereza was experimenting with making dry collodion plates by 'Barnes' albumen process', which turned out successfully, but two days later Nevil and Thereza were trying out the 'Shell lac collodion' process which Thereza noted was 'a failure thus far', but by this time the thoughts of the two experimenters seem to have been wandering from serious photography. Later that day, Nevil walked out with the whole family to Goppa, a wild rocky hillside with a dramatic view, where they were caught in a downpour and had to dry out by walking home. As the storm cleared, Nevil and Thereza could hear a cuckoo calling, which reminded Nevil of Dartmoor, so he regaled Thereza with fearsome legends of enchanted places that he knew on the moor. That evening at Penllergaer they all made music, played at 'Fortune' and told riddles and conundrums. The following day Thereza again brought out her microscope and they amused themselves by examining dirty water under it, and Nevil's final day at Penllergaer was spent with Thereza in the photographic laboratory. That night they all played a last 'grand game of Sir Vickery Eels'.

After Nevil had left, Thereza – who was of Quaker descent – felt that she should try and grapple with the strong emotions she found stirred up within her. 'My spirit', she confided to her diary, was 'saddened with the fight it had this day to maintain against my most corrupt nature', and she exhorted her soul to 'go crucify thy worldly thoughts and desires'. The following day being Sunday, Thereza listened to a sermon on temptation and disobedience and prayed for guidance through 'all the dangers which so easily beset me! keep me from my own coil and deceitful heart!'

Back in Oxford, Nevil, who found that thoughts of Thereza were still in the front of his mind, began to wonder where he could find a suitable better paid post, in order to be in a position to ask for her hand. He knew that his chances of finding such a post in Oxford were remote indeed, so the only thing was to look further afield, which he started to do at once.

Nobody in Oxford had fought harder than Nevil Maskelyne for better status and pay for professors, but he had to recognize that no single science chair produced a salary up to supporting a wife in anything like Llewelyn style. Max Müller noted that May that the battle for recognition for professors was still being hard fought, but that opposition to the cause remained strong, not least from Dr Pusey (with whom Max sat on committees) who could dominate all opponents except the indefatigable Jowett.

Benjamin Jowett and Henry Halford Vaughan had both been energetic campaigners for the status of professors but so little headway had been made that by June 1847, Vaughan, who had recently married, felt so disillusioned and financially insecure that he gave up the fight and resigned as Professor of Modern History at Oxford. His colleagues were appalled at his decision, because the Regius Professorship of Modern History was one of the better paid posts and Vaughan was a brilliant and popular young lecturer and first-class historian, as well as being among the leading fighters for university reform. His resignation would certainly be seen as a victory for the anti-reformers. Nevil Maskelyne wrote to Henry Halford Vaughan on 10 July to try and persuade him to change his mind, saying 'I do hope most truly, and so do all your friends, that you will prevail on yourself to think as we do. The moral effect of your retirement on the Professoriate will be calamitous.' On 18 June, Nevil Maskelyne wrote out a letter to the Prime Minister, Mr Gladstone, on behalf of Vaughan's Oxford friends (who signed it), imploring him not to accept the young professor's resignation. It was to no avail, for Henry Halford Vaughan's mind was made up, and the lively fair-haired historian was rarely to be seen in Oxford again.

Max Müller's choir. Left to right standing: Janie Skene, Miss Jelf, Mrs Jelf, Leslie and Zoë Thomson, Miss Jelf; seated; Max Müller

Despite the tense political drama bubbling away below the surface of Oxford life, the parties and picnics of the Oxford summer term blossomed as usual. On the musical front, Max Müller had formed a choir of 20 voices, which included those of Leslie and Zoë Thomson and the 'singing bird' Jelf sisters. Max Müller had taught them to sing Mendelssohn's *Lobgesang* and setting of Psalm 42, and they persuaded Nevil Maskelyne to photograph a nucleus of their choir – all long-standing friends of his – in the college garden. They used to give concerts in the hall of Queen's College, which Zoë would furnish up like a drawing-room for the occasion, with sofas, palms and rugs. Two of Professor Maskelyne's other old friends gained Oxford recognition that summer, with Charles Pearson winning the Poetry Prize and Matthew Arnold being appointed Professor of Poetry – a non-resident post which would allow him to go on living in London.

Nevil's own involvement with the life and struggles of Oxford made it hard for him to turn elsewhere for employment, but he had heard of a better paid post in London, so he resolved to put in for it. The job was a newly created civil service appointment for a Keeper of Minerals at the British Museum in Bloomsbury, which would start from the autumn and would have an assured salary with recently-won pension rights. For Nevil Maskelyne it would mean less freedom of movement, less holidays and a life in smoky London, but it would also mean the chance to try for the hand of Thereza Llewelyn. When he heard that the job was his, Nevil raised the question of his Chair of Mineralogy at Oxford, but both the museum and the university authorities were happy for him to continue as Professor of Mineralogy, giving two lecture-courses a year at Oxford.

Lady Louisa
Howard with her
daughter Winefride

Final details had still to be settled, but when he travelled down to Penllergaer in mid August with his sister Charlotte, Nevil must have felt a certain quiet confidence. Thereza on the other hand had been questioning herself to such an extent that she seriously wondered whether her duty in life did not lie here at Penllergaer, caring for the poor and needy of the surrounding hamlets and the education of the local schoolchildren. Nevil and Charlotte arrived on the same afternoon as several other guests, who included a geologist and travelling adventurer named Warington Smyth, who was to remain a good friend of Nevil's, and James Howard, brother to the Earl of Suffolk, together with his wife Lady Louisa Howard (Mrs Llewelyn's cousin and only daughter of the third Marquis of Lansdowne) and their young children, Winefride and Kenneth. Thereza was very much taken up with entertaining the guests, organizing the girls' school examinations and feast and perhaps even avoiding the main emotional issue, but she took a party to her observatory that night, and showed Charlotte Maskelyne various stars. During his stay Nevil worked on photography with John Llewelyn, while Thereza's time was mainly taken up with yet more guests arriving, and more school feasts and examinations (this time for the boys).

The atmosphere relaxed a little on 22 August, when most of the other guests left and Nevil and Charlotte were taken to Goppa for a picnic. The girls sketched, while the youngest Llewelyn children, Lucy and Elinor, made stepping-stones and threw rocks into the stream. The weather had been beautifully hot all week, and Nevil and Thereza had spent enough time together for Nevil to get some inkling of her misgivings and for Thereza to

Charlton Park house-party
Top right. Sons and daughters of the house. Probable order – standing: Henry Charles, Viscount Andover; seated: The Hon. Greville Theophilus, Lady Isabel Atherley and Lady Mary Howard
Top left. A group outside the front door at Charlton Park
Below. Hands of the ladies, with perhaps the face of Lady Victoria Howard, aged 13

take in the implications of his museum job. The intimate emotional situation in which she found herself still disturbed Thereza, combined with a terrible fear that she might one day be torn from her beloved home at Penllergaer. 'there are some feelings', she wrote in her diary the evening before the Maskelynes left, 'that you never impart to your dearest friend on earth, that you feel you have no right to impart, as your doing so would make them suffer with you; this is quite true!' The following day, close and thundery, Nevil and Charlotte left, having been invited on by their fellow-guest Mr Howard, to another house-party, at Charlton Park, the Wiltshire seat of his brother the Earl of Suffolk. The Suffolk family were related to the Howards of Norfolk and were lacking in neither blue blood nor hereditary cash at the time. Their great Jacobean house near Malmesbury stood like some grand operatic backdrop to the crinolined bejewelled guests assembled on the surrounding lawns. The sons of the house mingled somewhat languorously with the rest, sporting the latest in leisure clothing, while their lively youngest sister, Lady Victoria, had fun amongst the children and ponies.

While Nevil made the most of his stay at Charlton Park, he was still thinking of Thereza, and he managed to get back to Penllergaer in September in order to ask Thereza to marry him and to gain John Llewelyn's approval for the match. Thereza, who had managed to overcome some of her misgivings, accepted Nevil's proposal, and Miss Deutschik, the old governess who had known both Nevil and Thereza as children, saw fit to reveal that she had long ago had a premonition that these two were destined for one another. The wedding was planned for the following summer, even though Nevil would have preferred it sooner, but he was able to set out for his job in London in a new frame of mind.

Mineral Keeper

Nevil Maskelyne quickly found that while museum life was far removed from the academic power-juggling of Oxford, there was still plenty of opportunity for a good fight in the cause of the natural sciences. In those days the nation's natural science collections were housed on the first floor of the imposing neo-classical British Museum building in Bloomsbury, but over the past two decades the Department of Antiquities had been growing faster than the scientific displays, and the antiquarian side were raring to push out the scientists altogether. The fine pair of giraffes who stood at the head of the stairs looked down haughtily, as though to challenge any antiquarian who might contemplate getting rid of them and the departments they represented.

The minerals in the museum had not been cared for by a qualified mineralogist since the death of Mr König six years before, in 1851, and he had been Keeper of not only minerals but of plant, animal and fossil specimens as well. During the past few years while the minerals had lain neglected, the Department of Printed Books had been receiving lavish attention and it now held over a million volumes, housed under the magnificent dome of the newly completed library. This was the empire of Antonio Panizzi, the Principal Librarian, with whom Nevil Maskelyne was to hold many a spirited struggle, for the Principal Librarian was in effect the overall administrator of the museum, and a very powerful man who liked things done his way. It was Panizzi who insisted that the Keeper of Minerals should, like other senior museum staff, keep his top hat on at all times in the public galleries.

Since there was no laboratory nor scientific equipment of any kind in his department, Nevil Maskelyne faced a daunting task when he started to try and sort out the mineral specimens, almost none of which had labels to say

Antonio Panizzi,
Principal Librarian

where they had been found. The large reserve collection of minerals had no labels at all, so he delved into the departmental archives to find details of every mineral specimen, until after a few years they were all labelled for type and locality and the duplicates had been separated out for future sale. He wanted to get the minerals completely rearranged, and began wondering how the other big European museums displayed their mineral collections.

By December of his first year, 1857, Maskelyne was asking for an assistant to help him arrange the drawers of minerals, with a view to getting the whole collection catalogued. In February 1858 the assistant was found for him, in the shape of 21-year-old Thomas Davies – the son of the gallery carpenter – who turned out to be ideal for the job, because he developed an extraordinary talent for recognizing and memorizing the minute details of minerals despite having had little or no schooling and knowing nothing of mineralogy when he arrived.

Nevil Maskelyne's museum job rather curtailed his photographic activities, but he was out at Hounslow just before Christmas 1857, making another attempt at photographing the moon. This time it was through the efficient telescope of Warren de la Rue, a man of many parts whose house was comfortably out of London in those days when there were still apple orchards on the outskirts of Kensington, and the night sky was untroubled by the international air traffic of today. The photographic party were lucky enough to have much better weather than Nevil Maskelyne had suffered on a Bath rooftop exactly ten years earlier, so they had a good view of the moon and planets. 'My own dearest one', wrote Nevil to Thereza, 'I have seen such sights! However you are to come and see them as soon as you are Mrs N, if not before! Saturn with a power of 700 without a tremor! Rings and rings! . . . a very spectacle of wonder and delight. A wish as young as my youngest boyhood has been gratified. I only had one wish then and there – that you were there too . . . The moon under a 450 power was glorious! I found out my grandfather's mountain, Maskelyne, and had a good look at him. I looked too at the Mare Crisium, Piazzi Smyth's work.' Nevil was a good friend of the astronomer Piazzi Smyth, and was just writing an article about a trip Smyth

The moon, photographed through Warren de la Rue's telescope

had headed to Tenerife earlier that summer to carry out astronomical observations. Piazzi Smyth's brother Warington, the well-travelled geologist whom Nevil had met at Penllergaer, was showing increasing interest in Nevil's sister Antonia. Nevil continued his letter to Thereza 'You must come and work with us some night, De la Rue is an extraordinary fellow and has made every bit of his telescope himself.' Nevil remembered that an eclipse of the moon was due soon, so he urged Thereza to go to Basset Down to see it, 'for there you know it will be annular!!!!! Dearest, I can fancy you with all your headache, ploughing along through school children and people all looking hungry at you, and you happy in making *them* so.' Nevil knew that Thereza drew much of her confidence and satisfaction from her charitable work around the hamlets but he implored her 'Dearest Thereza, don't be unhappy about leaving Penllergaer. We will be so happy!'

Thereza's visits to Basset Down kept having to be put off – which Nevil found extremely frustrating – because Margaret Story Maskelyne, his mother, had been growing thin and wasted and the family had been told she had not long to live. Thereza sent some violets, which Nevil told her were as 'sweet as my recollections of you', but he added, 'Alas I can only talk of recollections and it seems as if my last kiss was taken when I was a boy'. Nevil wrote to Thereza that he found love made him thinner, but that he hoped that she was growng 'fat and jolly notwithstanding all this dreadful uprooting'.

Margaret Story Maskelyne did not last the winter out. Anthony was shattered at the loss of his beloved wife, and the estate, which had been in her name, had to be put into chancery to make it possible for Anthony to continue to gain his living from it during his lifetime – all of which gave Nevil, as his mother's executor, a good many worries on top of his museum work.

At Oxford, Nevil Maskelyne had been used to a good deal more freedom than he now experienced as Keeper of Minerals, and on 20 April 1858 he was particularly annoyed at receiving an internal circular informing him that he was strictly forbidden from allowing, let alone encouraging, photography within the museum. It had come to the notice of the museum authorities that three people had been taking photographs in the Department of Antiquities, and that not only was Maskelyne behind all this, but he had actually locked up part of the museum cellar for use as a photographic darkroom and processing laboratory. The following day he was further warned to stop using any kind of spirit-lamp or blowpipe or even a lighted taper in his museum office. This was all very well, but how did they expect him to analyse minerals when they would let him have neither a chemical laboratory nor even a room in which he could use the proper instruments to measure the angles of crystals correctly, in order to identify them? The forbidden blowpipe was a long tube through which air was blown from the mouth in order to direct the flame onto the mineral being investigated, mounted usually on a charcoal block. The effect was to increase the heat, and it was an essential tool for observing the heat-resistant qualities of certain crystals. Nevil Maskelyne was exasperated by the total lack of respect for his scientific needs, and he pointed out that he had been appointed to the job precisely because of his knowledge of the chemical analysis of minerals, but that he was now going to be allowed no facilities whatsoever for applying this knowledge.

There was of course a real risk of fire in the museum, which was why no gas lighting was ever allowed in the building, but even so, the official imagination fairly let rip on describing the horrors inherent in the use of Maskelyne's

spirit-lamp and lighted tapers. He was told of the 'possibility of accident
therefrom – in which the first touch of flame upon the thin glass would break
it; and supposing the wind to be in the N or NE such flame would be driven as
by the blast of a furnace, upon the thin wood and paper partition and thence
by the wooden door into the Gallery of Minerals. The deadly gases eliminated
by heat from many of the minerals would paralyse any efforts on the spot to
quench the fire – with probably fatal consequences to those who might persist
in such attempts.' Although the picture they conjured up was rather extreme,
the museum authorities did have a serious responsibility to protect the hordes
of people who now roamed the galleries in numbers quite unforeseen a few
decades before.

In fact the natural history galleries upstairs were more popular with the
general public than the larger Department of Antiquities below, and this in
itself caused friction within the museum because the keepers of the priceless
treasures downstairs were uneasy at the sight of all that orange-peel littering
the stairs, as the sandwich-eating crowds poured in to admire the Mexican
lap-dog and other curiosities in the galleries above. There was already talk of
the possible removal of the now fast-growing natural history collections – an
idea wholeheartedly supported by Panizzi, who was said by his friend George
Macaulay to be prepared to swop three mammoths for an Aldine edition any
day. Panizzi wanted his library to be the finest in the world, and the presence
of the untidy rocks, plants and stuffed creatures upstairs was no part of his
plan.

The general museum attitude to science was only too familiar to Nevil
Maskelyne from his battling Oxford days – in fact those days were not entirely
over. He was back in Oxford twice a week as usual during May and June 1858,
completing his summer term lecture series before his wedding. On meeting
his Oxford friends he found that Dr Acland had added yet more to his already
impressive string of university posts and was now both Regius Professor and
Clinical Professor of Medicine. Dr Daubeny had recently invited the explorer
Dr Livingstone to lecture in the Sheldonian Theatre about his African travels,
and Max Müller, like Nevil, was preparing for his own wedding. He was
marrying a niece of Charles Kingsley and had been grateful to Leslie Thomson
who had smoothed the path between the radical young German and his
future parents-in-law.

Nevil Story
Maskelyne, around
the year of his
marriage
(photographer
unknown)

The wedding of Nevil and Thereza took place on 29 June at Penllergaer, but after a week's honeymoon spent at the Llewelyns' smaller house, Ynisigerwn, among the waterfalls up a remote valley, the couple planned to make a wedding tour on the continent. Nevil had arranged to combine his annual holiday with several extra weeks to be spent studying the great mineral collections of the European museums, so as to discover how other mineralogists were classifying and displaying their specimens. Starting with the collection at the Ecole des Mines in Paris, which was classified by crystal geometry (or 'atomic structure', as Maskelyne himself described it), they travelled down through France to the Black Forest to see the Freiburg collection of minerals from the mountains, which were largely grouped according to their colour. After this they spent time among the mountain scenery of Switzerland, where Thereza could see and enjoy the natural habitat of the alpine plants she admired so much. Nevil and Thereza passed on through the spectacular southern Alps to Venice, but the next significant mineral collection they saw was at the Johannesburg Institute at Graz in Austria, where they made friends with Dr Wilhelm Karl von Haidinger, an alert and highly experienced mineralogist, familiar with minerals from all over Europe and thoroughly scientific in his approach to their study.

The Austrian Imperial Mineral Collection at Vienna, on the other hand, put empire before science and arranged its minerals according to the part of the Austrian Empire where each specimen had been found. It was in Vienna that Nevil fell ill with 'low fever' and had to take to his bed. Thereza, suddenly faced with finding him a doctor, looked one up in *Murray's Guide* and had to creep nervously 'alone up an unknown staircase to the flat where the doctor lived, and tell him my story in my very imperfect German. He was very kind however'. She was surprised, when this doctor called in a second opinion, to hear them discussing the patient together in latin.

The illness prolonged their stay in Vienna, but they received sympathetic help from a young Austrian mineralogist, W.J.Graïlich, who invited them out to his own country home outside the city, where they could relax in the company of his wife Caroline. This was a great comfort to Thereza, who now

Joseph Graïlich
(carte de visite)
(photographer
unknown)

realized that she must be pregnant, for Caroline Graïlich was expecting their
own first child soon. Hungarian-born Joseph Graïlich, who was just 29 – Nevil
was 34 – already had an impressive academic record behind him and was a
lively bright-eyed scientist doing vanguard work on crystal structure. He was
assistant curator at the Imperial Mineral Collections in Vienna and had just
been made Professor Extraordinary of Natural Philosophy as well, so he and
Nevil Maskelyne had much in common and spent time together discussing
optics and crystallography in great depth. It was the first time that Nevil
Maskelyne had found someone near his own age with whom he could discuss
crystallography as an equal, and learn by doing so. From Joseph Graïlich too,
he found out about the efficient precision optical instruments being used in
Austria for the study of crystals. By the time Nevil and Thereza were fit to
move on to study the mineral collections at Prague, Nevil Maskelyne and
Joseph Graïlich were firm friends.

Driving through Dresden late one night during the last part of their tour,
Thereza was gazing up from their carriage when she spotted 'a star where no
star should be'. It later turned out to be Donati's comet, which she had noticed
even before the Italian astronomer had publicized it himself. It was now early
autumn, and they returned to England by way of Bonn, where Nevil had been
asked by the British Museum to examine the private mineral collection of a
dealer named Dr Krantz, which was up for sale. Nevil found that the minerals
included whole series of felspars, silicates, beryls, sapphires, zircons, zinc
and metallic oxides, and when he returned to London he recommended the
purchase of a range of these specimens.

Nevil was able to walk to the British Museum every day from Gloucester
Terrace, scorning the horse-drawn omnibus which most of his colleagues took
to work. He had by now decided that the mineral collection should be reclassi-
fied according to the crystallo-chemical system of the mineralogist Dr Gustav
Rose. In October 1858 he made a start by rearranging the silicates, which had
been enriched by the recently acquired minerals from Dr Krantz. Another
exciting purchase that autumn was a huge Australian gold nugget from
Victoria colony in New South Wales, which had been named the Latrobe

nugget, after the current lieutenant-governor of the colony, and weighed 25 troy ounces, so its display in the museum may well have sent yet more eager prospectors out in search of such a golden prize. That autumn Nevil Maskelyne found himself receiving silver from Chile, spinel from the United States and various brilliant crystals from Iceland, which he may have had to take to Oxford for examination, having no facilities in London.

In Oxford, Nevil had been his own master, so it was hard for him to get used to life in the Civil Service; in fact he tried to ignore some of the constraints, but Antonio Panizzi was a match for the wayward young professor and for nine years the two of them were to exchange a stream of internal correspondence, rather in the manner of an ongoing duel. Panizzi liked to spot any weaknesses in Maskelyne's defences – like grammatical errors or faults of style, failure to submit invoices through the proper channels, and other deviations from the official path. Maskelyne in return always defended himself vigorously, giving as good as he got, but in the process, whether he liked it or not, he became better at grammar and style and began to master the art of the tactful latter. Panizzi was, as Thereza put it, 'much disliked', but she believed that the tolerable relations between the Principal Librarian and the Department of Mineralogy owed a good deal to the departmental records which she wrote out for Nevil in her own tidy hand.

The Story Maskelynes were approaching the date due for the arrival of their baby, and April Fool's Day 1859 was to prove a momentous day for them on several counts. Firstly their baby daughter Margaret was born, and this was an event of tremendous excitement and pride for Nevil. Secondly he had a long article published anonymously that day in the *National Review*, on 'the present state of photography', which was an account of processes used to date, couched in popular mid-Victorian flowery prose. He was currently secretary to a sub-committee of the Photographic Society preparing a more sombre report on this subject for the British Association.

Nevil Maskelyne's third contribution to 1 April 1859 was his Royal Institution Friday evening lecture on the nature of a crystal molecule. In his lecture he made it clear that he understood atoms to be the ultimate chemical units of matter, and he came down firmly on the side of the atomic theorists in thinking of atoms as being grouped geometrically in 'chemical clusters' (which some scientists were still confusingly calling 'chemical atoms'). these chemical clusters – judging by his earlier writings on the subject – corresponded in Maskelyne's mind with the core or nucleus of a molecule, like Gerhardt's radicle – the part which remained unchanged after double decomposition. He thought of these clusters as being further grouped into units which he described both as 'the ultimate crystal-units-of-mass' and as 'chemical molecules'. A molecule, he stated, was formed partly from atoms and partly from 'ether', a mathematically thought-up term to express the medium through which light waves could travel and in which atoms could move. Each molecule, said Nevil Maskelyne, was a distinct mechanical unit with its own centre of gravity and centre of volume. He and Joseph Graïlich had been corresponding on this subject and had come to the conclusion that the two centres were not one and the same.

The internal arrangement of the molecule of a crystal, said Maskelyne, was exactly the same as the completely regular arrangement of the molecules in relation to each other within that particular crystal – for the growth pattern of each kind of crystal was subject to rigid rules related to the angle at which each crystal face intersected with the next. By calculations, he stated, these angles could be related to particular axes, indices and parameters, to give the precise number of actual or possible planes for each type of crystal. Not only did the external facets of any crystal follow these planes of symmetry but, inside it, the molecules were neatly laid out along the planes of symmetry too.

In this same Royal Institution lecture he also explained that if, for example, a crystal was struck or was subjected to vibrations such as sound, it would resist such forces in a particular way geometrically related to its molecular structure. He mentioned Joseph Graïlich's discovery that while it was always easier to cleave a crystal along one particular plane of symmetry, its hardest facet was always at right angles to that plane. Concentrations of density followed the direction of the planes of symmetry too, and this density path influenced the magnetic properties of a crystal. In this context Nevil Maskelyne was resorting to Faraday's two terms paramagnetism and diamagnetism, and he also followed Faraday in saying that the transmission of electricity, heat and light produced 'electric tensions' between poles within the crystal. He did however add that the crystal itself contained static forces, related to its symmetry, which could modify the character, amount and direction of induced magnetism, electricity or heat.

One question which had puzzled Nevil Maskelyne since he had become interested in science in the mid 1840s was how heat could increase the volume of crystals. It was known that this increase in volume occurred, but at the time the phenomenon had been hard to understand, since crystals were still believed to be formed of 'continuous matter' and so to have no space between the molecules to allow for expansion or change. Although the French scientists Delafosse and Bravais had been thinking up ideas in the 1840s about space between molecules forming part of the structure of matter, the concept of non-continuous matter had been slow to catch on in scientific circles. It was acceptance of this concept which in 1859 allowed Maskelyne and Graïlich to understand that heat could increase the volume of a crystal without altering its system of symmetry or its original chemical content.

Graïlich and his assistant Viktor von Lang had been experimenting with the effect of light upon crystals, and Nevil Maskelyne had concluded from their work that two distinct factors inherent in crystals decided how they resisted external forces. Whereas heat, magnetism and vibrations such as sound were resisted by the arrangement and 'statical condition' of each crystal molecule relative to the next, light was resisted by what he termed the 'axes of elasticity within the molecule itself, that is, of the ether within it'. The elasticity of this mysterious ether surrounding the atoms was in itself determined, he said, by the action of 'atoms at rest' upon the 'ether particles in motion'. He decided that in the crystal systems then known as prismatic systems (orthorhombic), the ether particles must be vibrating in only one direction throughout the crystal – because in these crystals each molecule was arranged at the same angle relative to its neighbours, which caused the material particles of ether to constrain, or 'slow down' the velocity of wavelengths of light which entered the crystal. He added that oblique (monoclinic) crystal systems caused the light to be dispersed as well as constrained, which made the resistance of these crystals rather different.

The days running up to the Royal Institution lecture had been tense ones for Nevil because Thereza had been suffering tedious hours of pain at the approach of the birth of their baby daughter. When next he wrote to Joseph

Graïlich he told him of this distressing time, but Joseph Graïlich had developed more than enough troubles of his own, for he wrote back to tell Nevil that not only had he himself been seriously ill with a diseased lung, but over the Easter holidays his own baby daughter had started throwing convulsions which had recurred during most of two whole days. Caroline Graïlich had been terrified by these seizures, Joseph confided to Nevil, and he himself had felt so useless to her, being incapable of rising from his own sickbed to help her. Joseph's letter to Nevil was written in pencil this time, and towards the end the writing grew weaker and weaker. Later in May he had an operation for the removal of a suspected tumour – which he survived even though this was before the days of antisepsis in the operating theatre. It was, however, to have no lasting effect, and the planned visit of the Graïlich family to Basset Down that summer had to be postponed. They would, in fact, never come to England for, sadly, Joseph Graïlich the brilliant young crystallographer died in September 1859, and Nevil Maskelyne lost another good friend.

Crystallography had not been the only fast-moving field of science, for 1859 also saw the publication of Charles Darwin's book *The Origin of Species* which so shocked pious Victorian society, despite the numerous scientific lines of research which had so long pointed in the same evolutionary direction. To Nevil Maskelyne, Darwin's ideas would have come as no surprise, since he was so used to holding free discussions with those who, like himself, now upheld Darwin's Theory of Evolution – including Dr Daubeny, Viktor Carus, Thomas Huxley of the College of Mines, and Asa Gray, the American botanist who was to publicize Darwin's ideas in the United States. The American Civil War was just brewing up, but by the later 1860s Asa Gray was sometimes in London, when he would visit the Maskelynes and meet their friends over dinner.

Working at the British Museum was bringing Nevil into daily contact with a wide circle of outside scientists like John Tyndall, Professor of Philosophy at the Royal Institution, who was apt to make sudden demands for mineral specimens from the British Museum to serve his own researches in the field of physics – such as the large piece of rocksalt he wanted to use for following up the results of Melloni's experiments on radiant heat. Nevil Maskelyne, while heartily sympathizing with Dr Tyndall's aims, also felt that he would scarcely be acting as a good Keeper of Minerals if he let one of his superb mineral specimens go. Dr Tyndall, whose philosophy on the purpose of the British Museum was different, had a number of tough exchanges with Maskelyne on this sort of subject. Another scientific pillar of the Royal Institution, Sir Charles Babbage, was living in London in 1860, working out his ideas for mathematical machines – early computers – and he helpfully sent Maskelyne some useful specimens of 'exceedingly fine-coloured old glass' for making experiments into 'double-axed crystals and the law of dispersion in them'.

In October 1859 Maskelyne arranged for the British Museum to purchase a great array of minerals known as the Allan-Greg collection. Early in the nineteenth century an adventurer had spent several years in Greenland gathering rare minerals, which he finally sent off home to Britain by sea – a risky move as it turned out, for they were seized somewhere off the coast of Scotland by a privateer. When in due course the minerals came up for sale in Edinburgh they were bought for £13 by the collector Thomas Allan, who already possessed an exceptionally rich collection of British minerals. The Allan collection had then been amalgamated with that of another enthusiast,

R.H.Greg, to form the Allan-Greg hoard of over 9,000 good items. After purchasing them, the British Museum was able to present a very wide view of the earth's existing minerals and crystal forms.

The meteorite collection at the museum was flourishing by 1861 and Nevil Maskelyne kept receiving reports of showers and falls of these extra-terrestrial objects from every corner of the world. Nevil Maskelyne was the first to study fine transparent slivers of meteorite under the microscope and so identify not only many of the known terrestrial minerals, but some which were unknown on earth.

Curiously poetic-sounding minerals kept arriving at his British Museum study from all quarters, and Maskelyne noted them down as they came – 'an extensive series of beautifully crystallised zeolytes', for example, was sent back by the Chief Engineer of the Great Indian Peninsular Railway, and there was 'a Phenakite from Siberia' as well as a 'very beautiful Rubellite' and a 'green turquoise of large dimensions from the Summer Palace, Pekin', not to mention the Hungarian wagnerite, the beryls, sapphires, zircons, the 'crystals of erythrite of a rich crimson colour' and the more prosaic-sounding 'arsenico-phosphates of lead from Cumberland'. Nevil Maskelyne identified and named a number of new minerals himself, and he must have become very excited at times, as he unwrapped the packages which flowed in from those distant places, and felt the sharp sparkling stones on his hand.

One thing which frustrated Nevil Maskelyne beyond all else was his total lack of laboratory facilities for examining these rare treasures. Late in 1858, through his friend Joseph Graïlich in Vienna, he had bought a polarizing microscope, similar to the kind which Henry Fox Talbot had used for examining crystals in the 1830s. Through Joseph Graïlich too, Nevil Maskelyne had bought crystal models and a goniometer – the instrument which measured the angles between the facets of a crystal. Nevil Maskelyne used a reflecting goniometer with a microscope, but it is no wonder that he nearly went blind in one eye, even though he managed this method of classifying crystals with great accuracy. In the early 1860s he designed a special polarizing microscope with a graduated revolving stage, in which fine slices of greenish-white tourmaline served as a polarizing screen. This impressive brass instrument was delivered to the museum by the makers, Powell and Lealand, in 1863 and Maskelyne had a second one made for his own use at home, where the obvious advantage was that he could use it with artificial light.

His one overriding problem at the museum was the lack of light. The light bulb had not yet been invented and gas light was not allowed in the museum because of fire risk, so the sole source of light was the sun, which could only really be exploited for indoor use by placing a heliostat on a windowsill. This device would angle a magnified beam of sunlight into a room, but there were two problems – firstly the room had to face south, which the mineral gallery did not; and secondly of course it had to be a sunny day. In the mid nineteenth century, coal-burning London often suffered thick polluting fogs, and the museum sometimes closed altogether in the early afternoon for lack of light.

The smoking chimneys of London

Again and again Maskelyne tried to get the museum authorities to let him set up a room as a laboratory, at first suggesting a temporary one in the super-structure above the Elgin room, but then, seeing how hopeless it was to try and get facilities within the building, he asked for the use of an available house in nearby Great Torrington Street, even offering to pay the rent himself, but all to no avail, Meanwhile the activities of the museum's anti-natural-science lobby were increasing. But the scientists, Maskelyne among them, put up such a fight that they managed, for the time being, to prevent Parliament from passing a bill to divide the museum and send the natural history collections elsewhere. The scientists' gain was not to last long, and the constant threat of removal made for stress among the staff, so much so that Antonio Panizzi was heading for a nervous breakdown.

In those uneasy days of interdepartmental struggle, Nevil Maskelyne was only too grateful to gain an assistant in the shape of Viktor von Lang, who had been Joseph Graïlich's assistant in Vienna. Viktor von Lang arrived at the British Museum in 1862, full of enthusiasm and ideas, and he and Nevil Maskelyne, who had badly needed the stimulus of a scientific colleague, held many fruitful discussions, from which they published their *Mineralogical Notices* in 1863. Unfortunately for this useful scientific partnership, Antonio Panizzi, who returned that year after spending a considerable time in Naples convalescing from his breakdown, took exception to Viktor von Lang and had managed to engineer his removal from the museum staff by mid-1864 on grounds of 'lateness'. Von Lang returned to a professorship in Austria, his programme of museum work only part done. He and Maskelyne had assem-bled so much advanced knowledge that during 1865 they each wrote the substantial part of a book on crystallography. The following year, Viktor von Lang actually managed to publish his own book on crystal symmetry, which Henry Miers, one of Maskelyne's gifted Oxford pupils, recognized as contain-ing much material which must have arisen from mutual discussions at the British Museum

Professor Maskelyne's students of the 1860s all became familiar with the galley proofs of the book he was writing on crystallography which, said Henry Miers, introduced them to 'an attractive treatment of what was a new subject at the time'. The actual mathematical proofs of the angles possible between the planes of symmetry of a crystal were given by Maskelyne in his 1869 Oxford lectures, as W.J.Lewis, another student, later reported to Henry Miers; but it was Professor Gadolin, a Finnish chemist, who was to publish the same result, two years later. During the mid-sixties, Henry Miers used to attend informal mineralogy lectures given by Nevil Maskelyne in the house of the mathematician Henry Smith at Oxford. Maskelyne would lecture from a chair in the drawing room, with Henry Smith playing the part of student by asking questions and making useful comments, and young Miers used to notice how they were forever teasing away at mathematical problems together.

In 1860 Maskelyne requested five or six days leave from the British Museum to arrange a collection of minerals in the just-completed University Museum for the natural sciences at Oxford, because the British Association was again holding its summer meetings in Oxford that year, starting on 27 June. The meetings turned out to be probably the most dramatic ever – due to the celebrated debate which broke out between Samuel Wilberforce, Bishop of Oxford, and Thomas Huxley, fast-thinking supporter of Darwin's Theory of

Evolution. In the large library of the new University Museum, Dr Draper, a New York professor of natural sciences, had been addressing the Botany and Zoology section on the 'Intellectual Development of Europe', with reference to Darwin's theory that the law of natural selection determines the progress of organisms from one generation to the next. Wilberforce countered in an argumentative and eloquent style, asserting that not only was Darwin's theory founded on fancy rather than philosophy, but that he had been unable to produce a single instance of one species having changed to another, and the bishop concluded amid loud cheers that the theory was degrading to man. Professor Huxley's reply was calm, dispassionate and ice-clear in favour of the Theory of Evolution, but the content of his argument was naturally disturbing to most of his audience, who didn't like what they were hearing, because it tore from them much of the fundamentalist belief they held most dear.

The British Association meetings were once again graced by the presence of Prince Albert, and also by a young Russian nobleman– Prince Nikolai of Herzog, Duke of Leuchtenberg, a member of the famous Romanoff family of tsarist Russia. Mrs Jeune, wife of the Master of Pembroke, noticed the duke as a quiet, pleasing young man, and Nevil Maskelyne was particularly glad to meet and get to know him, because, at the age of 17, Prince Nikolai already had a passion for mineralogy. The fabulous wealth of the Romanoffs had left him relatively unaffected, and over the following years he several times came to dine with the Story Maskelynes, when in London visiting the British Museum mineral collections. He would always insist on leading Thereza in to dinner first – a gallant point of etiquette which she found amusing, but 'very natural in a Russian duke'.

Prince Frederick of Schleswig-Holstein was another occasional mineral-collecting visitor of theirs, but he was of a more outgoing character, sharing with Nevil and Thereza over the dinner table the anxieties he felt for his troubled principality. The Maskelynes by now had a wide circle of London friends and aquaintances, including the geologist Charles Lyell, who happened to give the first evening party to which Nevil took Thereza. Lyell, who had been hot on the trail of the story of the earth's formation some decades before, was now a firm supporter of Darwin's Theory of Evolution, and was searching among the flints of Europe for evidence of the emergence of tool-making man. Florence Nightingale they saw something of too, for she was living in London, and gave Thereza a little manual on the care of the sick. The Oxford don, Benjamin Jowett had started corresponding with Florence Nightingale from 1861, after meeting her at a house party given by Benjamin Brodie's father, the surgeon. From this, a deepening relationship had grown between them, so much so that by 1863 Benjamin Jowett was very often in London visiting her and had taken to administering the Holy Sacrament to her at intervals. She undoubtedly fascinated him with her strong personality and keen mind, and this stimulating but apparently platonic friendship was to last until Jowett's death.

Arthur Stanley was now Dean of Westminster, and Thereza recalled how the Story Maskelynes often crossed the park to visit him there. During the winter of 1862-3 Arthur Stanley had been chosen to accompany young Bertie, Prince of Wales, on a tour of the Middle East, following the death of his father, Prince Albert. After the funeral, a list of Prince Albert's favourite clergy had been discovered, with the name of Leslie Thomson, Nevil's one-time chemical analysis pupil, firmly at the top. Leslie Thomson was accordingly made a royal chaplain to Queen Victoria, which was a great advance in his already successful career in the Anglican Church. Arthur Stanley, confirmed bachelor that he was, surprised his friends on returning from the Middle East by getting married. His wife, Lady Augusta Stanley, used to devote all her energies to caring for him, even to the point of removing his *Times* from his hands in the morning, in order to read it aloud to him, so that he could not forget to eat his breakfast.

It was through the marriage of his sister Antonia to Warington Smyth the geologist, that Nevil gained some interesting new relatives, including his old friend the astronomer Piazzi Smyth who, sharing Nevil's enthusiasm for photography, was out in Egypt in 1865, taking pictures of the insides of pyramids with the aid of a magnesium flash. Warington Smyth was currently Inspector of Crown Minerals to the Duchy of Cornwall, so he and Nevil were able to work closely together on Cornish minerals. Nevil described several new minerals from Cornwall, including green 'waringtonite' and whitish-blue 'lyellite'. Warington Smyth's sister was married to the surgeon, William Henry Flower (who was later to become director of the British Museum of Natural History). Mr Flower, having been invalided home from the Crimean War, was now in charge of the Museum of Comparative Anatomy at the Royal College of Surgeons, where he used to enjoy explaining to Nevil and Thereza the new comparisons being made to suggest how one species of creature might have evolved from another – showing them the affinities between fins, feet and wings, or between a human leg and a horse's hoof. It was still a very novel way of looking at anatomy. Thereza with her more puritanical background was perhaps even more fascinated than Nevil, whose mind had been opened to the geological evolutionary debates since his teenage years. The post-Darwin era was dawning upon nineteenth century society.

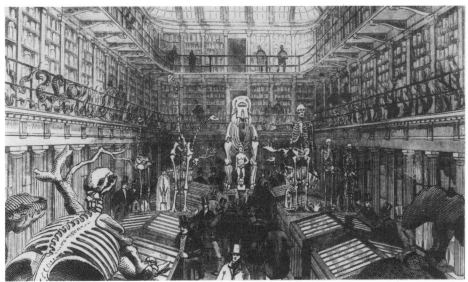

The Museum of Comparative Anatomy at the Royal College of Surgeons (from an earlier drawing)

It was in May 1864 that Nevil Maskelyne received an exciting letter from Russia, giving him details of the great Koksharov collection of minerals which was being offered for sale to the British Museum by Professor Nikolai Ivanovich Koksharov, son of the director of the St Petersburg Mining Institute and himself a leading authority on the Russian Imperial Mineral Collections. Nevil Maskelyne could see that he had an important decision to make on whether or not to recommend the British government to spend a considerable sum on its purchase, so he wrote to Professor Koksharov, from whom he discovered that his minerals included many specimens so rare as to put them on a scale quite unknown in existing European museums.

Maskelyne told the museum authorities that such minerals would add not only to the 'visible splendour of the London collection, but to its scientific value too', so he was authorized to make a journey to Russia to see the Koksharov collection for himself and to do any useful bargaining he could. Once over there, he was in the informed hands of Professor Koksharov and of 22-year-old Prince Nikolai, Duke of Leuchtenberg, who had just been made President of the Russian Imperial Mineralogical Society. As well as studying Koksharov's own collection, Maskelyne spent as much time as possible examining the Imperial Collections, but in the Hermitage he was sidetracked by the engraved gems from the ancient world and stopped, pondering, over a chalcedony scarab of a flying stork, wondering whether the craftsmen of these minute works of art all those centuries before, could even have been using a lens and engraver's wheel. While he was in Russia, Nevil Maskelyne managed to visit Moscow to inspect the minerals and gems in the cathedral treasury, and he also went to the great fair at Nijni Novgorod, where he bought wooden nesting dolls and eggs for his little daughters.

After some bargaining, he recommended the purchase of the entire Koksharov collection, and in 1865 the British Museum sent out a carriage to transport the 3,250 mineral specimens back to London. It must have been a rather tense security job for the men who brought the trundling horse-drawn load of Russian gold, Siberian diamonds, topazes and other precious stones across Europe, especially during overnight stops in out-of-the-way places.

Prince Nikolai of
Herzog, Duke of
Leuchtenberg
(carte de visite)
(photographer
unknown)

Once the collection had reached London, Nevil Maskelyne had to set about classifying and arranging it in his already overcrowded gallery.

The year 1866 saw scientific advances in the physical field, which included James Clark Maxwell's proof of the connection, long suspected by Maskelyne, between optics and electricity. The distinction had also at long last been proved between atomic weight and equivalent weight; more detailed work had been done on crystal angles and crystal hardness, and a new system had been devised for classifying meteorites – so Maskelyne was daily longing for facilities for those experiments he could have done so well. He was still very handicapped without a laboratory, but the prospect of getting one had diminished further, due to a recent fire in the museum bindery, which had set the Trustees on edge. Much analytical work had to be transported to his Oxford laboratory in Dr Acland's new University Museum, where he could analyse such awkward minerals as the 'silicates that do not gelatinize with hydrogen chloride', for which he had to set up such convoluted apparatus that it took him several paragraphs to describe it to the Royal Society.

As museums became more fashionable and collections grew in size, it was of course inevitable that some material would have to be rehoused. The collections in Oxford had certainly seen a good deal of reshuffling recently, and this included the contents of the Old Ashmolean Museum, above Nevil Maskelyne's former living quarters in Broad Street. The natural science collections from there had been transferred to the new University Museum, and Maskelyne's old basement home was converted to house the Arundel collection of marbles, from upstairs. During the course of these alterations, made in 1864, Maskelyne received news of a discovery made there by workmen, one of whom had driven his pickaxe through a wall below street level, into a small chamber containing an apparently historic horde of ancient wines and spirits. The workmen, after sampling the contents of their exciting find, fell to wondering about its origins. When details of the incident reached him, wrote J.Günther in 1923, Nevil Maskelyne became 'strangely excited' and exclaimed, 'They have broken into my cellar, the stupid idiots. If they had only looked at the other side, they would have seen my new oak door.'

The Voring Foss, a
Norwegian
waterfall

The year after his journey to Russia, Nevil took Thereza and his youngest
sister Agnes on holiday to Norway, setting off up the fiords by steamer from
Christiansand, taking to pony-drawn carioles when land got in the way, and
marvelling at the mighty waterfalls. During a stay at Vik they rode some sure-
footed ponies up a 'staircase of rock' to spend the night at a high-altitude milk
house where Thereza was surprised to find that 'the beds were covered,
entirely covered when we arrived, with everything belonging to the dairy,
and pans of milk were under them, whilst great cheese vats were on the
primitive kitchen fire'. When they took holidays at Thereza's old home at
Penllergaer, the Story Maskelynes sometimes took with them Dr Günther of
the museum's bird gallery, who was trying to create reconstructions of the
nests and favourite haunts of his stuffed birds, to liven up the displays. He
found Penllergaer a happy hunting ground, with its wooded lakes, farms and
hilly moorland.

Despite his efforts to build up his own Department of Mineralogy into the
best in the world, Nevil Maskelyne still had his critics – like the correspondent
to *The Times* of 1866, who felt that the mineral section of the British Museum
catalogue was no longer an adequate guide to the displays. On this point John
Ruskin leapt to Nevil Maskelyne's defence. Ruskin, who had been a friend of
Maskelyne's since the early days of the Working Men's College and the
planning stages of the University Museum, now lived with his mother at
Herne Hill. Nevil and Thereza used to visit them there, sometimes taking
their little girls for old Mrs Ruskin to see – and John Ruskin had, in 1862, given
the children a little illustrated book of German moral tales. John Ruskin could
respond to the criticisms of *The Times* correspondent with some authority, for
not only had he been a mineral collector from childhood (and presented the
museum with one of its finest specimens, the Colenso diamond) but he was
often in the mineral gallery in the mid 1860s, researching his book *Ethics of the
Dust*, which concerned crystals. He wrote to *The Times* that 'it is just because
Mr Maskelyne is doing more active, continual and careful work than, as far as
I know, is at present done in any national museum in Europe, because he is
contemplating gaps in the present series by the interrelation of carefully

sought specimens, and accurately reforming its classification by recently corrected analyses, that the collection cannot fall into the formal and placid order in which an indolent curator would speedily arrange and willingly leave it.' John Ruskin, who appreciated Nevil Maskelyne's affectionate nature and quick, alert mind, was himself a sensitive temperamental character, so as they grew older and Ruskin began to suffer manic-depressive phases, their correspondence was sometimes to show up the impatient side in them both.

Sparked off by his visit to Russia, Nevil Maskelyne's interest in gems had increased so much that he had become immensely knowlegeable about these precious or semi-precious stones with engraved or raised designs worked onto them with minute, delicate craftsmanship. He studied their history in detail, discovering their origins in the cultures of ancient Greece, Rome, Assyria and Egypt, as well as in the more recent civilizations of Mexico, Persia and India. His own knowledge of both classical literature and mineralogy backed up his gem studies and he was further helped by being in almost daily contact with the Department of Antiquities at the British Museum, where one of the world's finest gem collections was held.

He was soon to become an expert gem critic, and it was this skill combined with knowledge of minerals which took him to the Paris Universal Exhibition in 1869, as juror of the displayed gems, jewellery and precious stones. He found high-grade stones and elegant jewellery mixed up with ornaments and trinkets made from inferior materials, which made the judging rather difficult. He also noticed many examples of the diamond-cutters' extravagances, where they had cut much of the diamond away to pander to the current desire for sparkling parures, necklaces and sprigs of diamond geraniums, which he clearly found in dubious taste. The exhibition however was an undiluted success for Charlotte Maskelyne, whom Nevil and Thereza had brought with them to Paris, for Charlotte, now a middle-aged maiden lady and her father's châtelaine at Basset Down, had never been abroad before and was captivated by all she experienced – including the view of the old city roofs from her hotel bedroom, and all the foreign scents and sounds.

An unexpected request came in 1870 from the Duke of Marlborough, who wanted Nevil Maskelyne to catalogue his vast private gem collection at Blenheim Palace. Maskelyne visited the palace and gained permission to take the gems away so that he could work on them at home at 12 Gloucester Terrace. The duke seemed quite happy at the thought of his precious gems going off to stay with the Story Maskelynes, and Thereza welcomed them because it gave her the opportunity of becoming involved in Nevil's work, writing down the identification and description of each item as he examined them. Thereza enjoyed this kind of task and felt herself privileged in being able to share in Nevil's working life to a greater extent than many wives.

Thereza followed Nevil to Dover in the Easter holidays of 1869, when he was encamped above the cliffs with the Artists' Rifle corps of the British Museum volunteers – the militia being a popular way of supporting Queen and Country. She stayed with her sister nearby, taking her three daughters, Margaret, Mary and Terry down to the beach to play, while she sketched. She noticed a group of men wielding picks below the cliffs, and discovered that they had been employed to start digging the Channel Tunnel. Nevil and Thereza both remained enthusiasts for astronomy, and Nevil accompanied Piazzi Smyth that summer on one of his trips to make astronomical observations in Tenerife. In 1866, recalled E.M.Thomson, a meteoric shower had occurred, and even Leslie Thomson, now Archbishop of York, had written home to remind his dear Zoë to be sure to look out for the 'star shower', though he missed it himself through falling asleep. The Story Maskelynes on the other hand had spotted the shower on their way home from a dinner party, rushed home to change and made their way out to Paddington Green to watch the 'eruption of the countless stars' from those peaceful surroundings. Paddington Green is not a place you would single out today for making astronomical observations – with its horizons cluttered with high-rise blocks, elevated motorway and powerful street lighting.

Meteoric showers were of particular interest to Nevil these days because he was rapidly becoming an authority on meteorites. In 1870, aged 46, he was made Fellow of the Royal Society for his scientific achievements, and two years later he gave a Royal Institution Friday evening lecture under the title 'Whence came meteorites?' in which he argued that, while the origin of meteorites was not yet established, they were not, as some contemporaries suggested, pieces of the moon broken loose. In 1875 he wrote a paper saying that he had noticed that in the stonier meteorites – by which he meant the ones containing less nickel-iron – the alloy was richer in nickel and the accompanying silicates were richer in iron. In 1916, when a later scientist was to make this same observation, a physical law (Prior's Law) was based upon it. Maskelyne's museum correspondence was full of meteorite reports from far-flung corners of the world, and one piece of meteorite he acquired for the museum from Australia weighed 3½ tons and still stands in the British Museum of Natural History at South Kensington today.

Museums in general were on a boom – even the Working Men's College had decided to open one in London, and Nevil Maskelyne, who still lectured there from time to time, agreed to help them to arrange a small mineral museum at their current Great Ormond Street premises. Most of Maskelyne's former Christian Socialist colleagues had moved on, and the Working Men's College had by now fallen somewhat under the influence of the English Positivists, with their belief that the future of mankind lay with the development of science and technology. This influence came from Frederic Harrison, the pupil of the former Wadham tutor Richard Congreve, who was teaching at the college and writing left-wing articles for papers and journals. The English Positivists, associated as they were with trades unionists, could fairly claim to have been in at the start of the British left-wing intelligentsia.

In 1875 Nevil Maskelyne was invited by Joseph Collins of Truro to become a founder member of a national mineralogical society, but he declined, on the grounds that there were not yet enough really scientifically qualified mineralogists in Britain to justify such a society. Maskelyne evidently had other reasons behind his refusal though, which became clear when he finally mentioned to Mr Collins that he was himself assembling 'a small modest association of workers for dealing with some of the problems that concern mineralogical science'. Nevil Maskelyne's more select scientific group met for the first time at his own house, 12 Gloucester Terrace, on the afternoon of 4 June 1876. Professor Henry Smith summarized his own recent paper on the 'Conditions necessary for geometric symmetry'; Professor Antoine des Cloiseaux from Paris gave a reasoned explanation of why he thought that certain recently re-examined crystals should now be considered part of the oblique rather than the prismatic system, and Professor William Miller of Cambridge, the chairman, explained the special way in which he adapted his goniometer for making accurate measurements of awkward, heavy crystal specimens.

Professor Miller was particularly fond of this kind of ingenious home-made gadgetry, and Nevil Maskelyne later wrote of 'that interesting room' at Cambridge in which the shy professor surrounded himself with 'marvels of ingenuity . . . implements of observation fashioned out of the simplest materials – deal, cork, glass tube, wire – by the hand of their inventor, rough to look at but exact in their performance'. These menbers of the 'Crystallological Society', as it came to be known, were a rare bunch of experts who met several times a year for seven years, Nevil Maskelyne taking over as chairman in 1877 when Professor Miller grew too old to preside. The membership rose to 34, which included several prominent foreign scientists, like Emile Bertrand of the Paris Ecole des Mines, and of course Viktor von Lang from Vienna. Nevil Maskelyne was elected president of the Crystallological Society in 1881, and discussions started soon afterwards on whether or not to amalgamate with the once-scorned Mineralogical Society, which they eventually did, in 1883.

Nevil Maskelyne's scientific work was spread over a range of mineralogical subjects in the middle 1870s. He was trying to form double salts of silver nitrate, as well as studying the types of instrument used in crystallography, and forming an opinion on the causes of pitting on the surfaces of the 'stonier meteorites'. Maskelyne thought that the pitting occured at the spots where sudden heat entered the mass of the meteorite most readily, because those spots had held metals which were better conductors, fused most readily and allowed the heat to penetrate faster to the interior. The heat, he thought, fused the stone due to the high velocity of the meteorite at the moment it encountered the earth's atmosphere. M. Daubrée of the Paris Ecole des Mines, who came to stay with the Story Maskelynes in 1876, took a different view, and the matter aroused considerable discussion.

Maskelyne was asked to examine a group of very much larger stones than usual that year – the standing stones at Stonehenge in Wiltshire – in the hope that he could give a lead as to where they had come from. Maskelyne could give the exact nature of the rock forming the various stones of the prehistoric inner circle at Stonehenge, by examining them in fine microscopic sections, but he could give little clue to where they came from, because at that time there was still no complete public classified collection of the rocks of Britain, for comparison.

Helped by the fact that laboratory facilities and a laboratory assistant – Walter Flight – had at last been provided in a house near the museum, Maskelyne had been studying diamonds and the rocks from which they were formed. The fact that he had to be in the museum made it difficult to be in contact with his laboratory assistant to find out how the diamond experiments were progressing. These were the days of the great South African diamond boom, but Nevil Maskelyne as chairman of a Society of Arts committee stated that he regretted the British ardour for possession – remarking that while it might be a 'proud hope for an Englishman' that his nation should play the part of colonizing all these fertile countries, it might be questioned whether her dominions were not already too large, without extending her sway far into Africa. He noticed that South African diamonds existed in 'the throats of extinct volcanoes' and concluded that they had been formed under extreme heat and pressure within the rock itself.

Late in 1877 his interest in diamonds involved Maskelyne in something of a national news sensation which became known as the Hannay diamond controversy. He was initially asked to examine some particles of 'artificial diamond' made, it was claimed, in the workshops of a Glaswegian named McTear. By 1 January, Maskelyne had been able to prove that the particles were crystallized silicate, but the affair had already attracted publicity. He was asked to analyse yet another batch of 'artificial diamonds', this time from the workshops of Mr J.Ballantyne Hannay, again a Glaswegian but also a member of the well-established Chemical Society of London. Maskelyne himself was soon to spend three years as vice-president of the Chemical Society, and naturally respected his fellow-member, Hannay, whose specimens not only looked exactly like broken fragments of true diamond, but satisfied every one of the professor's tests for correct lustre, lamellar structure, surfaces of cleavage and refractive power. Nevil Maskelyne reported in *The Times* that there was no doubt that Hannay had managed to produce true diamonds. This statement caused professional horror among scientific men – who refused to believe that 25-year-old Hannay could have solved the problem of crystallizing carbon, something every chemist would have liked to achieve but considered physically impossible. Furious public controversy was also aroused because Maskelyne's verdict contained a threat to the entire flourishing empire of the diamond trade.

Descriptions of Hannay's methods indicate that he and his workmen had put enormous effort and skill into their experiments, exploding several furnaces on the way and claiming to create diamonds in only one out of nine attempts. Or was it all a hoax? Some would say that the controversy is still open today, for while in 1939 one scientist, using far more sophisticated equipment than Maskelyne's, found the Hannay diamonds to be genuine synthesized (artificial) diamonds, another experiment carried out in 1975 found them to be natural diamond. It could be argued that the impulsive Keeper of Minerals, correct though he was in identifying diamonds, might have been more prudent at the time to have fought shy of the headlines.

By this time John Ruskin had matured a plan to open a museum of his own at Walkley near Sheffield, for the education of working men. It was to be part of a grand design he had been working on for some years, to build an ideal society, starting from a nucleus – a 'guild of brethren' – who would fight for a merrier England. Part of Ruskin's wider plan was to recruit the cooperation of certain landlords, who would offer employment to members of his 'Guild of St George', and so be able to look out and see men engaged in honest toil on their farmlands, rather than the 'iron devils' of farm machinery.

In the year he was starting his museum, John Ruskin wrote to Nevil Maskelyne to provide him with some 'yes or no' answers to a set of question papers intended for display with mineral exhibits in the museum, but Maskelyne, who knew his friend's weaknesses, warily declined, suggesting that mineralogy was not so cut and dried as that. 'If you came to me', returned John Ruskin, 'to ask if a picture was in perspective – I should never tell you to go and learn perspective, but tell you positively – Yes or No. And *where* the error was. If I bring you an agate and ask you to tell me in what state its silica is and was, I expect you to tell me positively or put the stone aside . . .' Although they never resolved the matter of the question papers, Ruskin and the Maskelynes remained friends and the museum ran in Sheffield for some years before being taken over by the city council.

The British Museum natural history collections were now definitely due for early removal to the great new building being prepared for them in South Kensington. In early 1878 the British Museum was still closed on Tuesdays and Thursdays 'for cleaning', but this gentlemanly arrangement for keeping the general public at bay was soon to finish, for the doors were about to be opened every day, even to babes in arms (whose cultural needs seem to have passed unnoticed before). Nevil Maskelyne as an admirer of the classics, deplored the architecture of the new British Museum of Natural History being built at South Kensington for being too 'gothic', and he exchanged some sharp letters with its architect, Alfred Waterhouse, on his lack of provision for scientific work. He did not relish the move to the new museum, and various good reasons arose at that time to make him decide to move on. When the moment came for the natural history collections to be heaved out of the cuckoo's nest, the mineral collections were the first to go, but Nevil Story Maskelyne did not go with them.

The Yellow Banner

A warning had come to Nevil Story Maskelyne in 1876, when his father had suffered a long 'fainting fit' and had become largely bed bound. From this time Nevil had to hold himself ready to take over full responsibility for the Basset Down estate if his father should die. Thereza was often down in Wiltshire anyway, with the girls, whose health was thought to be suffering in the London atmosphere. From 1870 Nevil had rented Salthrop House from his father, so that they could escape to the downland air when they needed reviving. Salthrop House was a mellow Georgian stone house, only a quarter of a mile from Basset Down House where the whole family foregathered around Anthony Story Maskelyne every Christmas.

The festivities would start on St Thomas' Day, 21 December, recalled Thereza in her memoirs, when various parishioners of Lydiard Tregoz came 'a-Thomassing' to Basset Down for the time-honoured Wiltshire ceremony of 'Gooding', when each person received a groat, or four-penny piece. A bag of these coins was ordered ready, to join the many gifts of blankets and flannel winter clothing, made by Nevil's sisters Charlotte and Agnes. Due to the current agricultural depression, wages were again very low, but the cottagers this time knew how badly their wages compared with those of other workers, so they wanted better pay, not charity, and they became resentful of the paternalistic handout of alms and clothing. Thereza later recalled that once she and Nevil took over these arrangements, in the 1890s, the clothing distribution was dropped. After this the farm workers would send their children along to fetch the groat, rather than suffer the indignity of receiving alms in person, so the ancient ceremony had to be abandoned in favour of a local tea-party.

Salthrop House
in 1888

The Story Maskelyne family had a decorated Christmas tree, on which each candle had to be separately wired to its bough – a ritual carried out in Charlotte's bedroom, from which the scent of 'spruce fir, of heated hairpins and hot wax' was wafted out onto the landing. The days each side of Christmas Day were enlivened by visits from groups of handbell ringers just before dusk and by mummers' plays after dark. A team of handbell ringers consisted of a row of seven men with two bells each, linked to each wrist by a leather loop. Faced by their leader, they played the bells by a strong upwards wrist jerk which lifted the mouth of each bell to produce a rich musical chime. When the teams rang changes, the art was to pass the bells from one ringer to another, up and down the row of men.

The mummers would arrive later, carrying the oil lamps which had lit them there through the dark lanes, and they performed in the front hall at Basset Down, by the light of these lamps and the one dim lamp which hung from a hall beam. The actors represented strangely clothed characters who cavorted around under such names as Saint George, Slasher, the Valiant Soldier, 'Bull, Cut and Star', Father Christmas, Dr Faustus and Turkey Snipe (apparently derived from 'Turkish Knight'). Dr Faustus the Leech had an enormous pill, the size of a pigeon's egg, for reviving those who were struck dead during wooden sabre fights. The mummers' plays were somewhat meaningless burlesques by this time, and full of mumbo-jumbo, but this was because they had been passed down from such very ancient days, without ever being written down, that the words had become distorted. After their performance, the mummers were regaled with beer brewed by Mr Wood the butler in the Basset Down brewhouse.

The Story Maskelyne family ate their Christmas dinner beneath family portraits around an oval mahogany table, from which Mr Wood and a maid would whisk the white damask linen table cloth after the main courses, folding it lengthwise and lifting it over the heads of the diners. The dessert would be placed on the dark polished table, and a decanter of port wine set before Anthony Story Maskelyne. At the dessert stage, the children would be allowed in to join the adults in sampling the 'home-made conserves of quinces, damson cheese, sharp-tasting bilberries tied together in little bunches steeped in syrup, and a rich pound cake', but the children were probably the only ones to enjoy these sweetmeats to the full, because the adults had already sampled six courses.

Wiltshire life held much greater attractions for Nevil Story Maskelyne by the later 1870s, because he had been approached by a local Liberal party agent, who told him of the need for an able Liberal parliamentary candidate and asked him to stand for election to the constituency in which Basset Down fell – the Borough and Hundreds of Cricklade. this constituency included Swindon as well as the 'ragged hundreds', which were scattered districts beyond the north boundary of Wiltshire, and the area had been represented by a Conservative for years.

Several of Nevil Story Maskelyne's friends were already in politics. Charles Pearson, who had entered the Australian Parliament, was Education Minister for Victoria Colony, while Mounstuart Grant Duff had recently been made Under-Secretary for India and was soon to become Governor of Madras, but in 1871 he was back in Oxford laughing at Henry Smith's amusing stories, told with all the old charm and Irish humour. Nevil Story Maskelyne, who had been made an honorary Fellow of Wadham College in 1873, used to enjoy inviting Grant Duff or Smith to dine with him there when he was in Oxford lecturing. A Wadham contemporary named Wright-Henderson later recalled Maskelyne at dinner in hall with Henry Smith, still his closest friend, and told how Maskelyne used to take particular delight in 'starting paradoxes and in making statements about persons supposed to be hostile to Natural Science which it would be undesirable to repeat, and which he himself hardly pretended to believe. Henry Smith, with genial and kindly wit, defended the causes and the persons, but in a way somewhat more damaging than the blind invectives of his friend. The contrast between these two able men was very striking. Story Maskelyne was keen and eager and impatient of opposition; Smith was tolerant in those intolerant days, but his convictions were equally strong.' Maskelyne's brusque impatience, in the opinion of his Wadham contemporary, was 'due to the heat of controversy, for he had the air of a kind and courteous gentleman until he was roused'.

Henry Smith had himself tried and failed to be elected as parliamentary candidate for Oxford in 1878, but he had little time for electioneering, because in 1874, the year he had become President of the London Mathematical Society, he had taken on the job of Curator to the University Museum for the Natural Sciences, which was to prove tough and time-consuming, for not only had students learned to use the museum's facilities, but the general public were drifting into museums in a way they never had before. Nevil's other old Oxford friend, Max Müller, had in 1868 changed professorial chairs, from Modern Languages to Comparative Philology. Eight years earlier there had been a highly controversial election, when Max had put himself up for the vacant chair of Sanskrit – a field in which he was arguably the world expert – but he had been flung aside by the votes of the country parson electorate, for being a foreigner and a non-Anglican, and in the end an inferior candidate had gained the post. The electoral system had seen its changes since then, and Max Müller was a successful married academic, his house opposite Magdalen full of music – in fact he prided himself that his was the only house in Oxford in which Jenny Lind had consented to sing during her last visit to the city.

Henry Smith (*carte de visite*) photographer unknown

William Donkin, that other gentle musician at Oxford, had been working over the past years on partial and differential equations, publishing a number of papers on these and other mathematical aspects of astronomy, but the great book he had started to write on acoustics – combining mathematics and music – was not to be completed before his death in 1869. Viktor Carus, on the other hand, was at the height of a successful German scientific career in medical research and had translated Darwin's *Origin of Species* into German. Although Dr Daubeny had died, and with him a whole era of pioneer scientific discovery carried out by able gentleman scientists, Ben Brodie was still active in Oxford, hot in pursuit of a new 'Ideal Chemistry' or anti-atomic theory all his own, which took an original if involved approach to the old knotty problem of whether or not atoms existed as particles of matter. Nevil Maskelyne himself considered that recent experiments by Dr Tyndall at the Royal Institution had shown atoms to exist as unimaginably tiny particles – much smaller than had at first seemed possible – but Brodie pointed out that the existence of atoms as particles of matter had not been proved, so he preferred to back his own theory, rather than subscribe to abstractions about matter and space. On a lighter note – Robert Mansfield had long abandoned the old Christian Socialist habits and was living a giddy life among the British community in Pau, enjoying the horse-racing and the Pyrenean air.

It was the death of Anthony Story Maskelyne on 15 May 1879 which finally made Nevil decide to leave the British Museum. He had already been persuaded to stand for Parliament as a Liberal, and Anthony had put up £2,000 to support his son's attempt to become an MP – a career which Anthony could approve of at last. At the British Museum, Nevil had been frustrated by difficulties in recruiting qualified mineralogical staff, the new opening hours, lack of access to the laboratory and general official opposition to the needs of science, so he took up the new parliamentary challenge without many qualms. He saw that he would have to work to win the next election, so he started to get out and meet the voters whenever he could.

In towns, nearly half of all the men who actually occupied houses could vote, but in the country the story was different, for there the franchise extended only to the more privileged. Field labourers still had no vote, but the elections even so provoked a good turnout in a general atmosphere of merrymaking. Thereza recalled that Nevil Story Maskelyne, like many Liberals that year, took the personal initiative of explaining to voters what issues were coming before Parliament and what measures the Liberals intended taking on them. There was no nationally agreed party line for election campaigning in those days, but most Liberals singled out two main issues for attack – Disraeli's foreign policy and the current state of economic policy at home, both good bogeys to an excited crowd. It might be normal electioneering today, but at that time it was rather a new approach in country areas where haranguing had usually been aimed at persuading people to vote for the colour of your banner – Yellow for Liberal or Blue for Tory – based on family loyalties. In any case Story Maskelyne won his election and there was a nationwide swing towards the Liberals. The life of Member of Parliament and squire was so different to that of Keeper of Minerals that Story Maskelyne was later to recall that his father's death had been 'like a whirlwind that bore me from the museum and into the House of Commons'. In a certain way, he was to regret the stimulus of his scientific life, as he mentioned in a letter to Baldwin Spencer, of the Oxford Junior Science Club – 'I often look back wistfully to the pleasant days when the stream of life flowed between narrower banks and with more single aim, and when science was my principal pursuit'.

In the House of Commons, Nevil Story Maskelyne began a career which was to be active but, as his son-in-law was to put it, 'inconspicuous'. Never one for the limelight, he devoted himself to getting things done behind the scenes, concentrating on the spheres he knew best – science and technology, landlord-tenant relations and some of the sociological issues which had concerned him in his far-off Christian Socialist days. The landlord-tenant problem had grown more complex in the wake of Chartism, and Nevil wrote a report on the subject for the perusal of his Prime Minister, Mr Gladstone, who pronounced it to contain 'much good material'. Unfortunately Mr Gladstone was reaching that later phase in his life when he would make this kind of patronizing response to the efforts of his colleagues, without necessarily involving their ideas in his own policies. This habit was to lead to his alienation from fellow Liberal members and even to his ultimate defeat. An act had been passed in 1875, the first in a long succession of measures designed to protect the tenants of farmland, and during the reading of one of these bills on agricultural holdings Story Maskelyne upheld the right of an evicted tenant farmer to claim compensation and, if necessary, to take his case before an arbitrator. He also put in long hours of work in Wiltshire trying to 'put before our unhappy farmers there, the character of the bills before Parliament and to state in clear form what are the real issues as between landlord and tenant', but in the 1880s there was still a long way to go before tenants would feel secure on their farms.

The Story Maskelynes themselves were beginning to enjoy the comfortable country life and looked forward to being able to move into Basset Down House itself, once it was ready – for it was undergoing extensive alterations. Nevil, who liked entertaining and had been an enthusiast for food and drink ever since his schooldays at Bruton, was for many years chairman of the House of Commons Kitchens Committee – quite a powerful position in those days when Westminster was enjoying its heyday as a gentlemen's club. One of the many guests who enjoyed the hospitality of the Story Maskelynes at

Nevil Story Maskelyne. (Photo. Eliot and Fry)

Mary, the Story
Maskelyne's second
daughter
(photographer
unknown)

their home at Salthrop House was John Ruskin, who was there in the summer
of 1882, recuperating after one of a whole string of emotional breakdowns.
Thereza was relieved that he remained well during his stay – chatting and
laughing with the children who were staying at the time, and helping Mary
Story Maskelyne (the second daughter) with a colour sketch she was making
of some steps overhung with poppies.

Not long after his move to Wiltshire, Nevil decided to revive scientific
memories by taking up a long-standing invitation to visit the United States,
where he spent time at New Haven Connecticut, with Benjamin Silliman,
retired Professor of Chemistry from Yale University, whose father had been
Yale Professor of Chemistry and Mineralogy before him. Silliman's interests
had always been close to Maskelyne's, for they included meteorites, photography and the chemical analysis of minerals. Nevil Maskelyne met Charles
T. Jackson, a mineralogist and geologist at Boston, and also took up a warm
invitation to stay with Asa Gray, the great exponent of Darwin's Theory of
Evolution on that side of the Atlantic, who was Professor of Natural History at
Harvard and an eminent botanist. Asa Gray had a celebrated herbarium and
garden at Cambridge, Massachusetts, where he had assembled plants from
many parts of the world and conducted endless studies and experiments. He
presented Nevil Story Maskelyne with some walnuts from a tree in his own
garden, which were sent home for planting in the Hilly Cowleaze, a steep
meadow below Salthrop House. These nuts grew into great walnut trees,
several of which were still standing over a hundred years later. Asa Gray
wrote a number of books calculated to stimulate popular interest in plants,
and he was very concerned about the way botany should be taught in schools.
Nevil Story Maskelyne too spent twelve active years of this later phase of his
life as a member of a British Association committee on the teaching of science
in elementary schools.

He was also increasingly tied up with official duties, as president of the
Crystallological Society in 1881 and vice-president of the Geological Society
from 1882-3, and he was quite often out dining as the guest of other societies
such as the Royal Astronomical Society. One less predictable appointment he

received in 1883 was that of Deputy Lieutenant of the old county of Brecknock in South Wales, on the strength of having inherited the property his father had bought at Glanwysk. This entitled him to wear a splendid braided uniform with plumed cocked hat and epaulettes, in which he must have cut a fine figure before the eyes of his two maiden sisters, Charlotte and Agnes, who now lived at Glanwysk, where they occupied themselves with rearing Welsh ponies.

Basset Down House was ready for Nevil and Thereza to move into in the spring of 1885, just before the wedding of their daughter Mary to Matthew Arnold's headstrong nephew, Oakeley Arnold-Forster. Orphaned at the age of four, when his mother had died in India and William Arnold, his father, had died at Gibraltar on his way home. Oakeley and his brothers and sisters had been adopted and reared by their aunt Jane Arnold and her husband the Quaker Liberal politician W.E.Forster. Oakeley was now showing every sign of following Forster into politics, but Nevil Story Maskelyne did not entirely take to him as a match for Mary and had tried to discourage them from meeting. However Oakeley took a steady publishing job, and the wedding went ahead.

Oakeley, ardent and impulsive to the point of aggression, had already been deeply embroiled with Forster on the Irish question, which by 1885 had become the leading point of discussion in intellectual circles. Even the free-thinking Benjamin Jowett of Balliol College was against allowing the Irish to break away and rule themselves for, liberal though he was in many ways, he still felt that the first duty of any government was to preserve order and protect property – very much the kind of fear reaction which had, back in 1848, prompted many otherwise liberal men to police the streets of London against the Chartist petitioners. The popularity of Gladstone, which was already declining amongst his colleagues, was further reduced as Irish violence increased, but at this stage nobody could have envisaged Gladstone going so far as to advocate Home Rule for Ireland. Nevil Story Maskelyne was in any case concentrating on less contentious parliamentary measures such as the question raised in 1883 over the rights of New Forest commoners to a yearly supply of timber and firewood from the forest. He spoke up for the commoners, suggesting that 200 trees a year should be felled for their use, as part of their ancient rights. He also suggested that the beautiful forest should be preserved for the enjoyment and recreation of the general public – not necessarily a popular idea among his Westminster landowning colleagues in those socially divided times.

On a more technological note, Nevil Story Maskelyne spoke in the House of Commons on the need to remove fumes from the London underground steam railway in an efficient way, so that agreeable places like the Embankment Gardens should not be polluted. For the time being, he suggested a better-designed ventilation shaft with a pumping system, but he pointed out that it could be more effective in the long run to change the trains to electricity or to 'compound air' (an expression derived from Charles Mansfield, which hinted at the possibility of the internal combustion engine).

Electric lighting was just being introduced to England in 1883, so Nevil Story Maskelyne, no doubt remembering his frustrations over lack of lighting at the British Museum, threw himself into action on the side of the pioneers of electricity supply. An Electric Lighting Bill was being prepared, with the intention of granting licences to different private lighting companies who

Laying electric
cables in London

would each supply electricity to certain districts. The big city corporations, who were already obliged to supply gas (at a profit) to all their own districts, united to oppose the upstart electricity companies. The major railway, tramway and waterway companies also felt threatened by electricity, and the gas and sewerage industries fought the bill on the interesting grounds that the supply of electricity threatened their monopoly on breaking up roads and pavements for repair and pipelaying. Nevil Story Maskelyne and his fellow members of the Select Committee on electric lighting had a tough battle to gain the right to license electricity suppliers, but they won it at last on 2 August 1883, after a final stiff skirmish over who should light the Strand (won by the Swan and Edison companies) – so the Electric Lighting Bill became law.

Early in 1884, Nevil Story Maskelyne became chairman of the Select Committee on the preservation of the upper reaches of the River Thames for people's recreation. The matter particularly concerned him because his constituency lay on the extreme upper stretch of the Thames, and the river had become a pressing ecological issue now that the railways had taken all freight traffic off the water and the urban populace was taking to pleasure craft in ever-increasing hordes. Drifting down the river on a Saturday afternoon, they left unforeseen problems in their wake – for all the white water-lilies, once the glory of Henley, were now picked in bud for market, and the kingfishers were shot for ladies' hat feathers. Herons, sanderling, hen harriers, duck and moorhen were all considered fair game, and the trigger-happy trippers even shot swallows as they turned on the wing. Whole suburban trainloads of roughs were observed disgorging themselves into Thames pleasure boats at the weekend, and these Londoners were commonly armed with pistols, whereas provincial rowdies carried more cumbersome guns. The river had in fact become rather a hazardous place, due to the larking about and 'rude exertion of force' by these lads, who were also reported to indulge in indecent bathing at dusk – to the consternation of local residents. Further complaints included broken and burnt trees, vandalism to eel traps, mills and weirs, trespassing among backwaters and islands, riotous behaviour in boats, trampled fields and the wholesale destruction of swans' eggs. Story Maskelyne,

Pleasure craft on the Thames (contemporary *Punch* cartoon)

with his memories of the Working Men's College weekend walks, could sympathize with the working Londoner's need to enjoy the country air, even though his present landowning status made him see the other side as well. On the whole, the committee's greatest efforts were concentrated on making the river better for the trippers, by improving towpaths for walking, and increasing the number of public camping places, moorings and fishing areas and by taking many islands and backwaters out of private ownership, which released them for public amusement purposes. River policing, dredging, pollution and lock charges also had to be considered, so the committee sat 16 times that summer, and the bill had to be reconsidered the next year, before being passed on 14 August 1886.

In the meantime, Nevil Story Maskelyne was involved in pressurizing the government to grant a fund to the National Gallery to buy paintings by Raphael, Rubens and Van Dyck, which were to be sold from the Duke of Marlborough's private collection. He supported his cause by suggesting that first-class works of art attracted more visitors to museums and art galleries, especially artisan visitors, who would scrutinize these kind of works very closely, and so begin to cultivate a taste for painting. The National Gallery, said Maskelyne, was not a king's collection but a series of paintings consciously brought together by men who intended to show the history of art to ordinary people – but the campaign and petition organized by Maskelyne displeased Mr Gladstone and his closer colleagues, who had other uses for the money.

The railway employees of Swindon, however, found their M.P., Mr Maskelyne, a useful spokesman when he negotiated on their behalf with the Secretary to the Board of Trade to ensure that employees were included on all committees set up to enforce the Employers' Liability Act, and that employers should be stopped from using intermediaries as a means of avoiding conforming to the act themselves – a system exactly parallel to the old 'sweated labour' situation so prevalent in the days when Maskelyne had been involved with the setting up of the Working Tailors' Association. John Ludlow, the leading force from those early Christian Socialist campaigns, was just writing his memoirs of the movement, but he mentioned that he was deliberately leaving out any mention of former members of the movement who were still alive – who of course included Nevil Story Maskelyne. Probably Maskelyne feared that he had already earned himself a reputation for radical leanings and that mention of his name in connection with Christian Socialism could lose him vital votes in the next election.

Nevil was still Professor of Mineralogy at Oxford and gave a few lectures a year, but he was hoping that the Chair of Mineralogy would soon be put on a better footing so that he could hand it over to a properly paid resident professor. He still held fast to friends from many periods of his long life and a number of his old Oxford colleagues used to come and stay at Basset Down, reviving scientific memories for, although he was no longer in the experimental front line, he followed every scientific development with the same alert interest. He still took occasional photographs too, trying out George Eastman's recent invention of celluloid photographic film, which was taking over from glass as a negative base and was, in many ways, similar to Maskelyne's own cellulose-coated mica negatives of 30 years before.

It was late in 1885 that the Irish question started boiling up to a political head again in the House of Commons. Gladstone had resigned his government in the summer, after the Liberals had failed to unite over a budget vote, and a general election was called for November. Nevil Story Maskelyne had to refight his Cricklade seat – now renamed North Wiltshire – following a reshuffle of electoral districts to try and make them more equal – and this time he had to try and attract the votes of the newly enfranchised farm tenants. In a sense it was easy for him to attract their votes, because the tenants naturally hoped that the same Liberal government which had given them the vote would also be generous to them over financial conditions and tenacy rights. At that election, most country Liberal candidates were, like Maskelyne, returned to Parliament, but at the same time there was a decided swing against 76-year-old Mr Gladstone who had lost a lot of popularity last January when General Gordon was killed at Khartoum – the feeling being that if a British general was sent to British-occupied Egypt and then besieged in Khartoum, Mr Gladstone, who had sent him, should also have arranged for his rescue.

The result of the elections made Gladstone's position no easier, because the number of Liberals was now exactly equal to the combined Tories and Irish members; in fact he might not have been able to form a government at all, had it not been leaked out in January, by his son, that Gladstone was converted to the idea of Home Rule for Ireland. This leak encouraged the Irish members to give Gladstone just enough support for him to call himself Prime Minister and to form a Liberal government when Parliament reopened in February. On 1 April 1886, Gladstone introduced his Home Rule Bill in the Commons, an ill-timed move as it turned out, because the British people had lost faith in Gladstone's ability to control the Irish or any other situation, for they were especially afraid of Irish violence after hearing of recent uncontrolled insurgencies in more distant parts of the British Empire. By now too, Gladstone had lost too much popularity among his own party members, who had for some time resented the high-handed and paternalistic way he treated them and who felt betrayed at his failure to communicate to them that he had been thinking up an Irish Home Rule policy at all. Even the Irish members themselves started wondering whether the Conservatives might not be per-

Mr Gladstone's surprise card trick – Home Rule for Ireland (*Punch* cartoon)

suaded to offer them a better deal than the one being proposed by Gladstone.

That May, the comparatively liberal-minded Matthew Arnold – who had recently told his sister Fan, 'I should never myself vote for a Tory' – wrote a long article in the magazine *Nineteenth Century*, deploring Gladstone's Home Rule policy, his failure to administer law and order in Ireland and his lack of recognition for the protestant loyalists in Ulster. Matthew Arnold wrote that while he so admired the verve and brilliance of the celtic Irish, he thought that Gladstone would be mad to betray the Ulster protestants and leave two such disparate peoples to merge. Matthew Arnold was voicing not only the opinion of Victorian upper and middle class society, but the less predictable view of the scientific and literary fraternity.

That summer, when Mr Gladstone's Home Rule Bill was read for the second time in the House of Commons, 80 Liberal MPs voted it out, Nevil Story Maskelyne among them, and it has been suggested that many of these votes were more of a protest at being left out of the Prime Minister's confidence than a positive statement on Irish policy. In rejecting the bill, Liberal members defeated Gladstone's closest bid to give the Irish people the chance to rule themselves and they forced on him the choice of either resigning as Prime Minister or calling yet another general election. He chose to risk the election – which meant a stiff fight between the remaining Liberals who held firm with Gladstone, and those break-away Liberals who this time fought alongside the Tories in favour of Ireland staying united with the rest of Britain. Nevil Story Maskelyne was one of this latter group - the Liberal Unionists – and he won back his North Wiltshire seat under the new banner and took his seat in Parliament as part of a staid and secure joint majority of Conservatives and Liberal-Unionists which was to remain in power under Lord Salisbury until 1892.

Securely voted into Parliament and approaching his seventies, Nevil Story Maskelyne was rarely heard to speak in the House these days, but he was still an active committee man who was ready to put in a good deal of research on an issue which interested him. In 1887 for example, he joined in the debate on the educational funding of charity schools, by speaking of the misappropriation of certain funds intended for the education of the poorer classes, and he went on to press for free education for the poor all over the country. A school fee system was still operating in charity schools, and he knew from talking to his Wiltshire constituents that school fees were a burden to many agricultural labourers. Rather than diverting all the Charity Commissioners' money to free schools though, he wanted to see a small fund provided to allow certain gifted poor children to gain higher education through scholarships, raising themselves by way of the middle-class education system 'from the plough to the university'. Though not entirely socialist in its thinking, this plan was still rather ahead of its time in the Victorian summer of 1887, when the burgeoning suburban middle classes were generally content to keep higher education for themselves.

Parliamentary life left time for holidays, and the Story Maskelynes used to join the respectable flow of Victorian adventurers to Switzerland, France and Germany. In 1889 they took a tour round Normandy and Brittany, largely because Nevil wished to compare the Breton stone alignments at Carnac with the ancient stone circles at Stonehenge and Avebury in Wiltshire. Country life claimed more and more of his time, especially after 1889 when, as a result of radical policy, the county councils were formed, and he became a founder member of Wiltshire County Council. Nevil Story Maskelyne was chairman of the agricultural committee for many years and helped to set up the itinerant Wiltshire dairy schools, which aimed to improve butter and cheese making and general dairy practice. He was also chairman of the Bath and West agricultural show and an active member of the Wiltshire Archaeological Association, so it can have been no real disappointment to him in 1892 to lose his parliamentary seat, for he already had more than enough to occupy him.

It was the following year that the Story Maskelyne's youngest daughter Terry – reputed to have been able to multiply nine figures by nine figures in her head – married Arthur Rücker, a successful scientist who was shortly to become president of the British Association. Towards the turn of the century, Arthur Rücker brought some special chemicals to Basset Down and showed Nevil Story Maskelyne a new and exciting photographic process – the starch-grain lumière process for making colour slides – and they made some successful colour transparencies of yellow daffodils on a grassy bank at Basset Down. It was not until these quieter retirement years that Story Maskelyne at last put together his book, *The Morphology of Crystals*, which was published in 1895, the year in which he finally gave up his Oxford professorship after 44 years in the post. It had been reconstituted as the Waynflete Chair of Mineralogy, with proper salary and recognition, so he felt it was fit to pass on to Henry Miers, his former pupil and his successor as Keeper of Minerals at the British Museum of Natural History. When he resigned his professorship, 93 of Story Maskelyne's surviving friends and colleagues presented him with a portrait of himself holding a goniometer, but he was fast moving into that later area of old age when few of his real contemporary friends were left, and those who did survive, like John Ruskin, tended to be infirm.

Nevil and Thereza went up to the Lake District in 1895 to see Ruskin, now seriously ill, but they found his cottage haunted by tourists, and were themselves turned away at the door. Another old fighting comrade in rather better shape was Thomas Huxley, whom Nevil and Thereza used to visit from time to time at Eastbourne on the south coast. Thomas Huxley was still publicly engaged in verbal battles with Gladstone on aspects of Darwin's Theory of

A visit to Stonehenge by the Wiltshire Archeological Society.
Professor Story Maskelyne is second from right (photographer unknown)

Evolution, and Huxley's son had, like the Story Maskelynes' daughter, married a grandchild of Dr Arnold of Rugby. From 1897 to 1899 Nevil Story Maskelyne was vice-president of the Royal Society, which kept him in touch with the latest in scientific developments and, although he was now well into his seventies, he still gave the odd scientific lecture to the Swindon Mechanics' Institute.

At home he used to spend hours in his large book-lined library, working away with his grandson at cataloguing their gem collection. From above the old professor's desk, the portrait of Michael Faraday looked down with a benign and thoughtful gaze, flanked by one of Henry Smith and a now well-known photograph of John Ruskin with Henry Acland, taken shortly before they died. Young William the grandson would make notes for the gem catalogue while his grandfather turned a stick of scarlet sealing wax in the candle flame, ready to make a gem impression. When Nevil and Thereza celebrated their golden wedding anniversary in 1908 they were surrounded by the younger generation, and the aged gourmet of course laid on a sumptuous meal, producing as his final triumph of the feast a bottle from a case of Imperial Tokay once presented to him by the Emperor Franz Josef of Austria. At the age of 85, Nevil Story Maskelyne was still following the development of the use of electricity with keen interest and was noticed taking part in a public meeting in Swindon, but then, as Henry Miers was to remark, alertness had always been his main characteristic. He was kept in touch with politics by his son-in law Oakeley Arnold-Forster, who was now a cabinet minister in Balfour's government, but who had weak health and was to die in 1909, two years before his father-in-law.

When Nevil himself died at Basset Down in 1911 at the ripe age of 88, he left Thereza to live on there in the peaceful Wiltshire countryside for another 12 years in the household of her widowed daughter Mary. By the end of his life, Nevil Story Maskelyne had been heaped with accolades, which included his honorary doctorate of Oxford University, Fellowship of the Royal Society and the Wollaston Gold Medal of the Geological Society. He was honorary member of the Imperial Mineralogical Society of St Petersburg, the Society of

Natural History of Boston, the Academy of Natural Sciences in Philadelphia and the Royal Academy of Bavaria. As a young man he had earned the respect of the very earliest photographers, and he had introduced analytical chemistry to nineteenth century Oxford University. He had also done imaginative frontier work on early physics and chemistry and on the study of crystals and meteorites, and had built up the British Museum mineral collection until it was probably the finest in the world.

Nevil Story Maskelyne's achievements show that he played a considerable part in the Victorian era, and he himself wrote that he felt cheered to have 'lived through a great age' and to have 'known in different degrees so many of the vigorous men to whom that era is indebted for its splendour'. Those vigorous men had included Faraday and Buckland as well as Ruskin and Acland and the Liberal politicians of his later years, but they had also included the even less conforming set – the Wadham infidels, the Christian Socialists and the radical militant Oxford science professors of the 1850s – the rebels of their day.

Nevil Story Maskelyne and his friends had always cared far more for their relationships with other thinking people and for the frontiers of scientific discovery than they ever had for their own personal recognition, and it had been typical of the old scientist, faced with near-death in 1904 after a serious operation, to exclaim 'I must live, I want to know more about radium'.

Bibliographical notes

Wherever possible, quotations have been linked to the bibliography by author name, within the text itself. Anyone unfamiliar with a particular area touched upon by this book, but wanting to find out more, could try bibliography entries under the following names:

The Oxford Scene. Tuckwell, Cox, Rickards (the Skenes), Maclaine, Hughes, J.Butler, F.M.Müller, G.Müller, R.B.Mansfield, Faber (religion), W.R.Ward, G.Smith 1911, M.D.Jeune, E.M.Thomson (Leslie Thomson), H.L.Thompson (Lidell), Whateley (Baden Powell), Burgon (Hawkins), Lidell, Wadham College, Gardiner, Congreve, Liveing, F.Harrison (Congreve), Childers, Wright-Henderson.

Oxford Reform. Bill, W.R.Ward, Jowett, Abbott and Campbell (Jowett), G.Smith 1858, Tollemache (Jowett), Russell, Plumptre, Vaughan, Hawkins, Symons, Pope, Gaisford, Pattison, Devon.

Science in Oxford and elsewhere. Daubeny, Buckland, A.B.Gordon (Buckland), H.J.S.Smith, Gunther, Morell and Thackray, Brodie, Miers, Simcock, Acland and Ruskin, Atlay (Acland), Vernon, Bowen, Davis and Hull, King, Hartley, T.W.M.Smith (Brodie), Graham, Bragg and Porter, Brock and Knight (Brodie), C.B.Mansfield, E.W.Ward, Williams (Faraday), Williamson, Sherwood Taylor, Asimov, J.A.Thompson (V.Carus), M.H.N.Story Maskelyne.

Photography. Talbot, Hunt, Herschel, Gernsheim, Cundell, Schaaf, Schultze, Lee, Wood, Lyte, Arnold, Lassam, Allison, J.D.Llewelyn, Christies, M.H.N.Story Maskelyne.

Christian Socialism and reform. Christensen, Ludlow, C.B.Mansfield letters, Mayhew, Murray, Harrison, Grant Duff, Hughes, Llewelyn-Davis.

British Museum or mineralogy. British Museum, Cowtan, Crock, Graïlich, Miller, Grigson, Miers, Rucker, Von Lang, Koksharov, Revie (Hannay diamonds), Tyndall, M.M.Gordon (Brewster and the Koh-i-noor), Fletcher, Fock, Field, Des Cloiseaux.

Nevil Story Maskelyne's scientific and photographic paper of 1847 exists in full in manuscript only, although abbreviated forms of it were published by the Ashmolean Society and the British Association. The manuscript is in private hands.

Bibliography

Abbot, E. and Campbell, L. 1897. *Life and letters of Benjamin Jowett*. London: Murray.
Acland, H.W. and Ruskin, J. 1893. *The Oxford Museum*. London: Smith Elder.
Adelman, P. 1983. *Gladstone, Disraeli and later Victorian politics*. London: Longman.
Albert, H.R.H. Prince. 1847 MS. Letter to Wellington. Southampton University: Wellington papers, 2/255/15.
Allison, D. 1981. Nevil Story Maskelyne, photographer. *The Photographic Collector*, 2, 2: 16-36.
Arnold, H.J.P. 1981. *William Henry Fox Talbot*. London: Hutchinson.
   1981. Letter to *Brit.Journ.Phot.*, 128: 1163.
Arnold, M. 1885. *Letters of Matthew Arnold*, 1848-88, 2. London: Macmillan.
   1886. The Nadir of liberalism. *Nineteenth Century* 19: 645-63.
Arnold-Forster, M.L. 1949. *Basset Down*. London: Country Life.
Asimov, I. 1972. *A short history of chemistry*. London: Heinemann.
Atlay, R.B. 1903. *Sir Henry Acland, a memoir*. London: Smith Elder.
Bertrand, E. 1877. MS. Letter to N.Story Maskelyne. Brit.Mus.Nat.Hist.(Mineralogy).
Bill, E.G.W. 1973. *University reform in nineteenth century Oxford*. Oxford: Clarendon.
Bliss, P. 1854. Letter to the Vice-Chancellor. *Accounts and Papers*, 12.L.31. London: Government Blue Book.
Bowen, E.J. 1970. The Balliol-Trinity laboratories. *Notes and Records of the Royal Society*, 25: 2.
Bragg, W.L. and Porter, G. (eds) 1970. *Library of Science, Physical Sciences*, 1: 4-8, 55-8, 90-3, 201-4, 293-304. London: Elsevier.
British Association for the Advancement of Science. 1847. *Journal of sectional proceedings of 7th meeting*.
British Museum, Natural History. 1904. *The history of the collections contained in the natural history departments of the British Museum*,1. London: Trustees of the British Museum, Natural History.
Brock, W.H. and Knight, D.M. 1967. *The atomic debates*. Leicester: Leicester University.
Brodie, B.C. 1847. MS. Letters to H.H.Vaughan. Bodleian: Eng.Lett.d.440.
   1852. On certain allotropic changes. *Proc.Roy.Inst.*, 1: 201-4
   1853. On the formation of hydrogen and its homologues. *Proc.Roy.Inst.*, 1: 325-8
Buckland, W. 1849. MS. Letter to Greville (for Wellington). Southampton University: Wellington papers, 2/255/153.
   1850. MS. Letters to Dr Mantell. Mus.Hist.Science, Oxford.
Burgon, J.W. 1891. *Lives of 12 good men*. London: Murray.
Butler, J. 189?. *Memoir of George Butler of Exeter*. Bristol: Arrowsmith.
Carpenter, A.B. 1968. *The Dolphin*, magazine of King's School, Bruton. 100: 9-10.
Charlton parish register. 1831-49. MS. baptism registers, Suffolk family. Wilts. county archives.
Childers, S. 1901. *The life and correspondence of H.C.E.Childers*, Vol.1. London: Murray.
Christensen, T. 1962. *Origin and history of Christian Socialism*. Denmark: Universitetsforlaget i Aarhus.
Christie's, South Kensington. 1981. *Sale catalogue*, sale MPH 1806.
Collins, P.A.W. 1962. Dickens and adult education. *Vaughan College papers*, 7. Leicester: Leicester University.
Congreve, R. 1852-4 and 1858. MSS. Letters to his wife. Bodleian MSS. Eng.Lett. c181, f11.
Cooper, J. 1902. Wadham in the Thirties. *Wadham College Gazette*, 1: 254-65.
Cowtan, R. 1872. *Memories of the British Museum*. London: Bentley.
Cox, G.V. 1868. *Reminiscences of Oxford*. London: Macmillan.
Crock, J.M. 1972. *The British Museum*. London: Allen Lane.
Crosland, M.P. 1962. *Historical studies in the language of chemistry*. London; Heinemann.
Crowther, J.G. 1952. *Statesmen of Science*, Vol.5. London: Cresset Press.
Cundell, G.S. 1844. On a combination of lenses for the camera obscura.*Phil.Mag.*, 25: 173-5.
Curry, J.B. 1876. The diamond fields of Griqualand and their probable influence on the native races of South Africa, with notes by Story Maskelyne, M.H.N. *Journ.Soc.Arts*, 25:372-81.

Daubeny, C.G.B. 1836. On the action of light upon plants. *Phil.Trans.*, 149-75.
  1836. On the correlation of the sciences in Oxford. Oxford Tracts. 1829-48. Bodleian: GA Oxon 8° 659.
Davies, K.C. and Hull, J. 1976. *The zoological collections of the Oxford University Museum.* Oxford, pamphlet.
Denne, W.B., Story Maskelyne, M.H.N. and Dallas, W.S. 1862. The Enyclopaedia Britannica, 8th edition. *Westminster Review*, 72O.S.: 394-433.
Des Cloiseaux, A. 1859 and 1877. MSS. letters to N.Story Maskelyne. Brit.Mus.Nat.Hist. (Mineralogy).
Devon, 13th Earl of. 1852. MS. Letter to Lord Derby. Nat. Reg.Archives, Lanes 83. Knowsley papers, Box 8/1 OU affairs.
Doubleday, H.A.(ed). 1910. *Complete Peerage.* London: St Catharine Press.
F, A.D. 1968. Mr Abrahall. *The Dolphin,* magazine of King's School, Bruton. 100: 2-6.
Faber, G. 1957. *Jowett.* London: Faber and Faber.
  1974. *Oxford apostles.* London: Faber and Faber.
Faraday, M. n.d. MS. Letter to Barlow. Roy.Inst. FL 7-9.
  1971. ed. Williams, L.P. *Selected correspondence of Michael Faraday.* Vols. 1 and 2. Cambridge: C.U.P.
Farrar, W.V. 1965, Nineteenth century speculation on the complexity of the chemical elements. *Brit.Journ.Hist.Science*, 2: 297-323.
Field, F., with crystallographic note by Story Maskelyne, M.H.N. 1877. On ludlamite, a new Cornish mineral. *Phil.Mag.* ser. 5, 3: 52-7. *Proc.Crystallol.Soc.*, 1: 26-31.
Fletcher, L. 1879, 82, 85, 95. MSS. Letters to N.Story Maskelyne. Brit.Mus.Nat.Hist. (Mineralogy).
Fock, A., trans. and ed. Pope, W.J., 1895. *An introduction to chemical crystallography.* Preface by Story Maskelyne, M.H.N., vii-xii. Oxford.
Foster, J. 1891. *Alumni Oxoniensis*, Oxford: James Parker.
Gaisford, T. 1854. MS. Letter to Lord Derby. Nat.Reg.Archives, Lanes 83, Knowsley papers, box 8/2 OU affairs.
Gardiner, R.B. 1896. Registers of Wadham College, 2: 401,239,446.
Gernsheim, H. and Gernsheim, A. 1965. *A concise history of photography.* London: Thames and Hudson.
Giroud, A. & Co. 1839. MS. Letter to D.Ross. Lacock Abbey 39-65.
Gladstone, C. 1857. MS.Letter to H.Acland. Bodleian, Acland: d.68.
Gladstone, W.E. 1885. MSS. Letters to H.Acland. Bodleian, Acland: d.68.
  1886. Proem to Genesis. *Nineteenth Century*, 107: 1-21.
Gordon, A.B. 1894. *Life and correspondence of William Buckland.* London: Murray.
Gordon, M.M. 1870. *The home life of Sir David Brewster.* Edinburgh: Edmonston and Douglas.
Graham, T. 1842. *Elements of chemistry.* London: Baillière.
Graïlich, J. 1858-9. MSS. Letters to N.Story Maskelyne. Brit.Mus.Nat.Hist. (Mineralogy).
Grant-Duff, M.E., ed.Tilney Basset, A. 1930. *A Victorian Vintage.* London: Methuen.
Greswell, R. 1853. Letter to Lord Derby. Nat.Reg.Archives, Lanes 83, Knowsley papers, box 8/1 OU affairs.
Grigson, G. 1957. *Art treasures of the British Museum.* London: Thames and Hudson.
Gunther, R.T. 1904. *A history of the Daubeny laboratory.* Oxford: O.U.P.
  1923. *Early science in Oxford*, 1. Oxford: Oxford Historical Society.
  1923. *Early science in Oxford*, 11. Oxford: printed for subscribers.
Hansard, T.C. *Parliamentary debates*, ser.3, 1884-7. London: Cornelius Brick.
Harrison, F. 1899. Richard Congreve. *Wadham College Gazette*, 1: 127-31.
  1911. *Autobiographic memoirs*, 1. London: Macmillan.
Harrison, J.F.C. 1954. *A history of the Working Men's College.* London: Routledge.
Harrison, R. 1954. *Before the Socialists.* London: Routledge.
Hartley, H. 1955. Schools of chemistry in Great Britain and Ireland, 16, the University of Oxford. *Journ.Roy.Inst.Chemistry*, 79: 118-27.
Hawkins, E. 1854. MS. Letter to Lord Derby. Nat.Reg.Archives, Lanes 83, Knowsley papers, box 8/2 OU affairs.
Haydn, J. and Ockerby, H. 1890. *The book of dignities.* London: Allen.
Herschel, J.F.W. 1839-45. MS. experimental photographs with notes. Museum Hist.Science MS. 113.
  1840. On the chemical action of the rays of the spectrum. *Phil Trans.*, 1-59.
  1853. On the substitution of bromine for iodine in photographic processes. *Journ.Phot.Soc.*, 1: 70.
Hill, G.F. 1905. *Corpus of Italian renaissance medals.* Catal.Belli.4, no.6309.

H.M.S.O. Parliamentary papers . 1882. Electric Lighting Bill.
    1884. Preservation of the Thames Bill.
Hughes, T. 1873. *Memoir of a brother*. London: Macmillan.
    1900. *Tom Brown at Oxford*. London: Macmillan.
Hunt, E. 1854. corresp. to editor of *Bath and Cheltenham Gazette* (16 May).
    1854. MS. Letter to N.Story Maskelyne. Bath public library (archives).
Hunt, J.D. 1981. *The wider sea*. London: Dent.
Hunt, R. 1840. On the influence of iodine in photographic processes. *Proc.Roy.Soc.*, 325-35.
    1842. *On the art of photography*. Glasgow: Richard Griffin.
Jackson's Oxford Journal. 1844-64.
Jeune, F. n.d.. MS. Letter to A.Stanley. Bodleian: Eng.Lett.d.440.
Jeune, M.D. 1932. *Pages from the diary of an Oxford lady*. Oxford: Basil Blackwell.
Journal of Gas Lighting 1855. Anonymous article on the death of Charles Mansfield.
    [1855]: 85.
Jowett, B. 1857. MS. Letters to H.H.Vaughan. Bodleian: Eng.Lett.d.440.
Kargon, R.H. 1977. *Science in Victorian Manchester*. Manchester: Manchester University.
King, J. 1848. MS. A set of plans for Oxford University buildings. Bodleian: Top.Oxon.a.23.
King's School Bruton. 1911. *Register*. Somerset: privately printed.
    1968. *Four hundred years a school*. Somerset: privately printed.
Koksharov, N.I. 1866. Contributions to *Imperial St Petersburg mineral collections*. St
    Petersburg.
Küng, H., trans. Quinn, E. 1980. *Does God exist?* London: Collins.
Lassam, R.E. 1980. Nevil Story Maskelyne. *History of Photography*, 4, 2: 85-93.
Lee, J. 1840-55. MS. Hartwell House scrapbooks. Mus.Hist.Science, Oxford.
Liveing, S. 1926. *A nineteenth century teacher*. London: Kegan Paul.
Llewelyn, E. 1858. MS. Letter to A.Story Maskelyne. In private hands.
Llewelyn, J.D. 1855. MS. Letters to N.Story Maskelyne. In private hands.
Llewelyn, T.M. 1856-58. MS. Diaries and memoirs. In private hands.
Llewelyn-Davies, J. (ed). 1904. *The Working Men's College*. London: Macmillan.
Longford, E. 1972. *Wellington, pillar of state*. London: Weidenfeld and Nicholson.
Ludlow, J.M. 1852-3. MSS. Letters to C.B.Mansfield. Cambridge Univ. Library: Ludlow
    papers.Add. 7348/9.207-215
    1893. Some of the Christian Socialists of 1848 and the following years. *Economic Review*, 3,
    part 1: 486-end. Part 2: 24-42.
Lyte, M. 1853-4. Letters to the editor. *Journ.Phot.Soc.*, 1,2,3,4,: numerous pages.
Maclaine, W.O. 1837-9. MS. Letters to his family. Bodleian: MS.Top.Oxon.d.482.
Macray, W.D. 1890. *Annals of the Bodleian Library, Oxford*, 2nd ed. Oxford: Clarendon Press.
Mansfield, C.B. 1848-54. MSS. Letters to J.M.Ludlow. Cambridge Univ. Library: Ludlow
    papers. Add. 7348/9. 1-206.
    1852. MS. Letter to his sister Anna, 5 May. I.o.W. record office: Blachford papers, 8M57.
    1856. *Paraguay, Brazil and the River Plate*. Cambridge: Macmillan.
    1856. ed. Story Maskelyne, M.H.N. 1865. *A theory of salts*. London: Macmillan.
Mansfield, R.B. n.d.[1896]. *Chips from an old block*. London: James Blackwood.
Masterman, J. 1909. MS. Letter to N.Story Maskelyne. In private hands.
Masterman, J.C. 1963. *Social pioneers*, 16, John Malcolm Ludlow. London: C.U.P..
Maurice, F.D., ed. Maurice, F. 1905. *Life of Frederick Denison Maurice*. London: Macmillan.
Mayhew, H. 1849. Articles dated 24 Sept and 1 Dec. *The Morning Chronicle,* London.
    1980 and 1981. *The Morning Chronicle survey of labour and the London poor,*
    Vols.1 and 2. Horsham: Caliban.
Merriman, G.F.M., c.1908-10. MS. Notes and pedigrees, Maskelyne family.
    B.M.Add.MSS.39690-5.
Meyrick, F. 1905. *Memories of life at Oxford and elsewhere*. London: Murray.
Miers, H.A. 1911. Obituary on N.Story Maskelyne. *Nature*, 86:452-3.
Miller, E. 1973. *That noble cabinet*. London: André Deutsch.
Mineralogical Society, London. 1876-83. MSS. Minutes of the Crystallogical Society.
Mineralogical Society archives.
Morell, J. and Thackray, A. 1981. *Gentlemen of science*. Oxford: Clarendon Press.
Morton, V. with Lassam, R.E. 1979. *Nevil Story Maskelyne*. 32pp museum publication.
    Lacock: Fox Talbot Museum.
Müller, G. (ed). 1902. *Life and letters of the Rt.Hon.Friedrich Max Müller*, 1. London:
    Longmans Green.
Müller, F.M. 1850. MS. Letter to H.H.Vaughan. Bodleian: Eng.Lett.d.440.
    1884. *Biographical essays*. London: Longmans Green.
    1901. *My autobiography*. London: Longmans Green.

Murray, A.D. 1981. *John Ludlow, the autobiography of a Christian Socialist*. London: Frank Cass.

National Portrait Gallery. n.d. MS. Archives and pictorial records of contemporaries.

Oxford Magazine. 1903. Report on doctorate presentation ceremony.

Oxford University Commission. 1851. *Report and evidence to the Royal Commission*. London: H.M.S.O.

— 1852. *Report of H.M. Commissioners*. London: H.M.S.O.

Palmerston, H.J.T. 1854. MSS. Letters to Lord Derby. Nat.Reg.Archives, Lanes 83, Knowsley papers, box 8/2 OU affairs.

Pattison, M. 1850-4. MSS. Diaries and engagement books. Bodleian: MSS. Pattison, 11: 20, 98, 131,165.

Plumptre, E.H. 1852. MSS. Letters to Wellington. Southampton University: Wellington papers, 2/256/34 and128.

Pope, W,L, 1854. MS. Letter to Lord Derby. Nat.Reg.Archives, Lanes 83, Knowsley papers, box 8/2 OU affairs.

Quiller-Couch, A. 1913. Introduction. *The poems of Matthew Arnold*. London: O.U.P.

Registrum collegii Exoniensis. 1894. Entry for George Butler. Oxford: Oxford Historical Society.

Repertory of patents. 1841. 17: 170. London: H.M.S.O.

Revie, J. 1980. The case of the Hannay diamonds. *New Scientist*, 85: 59.

Rickards, E.C. 1902. *Felicia Skene of Oxford*. London: John Murray.

— 1916. *Zoë Thomson of Bishopsthorpe*. London: Murray.

Ross, A. 1846. MS. Invoices of camera sales. Lacock Abbey: 46-87.

Royal Astronomical Society. 1857-97. Club records, dining lists.

Royal Institution. 1847-50. *Index of managers' minutes*.

— 1874. *Royal Institution guard book*, 4: 130-2.

Rücker, A.W. 1912. Obituary, N.Story Maskelyne. *Mineralogical Society Magazine*, xvi, 74: 149-56.

— 1912. with Miers, H.A. Obituary, on N.Story Maskelyne. *Proc.Roy.Soc.*, A.86: xlvii-lv.

— 1912. Obituary, N.Story Maskelyne. *Trans.Chem.Soc.*, 101: 696-703.

Powis County Council. 1884. *Rules and standing orders, quarter sessions of the county of Brecknock*.

Ruskin, J. 1876 MSS. Letters to N.S.Maskelyne. Brit.Mus.Nat.Hist. (Mineralogy).

— 1866. Correspondence. *The Times*.

Russell, G.W.E. (ed). 1895. *Letters of Matthew Arnold*, 1. London: Macmillan.

Russell, Lord John. 1850. MSS. Letters to Wellington. Southampton University: Wellington papers, 2/256/19 and 54-5.

Schaaf, L. 1979. Sir John Herschel's 1839 Royal Society paper on photography. *Hist.of Phot.*, 3: 47-60.

Schultze, R.S. 1965. Photographic research of Sir John F.W.Herschel. *Journ. Phot. Science*, 13: 57-68.

Sherwood-Taylor, F. 1957. *A history of industrial chemistry*. London: Heinemann.

Simcock, A.V. 1984. *The Ashmolean Museum of Oxford Science, 1683-1983*. Oxford: Mus.Hist.Science.

— 1985. *Robert T.Gunther and the Old Ashmolean*. Oxford: Mus.Hist.Science.

Smith, G. 1858. On university reform. *Oxford essays*, 4: 265-87. London: privately printed.

— 1911. *Reminiscences*. New York: Macmillan.

Smith, H.J.S., ed. Glaisher, W.L. 1894. Biographical notices and letters. *Collected mathematical papers of Henry Smith*. Oxford: Clarendon Press.

Smith, T.W.M. 1979. MS. The Balliol-Trinity laboratories. Typed thesis for Part II Hons., School of Nat.Sc., Oxford. Balliol College library.

Somerville, M.F. 1846. with Herschel J.F.W. Effects of the spectrum on vegetable juices. *Proc.Roy.Soc.* (1846). 111-20.

— 1873. ed. Somerville, M.C. *Personal recollections of Mary Somerville*. London: Murray.

Sotheby, Wilkinson and Hodge. 1921. July sale catalogue. *The Story Maskelyne collection of ancient gems*. London: printed for Messrs Sotheby, Wilkinson and Hodge, auctioneers.

Stearn, W.T. 1981. *The Natural History Museum at South Kensington*. London: Heinemann.

Stirling, A.J. 1981. Early photography, general notes. *Journ.Roy.Soc.Arts*. 24: 737-40.

Story Maskelyne, A.H.M.R. 1823-44. MSS. Farm and household accounts and notes. Arnold-Forster papers , Wilts County Record office.

— 1830-47. MSS. Letters to N.S.Maskelyne. In private hands.

Story Maskelyne, Margaret. 1830-47. MSS. Letters to N.S.Maskelyne. In private hands.

Story (Maskelyne), M.H.N. 1845. MSS. Letters to H.Fox Talbot. Lacock Abbey: 45-161 and 45-175.

—— 1846-7. MSS. Letters to Margaret Story Maskelyne. In private hands.

Story Maskelyne, M.H.N. 1847. MSS. Letters to Anthony Story Maskelyne. In private hands.

—— 1847. MS. Paper on the bearings of photography on chemical philosophy. In private hands.

—— 1847. On the bearings of photography on chemical philosophy. *Proc.Ashmolean Soc.*, 2: 165-7. *Rpt.Brit.Assoc.* 17, (sect.2): 56-7.

—— 1850-5. MSS. Letters to J.M. Ludlow. C.U.L. Add.MSS., 7348/11/123-6.

—— 1849. On phosphates. *Proc.Ashmolean Soc.*, 2: 229-30.

—— 1851. On the connexion of chemical forces with the polarization of light. *Proc.Ashmolean Soc.*,2: 283-5. *Amer.Journ.Sci.*, ser.2, 12: 64-8.

—— 1852. On chemical replacements. *Proc.Ashmolean Soc.*, 2: 323-7.

—— 1853. On the oxidation of Chinese wax. *Proc.Ashmolean Soc.*, 5: 24-6.

—— 1853. *Report of the delegates for Oxford University Museum*. Pamphlet compiled by Maskelyne, signed by Cotton.

—— 1853. On a new plan for a camera. *Journ.Phot.Soc.*,1:39.

—— 1853. *Report to the president and governors of the general hospital at Bath*. Pamphlet. Oxford: privately printed.

—— 1854. Letter to Lord Palmerston. *Accounts and papers*, 12, L, 31. Government Blue Book.

—— 1854. The chemical history of silica. *Proc.Ashmolean Soc.*, 3: 41-2.

—— 1854. Letter to the editor. *Bath and Cheltenham Gazette*. Bath public library archives.

—— 1854-5. MSS. Letters to H.Fox Talbot. Lacock Abbey: LAM.105 and LA 54/60-9, 55/6.

—— n.d. MSS. Letters to P.Bliss. B.M.Add.MSS.34.582, f.644.

—— 1855. MSS. Letters to Brodie. University of Leicester: Brodie papers.

—— 1855. Investigation of the vegetable tallow from a Chinese plant, the Stillingia sebifera. *Journ.Chem.Soc.*, 8: 287-96.

—— 1855. On the history of the Koh-i-Noor diamond. *Proc.Ashmolean Soc.*, 3: 59-63.

—— 1855. The science and aesthetics of colour. *Fraser's Mag.*, 52: 503-16.

—— 1855. New metals. *Fraser's Mag.*, 52: 646-50.

—— 1857. On a prepared plate box. *Journ.Phot Soc.*, 3:198.

—— 1858. Tenerife, a summer above the clouds. *Fraser's Mag.*, 58: 35-46.

—— 1859. On the insight hitherto obtained into the nature of the crystal molecule by the instrumentality of light. *Proc Roy.Inst.*, 3: 95-106.

—— 1859. The present state of photography. *The National Review*, 16: 365-92.

—— 1859-66. MSS Letters to A.Panizzi. Brit.Mus.Nat.Hist.(Mineralogy) and B.M.Add.MSS.36719,f.87. 36723,f.502.

—— 1860. (with Hadow, Hardwich and Llewelyn, report of committee). On the present state of our knowledge regarding the photographic image. *Journ.Phot.Soc.*, 6: 308-12.

—— 1860. On diamonds. *Proc.Roy.Inst.*, 3: 229-33. *Chem.News*, 1: 208-13.

—— 1860-76 editions. *Catalogue of the collection of aerolites [meteorites] exhibited in the British Museum*. Pamphlet. London: British Museum.

—— 1862. On aerolites. *Rpt.Brit.Assoc.*, 32, sect.2: 188-91.

—— 1862-75 editions. *A guide to the collection of minerals*. London: British Museum.

—— 1863-4, with von Lang, V. Mineralogical notes. *Phil.Mag.*, ser.4, 25:39-58, 423-53; 26: 134-9; 28: 145-50, 502-8.

—— 1863-79. *Catalogue of minerals*. London. British Museum.

—— 1864. A new British mineral [langite]. *Phil.Mag.*, ser.4, 27: 316.

—— 1864. New minerals [waringtonite, lyellite] from Cornwall. *Chem News*, 10: 263.

—— 1865. Cornish minerals of the brochantite group. *Proc.Roy.Soc.*, 14: 86-9. *Phil.Mag.*, ser.4, 29: 473-6.

—— 1865. *The collections of the British Museum*. (reprint of 2 articles from the *Times* of 6 and 7 October, 1863). London.

—— 1866. On crystals of melaconite and on tenorite. *Rpt.Brit.Assoc.*, 35, sect.2: 33-4.

—— 1865-6. New Cornish minerals. *Chem.News*, 12: 277; 13: 10-11, 84.

—— 1866. MS. Letter to Mary Somerville. Bodleian: Somerville collection. SC 371, Box 21, FMSM-3.

—— 1866. Admiral Smyth. *Fraser's Mag.*, 73: 392-8.

—— 1866. Precious stones. *Edinburgh Review*, 124: 228-60.

—— 1866. Ueber die Krystallgestalt des Kupferoxides. *Verhandl. Russ.Kais.Mineralog.Gesellsch. St Petersburg*, ser.2, 1: 147-50.

—— 1866. Antique gems. *Edinburgh Review*, 124: 511-22.

1868. Gems and precious stones. *Reports on the Paris Universal Exhibition*, 1867, 2: 593-620. London: Government Blue Book.

1869. The chemical composition of Canaüba wax. *Journ.Chem.Soc.*, 7(22): 87-99.

1869. Mineral constituents of the Breitenbach meteorite. *Pro.Roy.Soc.*, 17: 370-2; *Chem.News*, 19: 182.

1869. Review of *Dana's Mineralogy*, 5th edn. *Nature*, 1: 161-3 and 186-7.

1869-70. MSS. Letters to H.S.Rawlings. Working Men's College archives.

1870. On the method of analysing silicates that do not gelatinize with hydrogen chloride. *Chem News*, 21: 27-8.

1870. Whence came meteorites? *Nature*, 2: 77-8

1870 and 77. MSS. Letters to H.R.Jennings. Working Men's College archives.

1870. *Catalogue of the Marlborough gems*. London: printed for private distribution.

1871. On the mineral constituents of meteorites. *Proc.Roy.Soc.*, 18: 146-57. *Phil.Trans.*, 160: 189-214; 161: 359-97.

1871, with Flight, W. Mineralogical notices. *Journ.Chem.Soc.*, 9 (24): 1-13.

1872. On andrewsite. *Rept.Brit.Assoc.*, 40, sect.2: 4-5. *Chem.News*, 24: 99.

1872. Localities of dioptase. *Rept. Brit.Assoc.*, 41, sect.2: 74-5. *Chem.News*, 24: 99.

1872. Meteoric stones. *Proc.Roy.Inst.*, 6: 513-7. *Chem.News*, 26: 61-2.

1872, with Flight, W. Mineralogical notices. *Journ.Chem.Soc.*, 10 (25): 1049-57.

1874, with Flight, W. Mineralogical notices. *Journ.Chem.Soc.*, 12 (27): 101-3.

1874, with Flight, W. 1874. On the character of the diamantiferous rock of South Africa. *Quart.Journ.Geol.Soc.*, 406-16.

1874. Doubtful minerals. *Chem.News*, 30: 250-1.

1875. On the crystallographic characters of nitrosoterpene. *Journ.Chem.Soc.*, 13 (28): 518-9.

1875. On andrewsite and chalkosiderite. *Journ.Chem.Soc.*, 13 (28): 586-91.

1875. Some lecture notes upon meteorites. *Nature*, 12: 485-7, 504-7, 520-3.

1875. MS. Letter to J.H.Collins. Mineralogical Society archives, London.

1875. Lectures on the morphology of crystals at the Chemical Society. *Chem.News*, 31: 3-4, 13-15, 24-6, 63-4, 101-3, 111-12, 121, 153-5, 200-2, 232. *Nature*, 9: 187-90. Reprint (1875) as a pamphlet, London.

1876. The Rowton siderite. *Nature*, 14: 272.

1876. The pitted surface of meteorites. *Phil.Mag.*, ser.5, 2: 126-31.

1876. Crystallography and mineralogy. *Handbook to the special collection of scientific apparatus*, 304-20. London: Brit.Mus.Nat.Hist.

1876. Crystallographic nomenclature. *Conferences held in connection with the special loan collection of scientific apparatus*, 304-20. London: British Museum.

1877. Notes on the optical characters of ludlamite. *Phil.Mag.*, ser.5, 3: 135-7. *Zeits.Kryst.Min.*, 1: 68-9.

1877. Additional notes on ludlamite. *Phil.Mag.*, ser.5, 3: 525.

1877. On the discrimination of crystals by their optical characters. *Chem.News*, 35: 152-4.

1877, with Russell, J. An attempt to form double salts of silver and other nitrates. *Proc.Roy.Soc.*, 27: 357-9.

1877. Indium in British blendes. *Nature*, 17: 5.

1877. Stonehenge, the petrology of its stones. *Wilts.Arch.Nat.Hist.Mag.*, 17: 147-60.

1878. A new mineral (liskeardite). *Nature*, 18: 426.

1879. Petrology. *Phil.Trans.*, 168: 296-301.

1879. Crystallography of the nitrosoterpenes of Dr Tilden. *Phil.Mag.*, ser.5, 7: 129-33; and 1882. *Proc.Crystallol.Soc.*, pt.2: 59-60.

1879. Enstatite rock from South Africa. *Phil.Mag.*, ser.5, 7: 135-6; and 1882. *Proc.Crystallol.Soc,*, 2: 60-2.

1880. The asserted artificial production of the diamond. *Nature*, 21: 203-4; *Chem.News*, 4: 4-5.

1880. Obituary on Prof. W.H.Miller. *Nature*, 22: 247-9.

1881. MS. Letter to W.E.Gladstone. B.M. Add.MSS.4473,f.131.

1884. President's inaugural address [on flints]. *Wilts.Arch.Nat.Hist.Mag.*, 21: 274-86.

n.d. [1880s]. MSS. Letters to Baldwin Spencer. Mus.Hist.Science,Oxford.

1885. President's address. *Wilts.Arch..Nat.Hist.Mag.*, 22: 136-9.

1885-6. MSS. Letters to Prof.T.Rupert-Jones. B.M. Add.MSS.42581, ff.120,122.

1886. Barbury Castle. *Wilts.Arch.Nat.Hist.Mag.*, 23: 180-94.

n.d. [1888?]. *The metals and minerals of the Bible*. Pamphlet. London: printed by Eyre and Spottiswood.

n.d. [1890?]. MS. Letter to R.T. Günther. Mus.Hist.Science, Oxford.

1891. The Koh-i-Nur, a criticism. *Nature*, 44: 555-9; 45: 5-7.

1894. *Lecture on Greek art*. Reprinted from *North Wilts Herald* of March 16, as a pamphlet. Wilts: privately printed.

1895. *The morphology of crystals*. Oxford: Clarendon Press.

1895. *Mineral veins and their history* (lecture to Jun.Engineering Soc., G.W.R. Mechanics Institute, Swindon). Pamphlet. Wilts: privately printed.

1895. The place name Cricklade. *Wilts.Arch.Nat.Hist.Mag.*, 30: 95-9.

1907. *A glossary of terms relating to the making of butter* (contributions to). Booklet. Trowbridge: privately printed.

Story Maskelyne, T.M. (née Llewelyn). 1856-8. MSS. Diaries. In private hands.

n.d. [1916?] Notes and pedigrees on the Story and Maskelyne families, and on N.Story Maskelyne. In private hands.

1923. MSS. Memoirs. In private hands.

Symons, B. 1854. MSS. Letters to Lord Derby. Nat.Reg.Archives, Lanes 83, Knowsley papers, box 8/2 OU affairs.

Talbot, W.H.F. 1839. *Photogenic drawings of W.H.Fox Talbot*. Pamphlet. London: British Association for the Advancement of Science. Lacock Abbey: 39–22.

1841. *Photogenic drawings*. Reprint from a memoir to the Royal Society. Lacock Abbey: 41-36.

1845. MS. Letter to W.L.King. Lacock Abbey: 45-148.

1854. MS. Letter to his solicitor J.H.Bolton, Lacock Abbey collection.

1854. MSS. Letters to N.Story Maskelyne. Lacock Abbey: 54-69.

Taton, R., trans. Pomerans, A.J. 1965. *Science in the nineteenth century*. London: Thames and Hudson. (orig.publ.1961. Paris, as *La science contemporaine*).

Thompson, H.L. 1899. *Memoir of H.G.Liddell*. London: Murray.

Thompson, J.A. 1903. Obituary on Viktor Carus. *Nature*, 67:613-4.

Thomson, E.M. 1919. *Life and letters of William Thomson, Archbishop of York*. London: John Lane, the Bodley Head.

Tollemache, L.A. 1904. *Benjamin Jowett, Master of Balliol*. London: Arnold.

Tuckwell, W. 1907. *Reminiscences of Oxford*. London: Smith Elder.

Tyndall, J. 1879. MS. Letter to N.Story Maskelyne. Roy.Inst. ref.Tyndall, case 6, packet 17.

Vaughan, H.H. 1854. *Oxford reform and Oxford professors*. London; J.W.Parker.

Vernon, H.M. and Vernon, K.D. 1909. *A history of the Oxford Museum*. Oxford: Clarendon Press.

Vincent, chemist. 1844. MSS. Invoices to N.Story [Maskelyne]. In private hands.

Von Lang, V. 1875 and 1877. MSS. Letters to N.Story Maskelyne. Brit.Mus.Nat.Hist. (Mineralogy) archives.

Wadham College. 1842-45. MSS. Battel bills, club subscription lists and book club purchases and requests.

Walker, R. 1848. MS. Letter to B.Symons. Bodleian: Oxford Tracts 1829-48. Bodleian: GA Oxon 8° 659.

Ward, E.R. 1955. Charles Blachford Mansfield 1819-55. *Discovery*, 16: 322-3.

1969. C.B.Mansfield, coal tar chemist and social reformer. *Chem.and Ind.*, 43: 1530-6.

1970. Charles Mansfield, a novel propellant. *Chem.and Ind.*, 45: 1432-3.

1977. Mansfield's patent gas or air light apparatus. *Chem.and Ind.* 12: 465-7.

Ward, E.R. 1979. Eminent Victorian: Charles Mansfield. *Chemistry in Britain*, 15, 6: 297-302.

Ward, W.R. 1965. *Victorian Oxford*. London: Cass.

Wellington, Arthur Wellesley, 1st Duke of. 1852. MSS. Letters to Lord John Russell and E.H. Plumptre. Southampton University: Wellington papers, 2/256/23-30 and 127.

Westropp, H.M. 1869. On the nature and composition of the Murrhine vases of the ancients (with observations by N.Story Maskelyne). *Proc.Soc.Antiq.*, ser.2, 4: 222-4.

Whateley, E.W. 1884. *Personal and family glimpses of remarkable people*. London: Hodder and Stoughton.

Williams, L.P. 1965. *Michael Faraday*. London: Chapman and Hall.

Williamson, A.W. 1853. On Gerhardt's discovery of anhydrous oxygen acids. *Proc.Roy.Inst.*, 1: 239-42.

Wood, R.D. 1975. The calotype patent lawsuit of Talbot v.Laroche, 1854. Typed pamphlet. Lacock: Fox Talbot Museum.

1980. Latent developments from gallic acid. *Journ.Phot.Science*, 28, 1: 36-42.

Working Men's College. *W.M.C.Mag.*, 1: 79; 2: 191; 3: 123, 133.

Wright, D.G. 1970. *Democracy and reform, 1815-1885*. London: Longman.

Wright-Henderson, P.A. 1911. Obituary on N.Story Maskelyne. *Wadham College Gazette*, 3, 42: 433-5.

Index